BRADFORD
IN THE GREAT WAR

BRADFORD
IN THE GREAT WAR

EDITED BY
MIKE WOODS & TRICIA PLATTS
BRADFORD WORLD WAR I GROUP

SUTTON PUBLISHING

First published in the United Kingdom in 2007 by
Sutton Publishing, an imprint of NPI Media Group Limited
Cirencester Road · Chalford · Stroud · Gloucestershire · GL6 8PE

British Library Cataloguing in Publication Data
A catalogue record for this book is available from the British Library.

ISBN 978-0-7509-4818-6

The book writing team of the World War I Group at the Mechanics' Institute Library, Bradford. Left to right: Geoff Barker, Tricia Platts, Gerry Beevers, Mike Woods, Patricia Featherstone, Joyce Appleby.

Typeset in 10.5/13pt Galliard.
Typesetting and origination by
NPI Media Group Limited.
Printed and bound in England.

Contents

	Acknowledgements	vi
Preface	Piecing Together the Story of the Great War *Mike Woods*	vii
Introduction	The Great European Shake-up *Mike Woods*	xi
1.	Behind the Headlines: Bradford in 1914 *Tricia Platts & Mike Woods*	1
2.	Merchants, Hawkers & Tingalarys *Tricia Platts*	12
3.	Bradford's Fighting Men *Gerry Beevers, Tricia Platts, Geoff Barker & Joyce Appleby*	24
4.	Soldiers' Stories *Gerry Beevers & Tricia Platts*	46
5.	The War Service of J.B. Priestley *Alison Cullingford*	65
6.	Bradford's Textile Industry 1914–18 *Mike Woods & Tricia Platts*	81
7.	Manufacturing Industries *Geoff Barker, Mike Woods & Gerry Beevers*	98
8.	Low Moor Explosion *Tricia Platts*	111
9.	Military Hospitals and Convalescent Homes *Patricia Featherstone*	123
10.	Can We Help? *Tricia Platts*	146
11.	Women, Peace and Politics *Mike Woods & Tricia Platts*	159
12.	Aftermath *Tricia Platts*	178
Appendix 1	Transcript of Connie Gallilee's Recollections	197
Appendix 2	Timeline of Events in Bradford	199
Appendix 3	Websites	201
	Bibliography & Further Reading	203

Acknowledgements

This book has been compiled by members of the World War 1 Group at the Mechanics' Institute Library, Bradford. The writers are indebted to all the members of the group for their suggestions, encouragement and support and to the staff of the library for helping search for sources and for overlooking extended loans on vital reference books!

Particular thanks go to Graham Hall, a fellow member of the World War 1 Group. He has sourced numerous photographs and postcards from his extensive archive and has also helped with tracking down information, either from his own collection of books about Bradford, or from his knowledge of sources at the Bradford Industrial Museum. The Graham Hall Archive is a treasure trove into which we have had the good fortune to delve.

We have also been helped by staff at Bradford Central Library, Bradford Industrial Museum, Bradford University Library, Kirklees Library, Huddersfield University Library, West Yorkshire Archives, Manchester Archives, National Archives at Kew, the Imperial War Museum, the Regimental Museums of the Prince of Wales's Own West Yorkshire Regiment, the Duke of Wellington's Regiment, the KOYLIs and the Devon and Dorset Regiment. John Nicoll kindly made available to us information gathered for his website and his collection of photographs of Low Moor. The *Telegraph & Argus*, *Shipley Times* and many other local newspaper archives have been opened to us.

Several authors have given specific permission to quote from their work and Bob Duckett has been particularly helpful. We have endeavoured to credit all our sources but many anecdotes and stories are by now apocryphal. While we have checked the authenticity of these it is not always possible to establish their true origin. We thank all those individuals who have allowed us to publish memories of their families and hope that by so doing, these memories will not be lost to succeeding generations.

The Lord Mayor's Community Chest advanced funds which have helped enormously in meeting our many expenses.

Dr Mike Woods, who sadly died in July 2006, was the driving force behind the concept of this book. A man of vision and ideas, Mike inspired members of the Bradford World War 1 Group to embark on a project which carried considerable challenges. His determination and enthusiasm brought the manuscript almost to completion and it has been as a tribute to him that other members of the group have finished the project.

Requiescat

Preface

Mike Woods
Piecing Together the Story of the Great War

History is not dead and evidence of our particular page in history, Bradford during the Great War, is all around us. With a little thought and simple research we can all interpret the evidence which might be contained on war memorials, in street names or dusty old mementoes, thereby revealing all kinds of personal or local links with this world-shaking event.

It is unspeakably moving to visit the Somme battlefields for the first time and a little further reading, for example Martin Middlebrook's *First Day on the Somme*, can personalise the experience. For me, it was the area around Montauban where I was to read that Battalions of the City of Liverpool had been active, and this reminded me of a faded photograph which had pride of place on mother's mantelshelf in Liverpool and was now on mine. The young soldier, in the uniform of the Liverpool Scottish Regiment, could well have crossed those very same fields near Montauban. His eldest daughter was happy to share with me her transcription of his diary of the period, which added richly to my knowledge of the Great War. This man survived the war and lived to a good age but his wife, who had worked in munitions, predeceased him by some years as the TNT with which she had worked gradually poisoned her.

The photograph on the mantelshelf: Pte Herbert Faulkner, 1/10 Battalion (Scottish) King's Liverpool Regiment.

In Baildon, near Bradford, there is a sweetshop not much larger than a kiosk. It is a wooden structure and, amazingly, is supported on small wheels, now embedded in the tarmac. The present owner

Robinson's sweet shop, Baildon. Note the wheels beneath the wooden structure.

explained that at the end of the Great War the local Veterans' Association had the shop constructed to provide a livelihood for a returning soldier. As it was wheeled it was not subject to rates. The local studies section of Baildon Library confirms the story and provides further information about this Veterans' Association.

Near the sweetshop there are three streets named after battlefields from the Great War. Menin Drive, Hazebrouck Drive and St Eloi Close were built on land acquired by the Veterans' Association to provide housing for returning troops. Baildon also has a Roll of Honour, which bears the names of the men of the township who served in the war. It is housed in the old Soldiers and Sailors Club, now renamed Shroggs after the field on which it is built.

Baildon street signs recalling the Great War.

The former District Nurses' Home, built as part of Baildon's memorial to the Great War.

It is estimated that there are over 850 memorials in the Bradford area. They are painstakingly listed in handwritten documents in Bradford Central Library. Memorials in general are the most visible reminders but not all are stone monoliths or cenotaphs. In Esholt a village hall was built as a memorial and Baildon dedicated the District Nurses' Home in memory of the war.

Shipley has a fine example of a memorial garden with a cross of remembrance and the people of Greengates chose a prominent roadside position for their magnificent winged statue. It was unveiled during a royal visit in 1923 by the Prince of Wales and the Duke of York (the future kings Edward VIII and George VI). In striking contrast, but almost equally moving, is the only remaining visible evidence of Tong Village. Its war memorial now stands in farmland.

We hope that this book might inspire our readers to notice, search out, investigate and question all the resources which cities, towns, villages and family albums afford. Our book is a joint effort by members of the Bradford World War I Group, which meets monthly at the Mechanics' Institute Library. Joining a group is a sure way of finding like-minded souls to spur on your research!

The war memorial at Greengates.

Introduction

The Great European Shake-up

Mike Woods

The study of history is the study of change, but, between 1914 and 1918, the pace of change accelerated dramatically across Europe and indeed the whole world. The changes were seen in empires, politics, diplomacy, armed forces, industry, the role of women, the structure of societies and the beliefs and outlook of individual people. In 1914 the triangle formed by Great Britain, France and Germany (soon to become the Western Front) was a centre of world influence. By the end of the war America, Japan and Russia were emerging as world powers.

Douglas Haig, commander of British forces in France and Flanders for much of the war, claimed that battles fought beyond France and Flanders were merely 'side-shows', and this view prevailed at the time. The Eastern Front, so significant in the

A view of Forster Square, *c.* 1914. Note the horse-drawn and mechanised transport and the absence of private cars.

Second World War, occupied only one-quarter of Germany's armies at its peak, and none were engaged there by 1918. The success of the allies' campaigns in the Far East clipped Germany's expansionist wings but raised the aspirations of Japan and could be claimed to begin the long trail to Pearl Harbor. The Middle Eastern and Turkish campaigns changed little at the time but laid the foundations for striving and unrest in years to come.

Even without the Great War, the grand but fading empires of Austria-Hungary, Tsarist Russia and the Turkish Ottoman may well have descended into final decline. Germany, ruled by an ambitious and impatient Kaiser, might well have become the dominant European power had he not handed government to his generals and the war then destroyed Germany's industrial successes. Allenby's entry into Jerusalem and Damascus finally brought down the tottering Turkish Empire and changed that region for the foreseeable future, producing the conflicts and terrorism that we are still involved in today. The British Empire, controlling one-third of the world's land space at its Victorian zenith, might have been overtaken in time by America, but all this is speculation.

From a twenty-first-century viewpoint it can be difficult to imagine the cobbled streets and mill chimneys of Bradford in 1914, and to comprehend the rapid changes which were being brought about by the city's industrial pioneers. While mechanised vehicles were gradually overtaking horse-drawn transport, the Great War sped up the process. Of the heavy horses which returned from the battlefields many succumbed to the horse flu which matched human flu in its destructive effect in 1919. As a consequence, the war saw many cartage businesses disappear but memories of the horse transport era can be seen in the Bradford Industrial Museum, which is housed in the old Whitehead Mill, Laisterdyke.

Trolleybuses were introduced to Bradford in 1911 and a wide range of other mechanised transport was rapidly appearing on the streets, development being spurred on by the demands of wartime. The Industrial Museum also displays a three-wheeled curiosity called a Scott Sociable. Manufactured in Bradford by Scott Motors, this was developed out of a battlefield scout car.

Based at Scott Motors were brothers Ben and William Jowett. They began making V-twin engines for driving machinery and some of these found their way into local cars as replacements for other makes. In 1904 they had begun producing cars and became the Jowett Motor Manufacturing Co. However, the factory was still fully occupied making Scott motorcycles and their first vehicle was tested for four years before production started. This car used an 816cc flat-twin water-cooled engine and three-speed gearbox with tiller steering. The body was a

BENJAMIN JOWETT
Born in Bradford 24 March 1877.
Died in Bradford 1963.

WILLIAM JOWETT
Born in Bradford 17 June 1880
Died in Bradford 1955

The brothers who founded Jowett Cars and were pioneers in car design for half a century.

An admiring crowd pose for the camera beside a Bradford trolleybus with its driver and conductor. Bradford was the first city to introduce this form of public transport.

lightweight two-seater. Twelve vehicles were made before an improved version with wheel steering was launched in 1913 and a further thirty-six were made before the outbreak of war.

As with many other businesses, the factory was then turned over to munitions manufacture and production of vehicles for military use. Some Scott motorcycles were used by the Motor Machine Gun Service on the Western Front but they were shown to be insufficiently robust for active service. After the war, the renamed Jowett Car Co. moved to their Five Lane Ends factory at Springfield Works, Idle, and became one of the city's major employers until closing in 1954. (The site is now a Morrison's supermarket.)

Perhaps the most dramatic technological developments came in air travel. It was in 1903 that the Wright brothers made halting hops of a few hundred metres. Only sixteen years later, in 1919, a British wartime bomber plane, the Vickers Vimy, flew the Atlantic. Bradfordians were entertained by their first sighting of an aircraft on 1 August 1913. Gustav Hamel, a young aviator, touched down in the Clock House estate near Lister Park. The watching crowd was relieved when the plane managed to stop only 5yds from the wall at the end of the field. Level ground was, and still is, in short supply in Bradford and two trees had to be cut down to make room for Hamel's landing.

One year later war was declared and Hamel's rickety plane, or its equivalent, had to be turned into an efficient battlefield asset. Helping this happen were Bradford industrialists. Christopher Pratts (furniture manufacturers) provided the wooden frames and the planes were built by Phoenix Dynamo Manufacturing Co. Ltd of Thornbury. Details of their achievements can be found later in this book.

The people of Bradford had more immediate concerns in their daily lives. The cost of living rose inevitably and steeply in the war years. In 1914 Cadbury's milk chocolate was a penny a bar and an Army private was paid 1s 1d per day. In 1914 Thomas Cook offered a fifteen-day grand tour of Switzerland for £30 but by 1919 prices had virtually doubled and increases in the costs of household basics such as flour, sugar and soap powder were pressing concerns. It is a salutary exercise to examine the attitudes of Bradford men and women; the qualities which enabled them to cope with wartime conditions.

Belief in King and country, the Empire, social class, playing the game and maintaining a straight bat were characteristic of the population of Britain in 1914. Queen Victoria, almost to her own surprise, was a genuinely popular monarch and her portrait hung in homes across the land. Her grandson, King George V, came to the throne in 1910 and sustained the nation's pride in the Empire which remained depicted in pink on every schoolroom map. Great statesmen and empire builders, such as Clive of India, Cecil Rhodes in Africa and Kitchener of Khartoum remained significant figures in the public memory, and men and women from across the Empire were only too ready to 'rally to the flag' and 'come to Britannia's aid in her hour of need'.

Awareness of class also remained strong in 1914, as was the belief in a woman's place being in the home. Both these were profoundly shaken by the Great War. The role of women was to change radically and will be treated in more detail later in this book. In the trenches, products of the upper classes continued to lead those from the working class. The new middle class, often rising up the social scale through trade or success in the professions, was caught somewhat uncomfortably in between. At the end of the war there was often some difficulty in placing those men who had been commissioned in the field because of the confusion about their origins. In 1918 when Bradford Chamber of Commerce was devising ways of reintegrating officers into management, the problem of officers who were not gentlemen and gentlemen who were not officers gave rise to confusion and debate.

Contemporary accounts of life in the trenches often reflect the nation's attitude to class divisions and do not appear to challenge the quality of leadership given by the upper-class products of the public schools. This account of the Somme, written by a young officer one year after the carnage is from the *Yorkshire Observer*:[1]

A story is told of one, a mere youth from school, just out of his teens and the grandson of a local knight and merchant prince. He led his company unmindful of danger and numerous wounds but was finally compelled to retire having received nearly the full discharge of an enemy machinegun.

Another was last seen with an impromptu bandage round his head, smoking and swinging a cane, without any seeming display of histrionics. The officer was the first of his party out of the trench and helped all the men out.

One subaltern, a local solicitor who sustained a fractured leg, roundly abused a non-commissioned officer when he offered assistance. Another subaltern, who had connections with a local newspaper, cheered the men on while he lay unable to advance being mortally wounded.

The writer heard one wounded officer giving detailed orders to a depleted machinegun team from a trench just in front, under the fiercest barrage. The men too were splendid, as one can only expect from such inspiring examples of courage.

At home and abroad men and women continued to display enormous fortitude in the face of hardship coupled with a respect for manliness. On the Home Front families suffered shortages, worked longer hours and faced bad news and good with all the courage they could summon. The stoicism of the men who endured the unspeakable horrors in the mud of Passchendaele, the insanity of the men pushing past their fallen colleagues to throw themselves against the uncut wire on the Somme, the dumb loyalty of both sides at Verdun reflects a generation programmed to withstand suffering.

Legend has it that the 'Tommies' were named after a soldier of Wellington's time. The Iron Duke was reviewing a badly wounded soldier, who gave his name as Tommy Atkins. When asked if he was suffering, he told the Duke, 'All in the line of duty, Sir'. This attitude persisted in rank and file throughout wartime.

In the early twentieth century weakness and effeminacy were frowned upon, homosexuality was punished by law and emotional responses were expected only in women. Among the working men of Bradford this could not have been more true. Yorkshire grit is stronger than the rock on which the city is built; it is an expression of manliness as lived in Bradford and, during the Great War, it helped hundreds of men (and women) carry on. But then as now, men needed to express some 'unmanly' feelings and did so, perhaps disguised as cheeriness in letters home or, more privately, in poetry. Herbert Read DSO, MC, served as a Captain in the Yorkshire Regiment for four years. His poetry captures the reality of men's lives in the trenches:

> My men go wearily
> With their monstrous burdens.
>
> They bear wooden planks
> And iron sheeting
> Through the area of death.
>
> When a flare curves through the sky
> They rest immobile.
>
> Then on again,
> Sweating and blaspheming–
> 'Oh, bloody Christ!'
>
> My men, my modern Christs,
> Your bloody agony confronts the world.[2]

In describing the agony of his men Read paints a picture far removed from Yorkshire grit:

> Bloody saliva
> Dribbles down his shapeless jacket.
> I saw him stab
> And stab again
> A well-killed Boche.
> This is the happy warrior,
> This is he . . .[3]

How different this to the comic books and public school spirit of 'playing the game'. Kipling's poem 'If' summarises this urge to survive and smile through many vicissitudes.

> If you can force your heart and nerve and sinew
> To serve your turn long after they are gone,
> And so hold on when there is nothing in you
> Except the Will which says to them: 'Hold on';
> Yours is the Earth and everything that's in it,
> And – which is more – you'll be a Man my son![4]

Even as late as July 1916 Captain Neville of the East Surreys began his advance by kicking a football towards the German lines. The ball was clearly labelled: *The Great European Cup, The Final, East Surreys v Bavarians, Kick-off at Zero Hour 1 July 1916.* Of course, it wasn't a game and Captain Neville and many of his men were killed that day near to the 'jump-off' point.

There was a long British tradition of the younger sons of aristocracy and gentry buying their commissions in the military. By 1914 this had ceased but the officer class continued to be drawn from the well educated, often well born in the mould of *Boys' Own* adventurers. The preferred service was the Royal Navy, which was seen as the 'iron walls' of the Empire. Even very senior Army men were not slow to express their preferences. Sir William Robertson, who rose from the ranks to become Chief of the Imperial General Staff in December 1915, is recorded as saying to his son, 'I would rather bury you than see you in a red coat.' Recruitment for the Navy was so successful that an excess of men was channelled into the special battalions of the Army.

These ideals of fortitude in adversity, service to the country and respect for class boundaries continued to prevail at home, reinforced by positive reports of far-away actions in the press. However, men returning from the trenches brought a changing set of attitudes. When on leave they found themselves strangers in what had become a foreign land. Many were often relieved to return to the certainties of the front line. In *Goodbye to All That*, Robert Graves writes:

> England looked strange to us returned soldiers. We could not understand the war-madness that ran wild everywhere, looking for a pseudo-military outlet. The civilians talked a foreign language; and it was newspaper language. I found serious conversation with my parents all but impossible.[5]

Similar issues were experienced by German soldiers. In *All Quiet on the Western Front*, E.M. Remarque describes the hero, Paul Baumer, being shunned when he tries to describe to his old professor (who is instructing his class in the old values) how the world has changed.

In 1914 Bradford had no fewer than five local newspapers. Each provided a distinctive political voice ranging from Tory and establishment Liberal to the growing Labour Party. The *Bradford Daily Telegraph*, the *Daily News*, the *Daily Argus*, the *Bradford Pioneer* and the *Yorkshire Observer* are all available on microfilm at the Central Library and, if eyesight is good, they provide a rich source for the study of change in our city.

At the beginning of the war, the *Telegraph* and the *Bradford Pioneer* were near-pacifist in attitude. This was a view endorsed by Fred Jowett, a leading activist of the Independent Labour Party.

On 2 August 1914 he wrote, 'This is the greatest war this world has ever seen. I hope Great Britain will not be drawn into this crime against civilisation.' The *Argus* worried about 'letting our European friends down' and the *Yorkshire Observer* was concerned about the growth of the Labour Party and Trade Unions. All the papers reflected the business community's worries about the loss of trade which the war might bring. There seemed to be very little optimism that the war could bring opportunities and there was even less awareness of the sacrifices which would be demanded.

J.B. Priestley, son of a Bradford schoolmaster, described Bradford in 1914 as 'at once one of the most provincial and yet one of the most cosmopolitan of English cities.'[6] Despite a worldwide reputation for its textiles, Bradford remained in the shadow of Leeds, being on a branch line of the rail service to London and lacking the mixed trades upon which Leeds thrived. Priestley goes on to describe the 'curious leaven of intelligent aliens, chiefly German Jews and mostly affluent'. This section of the city's population produced men of great distinction including the composer Frederick Delius, two renowned painters and a well-known poet, in addition to the industrialists and entrepreneurs who helped make Bradford rich.

Priestley recognised that the Great War brought to an end 'a kind of regional self-sufficiency'. He describes his father as having never read a London newspaper and being unconcerned about what happened 'down south'. And yet the powerful local political and cultural tradition was something of an Indian summer, 'the last majestic flowering of nineteenth-century provincial life that had made Bradford one of the great cities of Victorian England'.

By 1914 Bradford had grown from a small industrial and market town to the international centre for the production of mixed fibre cloths and the marketing centre for the textile products of the West Riding. Textiles were dominant and have a separate chapter in this book. One-third of working men and two-thirds of working women were employed in the industry. However, even though it might not have been widely recognised at the time, textiles in Bradford were already in decline. As 80 per cent of wool staples were imported it was clear that war disruption on the high seas could only hasten this decline. Other industries barely survived the war, including coal mining, iron ore working and engineering companies supporting the textile industry. An exception was the burgeoning electronics industry, which in the Second World War produced radar, then Baird televisions, Microvitec and, most recently, PACE, which emerges as one of the few standard-bearers of Bradford's industrial heritage.

Bradford newspapers reported the early signs of the war affecting life in the city. On 31 July 1914, the day of Russian mobilisation, there was panic-buying of flour in Bradford and the price rose by 2s per stone. On 3 August, 'watched by a small crowd', naval reservists quietly departed while, on the same day, there was a run on the banks and the government, not noted for interference, allowed for a temporary suspension of debts. Landladies in Scarborough reported a major fall-off in visitors despite lovely weather. The papers claimed that Whitby, Bridlington and Filey had suffered a 25 per cent drop in business. Some firms put employees on half pay and rent for company housing was stopped in some areas. Flour prices rose again, as did those for sugar, and War Relief organisations sprang up.

As described elsewhere in this book, the men of Bradford, the principal providers, were quick to volunteer. The city's pride in its menfolk was matched only by the distress of those left behind.

Notes

1   *Yorkshire Observer*, August 1917
2   From *My Company* by Herbert Read
3   From *The Happy Warrior* by Herbert Read See www.fordham.edu/halsall/mod/1914 warpoets.html#read
4   See www.fordham.edu/halsall/mod/kipling-if.html
5   Robert Graves, *Goodbye to All That*, Jonathan Cape 1929
6   J.B. Priestley, *Postscripts*, Heinemann, 1940

ONE

Behind the Headlines: Bradford in 1914

Tricia Platts & Mike Woods

In 1914 Bradfordians were a well-informed lot: there were four daily newspapers and a weekly, the *Yorkshire Observer Budget*! To look through them helps cast light on the interests, activities and concerns of citizens in the months leading up to the outbreak of war.

The newspapers provided far more than local, national and international news. Advice on dressmaking, rabbit and poultry keeping and medical self-help was informative and well illustrated. Advertisements often seemed to concentrate on unmentionable female complaints, luridly portrayed. Serialised novels, the *Archers* and *Coronation Street* of the day, were a good reason to continue buying the paper of choice. Unfortunately, serialisations in *The Yorkshire Observer Budget* were more Mills & Boon than Dickens and titles such as *Held in Bondage* failed to live up to their promise and, by modern standards, are very tame.

But what of the headline news in August 1914? In terms of research, scrutinising microfiche images of newspaper columns in Bradford Central Library is a pretty daunting task and, other than for certain events of national importance, most of our research has focused on the *Yorkshire Observer Budget*.

'BRADFORD 2 ARSENAL 0: 16,000 PEOPLE WATCH THRILLING CUP TIE'

In 1914 Bradford was a powerful force in Association Football with two teams in the top division (now the Premiership). Bradford City Football Club (claret and gold) had played their first league game on 1 September 1903 in the second division. By 1908 they were promoted to the first division, rising to fifth place in 1911. This was also the year in which they won the FA Cup, beating Newcastle United 1–0 in the replay at Old Trafford, Manchester.

When the team returned to Forster Square station they were greeted by a brass band and thousands of Bradfordians. The trophy was returning home: it had been made by the Bradford jeweller, Fattorini, and was displayed with double pride at the celebration dinner in the Midland Hotel.

Bradford City's FA Cup winning squad of 1911/12. 'We've got Dicky Bond' was scrawled on a board and held up for Bradford Pals to read across no-man's land in 1916. Bond is seated front right.

The second Bradford team was founded in 1907 and, to distinguish itself from Bradford City, adopted the name of its ground: Bradford Park Avenue. It entered the second division in 1908 and reached the quarter-final stage of the FA Cup in 1912/13. At the end of the following season the club was promoted to the first division where the team inevitably met their Bradford City rivals. Just under 30,000 saw the local derby match and after the return leg Park Avenue finished the season in their best ever ninth position.

Players from both teams enlisted when war began. Outstanding among them was the famous Bradford City and England international player Dicky Bond, who enlisted with the 2nd Bradford Pals in April 1915 with fellow team member Harold Walden. Walden was quickly commissioned and for a time served as adjutant. He was transferred to the 20th Reserve Battalion in August 1915. Dicky Bond was captured by the Germans at the end of July 1916 and, with Walden, resumed his playing career after the war ended.

Nine members of the City side were killed in action. They included the central defender Bob Torrance who had played a vital role in winning the FA Cup in 1911, and Jimmy Speirs who had been team captain. They both lost their lives in 1917. Jock Ewart, the City goalkeeper, was badly shell-shocked but managed to play again.

From the Bradford Park Avenue club came Donald Simpson Bell. When war broke out, Bell, with the club's consent, immediately enlisted as a corporal. He was commissioned in 1915 in the Yorkshire Regiment (later the Green Howards).

He was serving on the Somme on 5 July 1916 at Horseshoe Trench when he was awarded the Victoria Cross. The citation[1] describes the action:

> . . . very heavy enfilade fire was opened on the attacking company by an enemy gun. Second Lieutenant Bell immediately, on his own initiative, crept up a communication trench, and then, followed by a corporal and a private, rushed across the open under very heavy fire and attacked the machine-gun, shooting the firer with a revolver and destroying the gun and the personnel with bombs. This officer lost his life five days later performing a very similar act of bravery.

Donald Bell was the only professional footballer to be awarded the Victoria Cross.[2]

Bradford Park Avenue player Donald Bell was awarded the Victoria Cross for his bravery at Horseshoe Trench on 5 July 1916. He was killed a few days later.

'MOTOR ENGINEER EDWIN BINNS DRUNK IN CHARGE OF MOTOR CYCLE'

Motorcycles (many with sidecars) were manufactured locally by Scott Motors and were a favourite mode of transport for the aspiring man. Bradford's streets also boasted trolleybuses (the first in the country, introduced in 1911), tram cars and buses as well as some motor cars. Horse-drawn transport was still the norm for the movement of wool and cloth but Edwin Binns's offence was becoming more common. Other offences included the attempted derailment of a train by a seventeen-year-old boy 'from respectable parents' and a footballer in court on a bribery charge. Some newspapers pointed the finger at Leeds picture houses as the cause of the crime wave.

In 1914, Bradford Police Service had 443 officers, an increase of five on the previous year, and they produced the following list of offences for the *Budget* to publish:

Indictable offences	1,296 (male:female, 4:1)
Offences against the person with violence	50
Offences against property with violence	203
Offences against property without violence	985
Drunkenness and attempted suicide	53
Sent to prison	124
Sent to reform school	14
Sent to industrial school	5
Whipped or probation	208
Inebriate reform	6

Crowds enjoy a weekend stroll in Manningham Park. The bandstand was a focal point.

'BRADFORD PERMANENT ORCHESTRA BIG SUCCESS'

Public entertainment in Bradford was very well supported and covered a wide range of interests from barrel organs and street musicians to picture houses, music halls and brass bands. Saturday afternoons were often spent in one of Bradford's parks listening to a brass band on the bandstand.

As early as 30 July 1892 the *Bradford Observer* had reported attempts by W.B. Sewell to establish a permanent orchestra with a management committee and list of vice presidents. In its first season there was a deficit of £50 and the musicians were not paid. In the second season half salaries were paid and £15 profit made. The first performance with the Bradford Festival Choral Society was *Elijah* in November 1894 and from 1895 it became the Bradford Permanent Orchestra. The President of the Festival Choral Society said:

it is a matter of pride that there is such a body of instrumentalists in the town. Formerly the Society had to go to all the points of the compass to get together a scratch band, but the town now has a permanent orchestra. The manner in which the members of this body acquitted themselves at the last two concerts of the Society is worthy of commendation in every way. With the exception of Manchester I do not think there is another town in the north of England that possesses such a combination. I hope the Bradford Permanent Orchestra will flourish and go hand in hand with the Festival Choral Society for many years to come.

Sewell, G.F. *History of the Bradford Festival Choral Society*, 1907

The Bradford Permanent Orchestra pictured in St George's Hall, 1914.

The magnificent façade of the Alhambra Theatre pictured immediately before its opening in 1914. The billboard announces the programme for the first week and includes an appearance by Nellie Wallace.

The Alhambra Theatre (opened in 1914) and St George's Hall were cultural centres but music halls[3] and picture houses continued to be the main centres of popular entertainment.

St George's Hall doubled as a cinema and concert hall, and nearby was the Electric Theatre de Luxe which in 1914 renamed itself the Theatre de Luxe.[4]

The Bijou Orchestra was resident at the Theatre de Luxe adding sophistication to the establishment.

This was housed in a former art gallery off Bridge Street and was operated by the Pathé Frères Co. which had established an office in Bingley. In February 1914 the *Bradford Daily Argus* reported on its latest, rather novel programme:

H. Leacey, the manager of the Theatre de Luxe, is full of original ideas and his latest is a programme made in the form of a fan. The pictures, with accompanying musical items, for the first part of the week are printed on one side, and for the second part of the week on the reverse side. It is quite a dainty novelty.

When the war began in 1914 the Theatre de Luxe announced that 'Café' (Collinson's) would be served from 1.30 p.m. to 9.30 p.m. free of charge. This initiative followed Pathé Frères' practice in their French cinemas. Collinson's coffee was regarded as a luxury and must have generated considerable interest as did the continuous showing of films, another initiative introduced by the management.

The Picture House, situated a stone's throw from the Town Hall at the beginning of Thornton Road, had been developed from a former warehouse and was most luxuriously appointed. It was claimed that the Turkish carpets in its Grand Café were those used on the Royal Yacht, which had taken the King and Queen to the Delhi Durbar in 1911. In the basement were a billiard hall and the control centre for the central heating and air-conditioning systems. The Picture House claimed to be 'The world's Premier Pictures with elegance, refinement and comfort. Latest

The exterior of the Picture House belies the magnificence of the interior. The name 'Forum' was added in the 1920s.

flicker-free apparatus installed.' The silent films were accompanied by a small orchestra.

While many cinemas occupied old, converted premises, the Regent Picture Theatre was purpose-built. Standing at the city end of Manningham Lane it was a magnificent building. Clad in white faience tiles it stood four storeys high and was described as 'French Classical' in style. Its interior was equally magnificent with sweeping marble staircases and pillars, gentlemen's smoking room and top-floor Winter Garden where luncheons and teas were available. The Regent was opened by the Lord Mayor on 30 September 1914 and the Grand Patriotic Concert which followed was attended by Sir William Priestley MP, Sir Arthur and Lady Godwin and the Belgian Consul, Henry E. Gerhartz. The Bradford Musical Union, the Yorkshire Military Band and the Bradford Bohemian Dramatic Club were among the groups providing entertainment. In his speech, Sir William Priestley spoke of the war and 'trusted that when better times come the Regent will continue to be a real home of culture'.

The Palace and Empire theatres provided music hall entertainment which was at the height of its popularity before 1914. The Empire, standing almost opposite the Alhambra Theatre, was thought to provide rather better quality acts than its rival the Palace. Artists performing there included W.C. Fields, Marie Lloyd, Little Tich and a young Charlie Chaplin.

The Theatre Royal on Manningham Lane, a favourite haunt of the young J.B. Priestley, whose early writing included reviews of productions at this venue.

Opened in 1899, the Empire Theatre held daily concerts given by the All-Ladies Orchestra of Miss Gabrielle Hope and visitors could also take refreshment in the Moorish Tea Rooms and Lounge. After twenty years of stage entertainment, it reopened as the Empire Picture House in February 1918. It began with a screening of *Sweetheart of the Doomed* starring Louise Glaum but just how many sweethearts of doomed young men of Bradford saw the film is not recorded. It could be seen as an insensitive title for those last months of the war but the supporting 'comedies and dramas' on the programme might have provided some relief from the wartime gloom.

In Manningham Lane was the Theatre Royal, the place for serious drama. It was here that Henry Irving made his last appearance. On Friday 13 October 1905 he was taken ill on stage and died in the foyer of the Midland Hotel. A regular audience member at the Theatre Royal was the young J.B. Priestley who wrote reviews of the plays for the *Bradford Pioneer* (the newspaper of the Independent Labour Party). Later, Priestley was to write about standing in the queue for the Theatre Royal, a description which must have reflected the feelings of many a Bradfordian eager to be transported from the everyday to the fantastical world of the stage:

In those days actors looked like actors. . . . There was no mistaking them for wool merchants, shipping clerks and deacons of Baptist Chapels. . . they swept past us, fantastically overcoated, with trilbies perched raffishly on brilliantined curls, talking of incredible matters in high tones . . . vanished through the stage door, to reappear, but out of all recognition, in wigs and knee breeches.[5]

'GERMAN AMBASSADOR PRINCE LICHNOWSKY GUEST OF BRADFORD CHAMBER OF COMMERCE'

The importance of the Chamber of Commerce in a manufacturing city such as Bradford cannot be overestimated. Many Bradford companies were mutually dependent and even rival firms shared common interests, which served to make the chamber a well-subscribed, much-respected body. In other chapters of this book there will be a closer examination of the work of the Chamber of Commerce and also the significant role played by members of Bradford's German community in maintaining the economic importance of the city on an international platform. The presence of Prince Lichnowsky[6] is further evidence of the influence which German merchants could wield in drawing international figures to the city.

'PRINCESS REFUSES TO PAY HER DOG LICENCES'

The princess in question was Princess Sophia Duleep Singh,[7] a godchild of Queen Victoria who was a leading light in the women's suffrage movement and made several court appearances in this connection. During the war she organised patriotic flag days for Punjabi troops in London and visited wounded Indian soldiers in Brighton Pavilion, obliging some of them with signed photographs of 'Maharajah Ranjit Singh's grand-daughter'. Why she should be in Bradford with her dogs is not known but in April 1914[8] Bradford Moor golf course had been damaged by suffragettes and in May 1914 a militant attempted to blow up a reservoir near Dewsbury. Maggie Newbery[9] recalls the Suffragette Movement having a meeting room on Manningham Lane:

> Whenever we were passing, if there were signs of activity there, we would walk very quietly up to the door, open it quickly and all yell together, 'Votes for women' in a derisory way. It was one way of letting off steam.

Bradford newspapers covered a wide range of national and international stories during the war years. One was about Irish Home Rule, which was of great interest to Bradford's many Irish immigrants. In a speech in St George's Hall, Bradford, in 1914 Winston Churchill, the First Lord of the Admiralty, reiterated his previous statement that he would never coerce Ulster to come under a Dublin Parliament but would do all that was necessary to prevent Ulster stopping the rest of Ireland having the parliament they desired. He went on to say, 'I believed this was sound and right and, in support of it, I was certainly prepared to maintain the authority of the Crown and Parliament by whatever means were necessary.' By 18 September 1914 Home Rule became law with the Protestants of Ulster poised to defend themselves against integration into a United Ireland.

A correspondent of the *Bradford Observer* even considered, wrongly as it transpired, that one good thing about the coming of war was that the troubles would be shelved for the duration. Later in the war the Easter Rising of April 1916 and its bloody aftermath were reported in detail in the Bradford papers. Despite this turbulent background, the memorial to the men of the 36th (Ulster) Division commemorates both the Protestants and the Catholics who died on the Somme in 1916.

Bradfordians were also able to follow the other big stories of 1914 to 1916 – for example the Shackleton and Mawson expeditions to Antarctica were full of derring-do. Sir Douglas Mawson's Australasian[10] expedition successfully claimed 2.5 million square miles of Antarctica for Australia. Mawson was born in Shipley in 1882 but lived in Australia from boyhood. He had previously been a member of Scott's Antarctic expedition. Mawson departed from Hobart on the *Aurora* on 11 December 1911 but his 'adventure' saw him endure dramatic hardships: the dog team was eaten one by one and when his surviving companion, Dr Mertz, died, Mawson was left to struggle on alone. He eventually reached his base camp in February 1913. It was a year later before the party was able to sail into Gulf St Vincent on 26 February 1914.

Visitors to Bradford from overseas were reported by the papers. For example, there was 'a large audience' at the Wesleyan Room for a lecture on sleeping sickness in Rhodesia, and a visit from a Ugandan Chief in May was avidly reported. Reports of civic visits by members of the German aristocracy (many of them Queen Victoria's relatives) and pictures of St Petersburg and Berlin in the snow were also published.

As soon as war was declared the young men of Bradford swarmed to recruiting stations at the Mechanics' Institute and at Bradford Moor and Belle Vue Barracks. The jobs they left behind were not vacant for long. Women came forward to do work of all kinds. In *The Garnett Story*[11] E.P. Dobson writes:

> For the first time in history, women played a great part in wartime production . . . the firm was able to rely on women and girls who were direct inheritors of the woollen and worsted tradition . . . they understood their menfolks' pride in producing 'a bit of right good stuff'.

Some managers expressed surprise that the women 'were as skilled and diligent' as the men they were replacing. At Garnett's normal production ceased abruptly in August 1914 and the automatic looms installed in 1913 went over to the production of Service Cloths to meet Army contracts.

As the war went on, the local papers inevitably carried news of casualties in stark contrast to the news of military achievements printed alongside. The casualty lists were particularly lengthy in July and August 1916 after the Battle of the Somme. Of the 2,000 men in the two Pals Regiments, only 223 survived the battle and Bradford newspapers made very sombre reading. These were not the only regiments losing men in large numbers. The age profile of serving men would suggest that each one predeceased his parents and many would also have been young married men, leaving a widow and possibly children. Sons-in-law, grandsons, brothers, nephews, cousins, neighbours, work colleagues and members of church congregations and sports clubs represented a network of grief which would have affected every family in the city.

Writing in 1933, J.B. Priestley reflected on the loss to the City of Bradford wrought by the war years. While speaking of his sense of personal loss Priestley must also have reflected the feelings of the whole of his generation of Bradfordians:

There are great gaps in my acquaintance now; and I find it difficult to swap reminiscences of boyhood. 'The men who were boys when I was a boy' the poet chants; but the men who were boys when I was a boy are dead. Indeed they never even grew to be men. They were slaughtered in youth; and the parents of them have gone lonely, the girls they would have married have grown grey in spinsterhood, and the work they would have done has remained undone.[12]

Notes

1   See www.webmatters.net/france/ww1_bells_redoubt
2   See www.members.tripod.com/~midgley/midgleyana. This site also has a photograph of the memorial to Donald Bell. It stands on the Mametz road out of Contalmaison and was unveiled on Sunday 9 July 2000, the day before the 84th anniversary of Bell's death, which occurred a few metres from where the memorial stands
3   For a description of the heady atmosphere of the Bradford Theatre Royal see P. Holdsworth's *The Rebel Tyke: Bradford and J.B. Priestley* (Bradford Library, 1994)
4   See Colin Sutton's excellent illustrated account of Bradford cinemas at www.kingsdr.demon.co.uk/ Cinemas/tattler.htm
5   J.B. Priestley, *English Journey*, William Heinemann, London, 1934
6   Prince Lichnowski was German Ambassador in London. His memoirs, 1912–1914 can be read at: www.lib.byu.edu/wwi/1914m/lichnowy.html and provide interesting insights into his anglophile stance
7   Christy Campbell, *The Maharajah's Box*, Harper Collins, 2000
8   See www.bradfordtimeline.freeserve.co.uk
9   Maggie Newbery, *Reminiscences of a Bradford Mill Girl 1980*, City of Bradford Metropolitan Council Libraries Division
10 See www.south-pole.com and www.mawson.sa.gov.au/ie.htm
11 E. Philip Dobson, *The Garnett Story*, William Sessions and Co., York
12 J.B. Priestley, *English Journey*, William Heinemann, London, 1934

TWO

Merchants, Hawkers & Tingalarys

Tricia Platts

The population of today's Bradford is a rich ethnic mix with a particularly strong representation from Asia. However, workers from Pakistan and India only started arriving in significant numbers after the Second World War and were barely present in the city in 1914. Throughout the nineteenth century the population of Britain was increased by the migration of peoples from all over the world. Victorian Bradford with its booming economy and promise of employment, even wealth, became the destination of Europeans as well as men and women from countries of the Empire. Thus Bradford has a long history of welcoming overseas workers who all played a part in the city's increasing prosperity.

Postmarked Bradford and sent to Switzerland this rare card could have been penned by Delius Senior himself. The order for cloth which it carries is in a mix of German and English.

In the earlier part of the nineteenth century, the rapidly expanding mills of Bradford attracted hundreds of workers from Ireland. By 1851, 8 per cent of Bradford's population was Irish: 8,700 in a total population of 103,800. This was a higher figure than any other West Yorkshire town and with a higher proportion working in wool manufacturing: 26 per cent in Bradford compared with 23 per cent in Leeds, 8 per cent in Sheffield and 6 per cent in Dewsbury. Manchester Road in Bradford became known as 'the Irish Channel'.

The census enumerators' manuscripts[1] and the 1851 census[2] show the valuable part these workers played in the success of the city's emerging industries. However, the pattern of employment also indicates the relatively weak economic position of the Irish immigrants. For example, there was an above average proportion of Irish workers in stuff, woollen and worsted manufacturing but fewer Irish were shopkeepers. Many more charwomen and washerwomen were Irish but fewer Irishmen were building craftsmen. Positions in commerce, local government, the police, banking and finance and skilled crafts were rarely held by Irish workers, but the Irish community produced eight times more hawkers and pedlars and six times more general labourers than the average for the city. A partial explanation can be found in the extremes of poverty and literacy from which the Irish nation as a whole had suffered. The Census of Ireland of 1841[3] reveals the proportion of the population who could neither read nor write to be 43 per cent. The figure was higher in the western counties, rising to 79 per cent in County Mayo.

By the turn of the century some of these discrepancies had been adjusted. Children of Irish workers had been included in the Bradford school system for fifty years or more, and would have benefited from the introduction of school meals, health checks and improved housing conditions. Names on the 1914 enlistment rolls of Bradford regiments include many of Irish origin and the occupation listed for each man shows how employment patterns were changing: Conroy (seal finisher), Hogan (insurance agent), McConnell (draper), McCormack (clerk), McCully (horse driver), McMann (tailor), O'Brien (commission agent), O'Connor (packing case maker), O'Donnell (dyer's labourer), O'Neill (dyer's labourer), O'Sullivan (French master).

There are also many names of Irish origin among those killed in the Great War, including Thomas Moroney (killed in action 3/5/1917), Cpl George McCormack (killed in action 3/5/1917), John McMahon (killed in action 1/7/1916). Private Bernard Coyne of the 1/6th Battalion, West Yorkshire Regiment, the Bradford Territorials, was the grandfather of Bradford World War I Group member Patricia Featherstone (see Chapter 9).

Bernard Coyne was born in 1878 in Castlereagh, Ballinlough, County Roscommon. He was one of seven children. Two of Bernard's older brothers settled in England, Martin in Liverpool and John in Halifax where Bernard joined him in 1900. In 1906 Bernard was

The gravestone of Pte B. Coyne in Mill Road Cemetery, Thiepval. 4592 Bernard Coyne of the 6th Battalion, West Yorkshire Regiment (Prince of Wales's Own) died on 1 July 1916.

married in St Mary's Church, East Parade, Bradford, to an Irish girl from County Leix. Bernard worked as a gas fitter until 1915 when, at the age of thirty-seven, he enlisted in the 1/6 Battalion of the West Yorkshire Regiment.

Bernard was trained as a bomber: older men with steadier nerves were often selected for this most dangerous of tasks. Bernard was killed on the first day of the Somme and buried in Mill Road cemetery. His wife and three daughters were visiting family in Ireland at the time of his death and, because of peculiarities in the Army pension system, she received no pension. The family still does not know why the pension was denied, but Bernard's widow, Anne, worked as a cook at the Ear and Eye Hospital until she reached the age of seventy-four and was crippled with arthritis. Bernard's name appears on the war memorial inside St Mary's Church where the last Mass prior to closure was celebrated in November 2006.

Two groups of European migrants began arriving in Bradford almost simultaneously, from Germany and Italy. There were many 'dried-up' villages, particularly in northern Italy, so-called because a lack of work and opportunity for advancement led to the population draining away. Frederick Taglione[4] names Joseph Cadamateri as probably the first Italian immigrant to Bradford. He arrived as an eighteen-year-old in 1865 and, rather than finding millwork, he bought a handcart, made ice cream and sold it on the streets. From this lowly beginning he built up Caddy's Ice Creams, which was still going strong in Dewsbury 133 years later. As a result of his success, Joseph was able to set up in business each one of his fourteen children!

Between 1876 and 1920 several hundred Italians arrived in Bradford from Milan, Turin, Naples, Rome and Florence. Names in the city took on a continental flavour: Mollicone, Sinicola, Duce, Tenzio, Cappavani, Donatelli, Verrechi, Minchella, Steffanuti'a and Romani among others. By 1920 there were two Italian Consulates in the city, one on Canal Road and the other on Manningham Lane.

Many Italians worked in textiles, iron foundries and on the railways but others demonstrated a more entrepreneurial spirit. On North Wing (behind the Cathedral) Carlo and Madeleine Duce had a fleet of barrel organs, known as Tingalarys. Tomasso re-tuned barrel organs and also updated the repertoire by installing new tunes. Tenzio, on Paper Hall Street, ran a successful business in repairing and reconditioning these machines, making a living sufficient to bring up a family of nine children.

Other small businesses included Chicona's savoury shop on Cavalier Street. Chicona was able to purchase a return train ticket from Bradford to Rome for £5 and travelled regularly to replenish his stock of Italian delicacies. In Otley Road was a shop owned by Montilano, a chef from Milan. He sold pasta, macaroni, spaghetti and special sauces. Montilano came into his own when employed by the Midland Hotel for a week to prepare meals for trade delegations of Italian and German wool buyers and architects. He served up to 150 meals each day but seemed content to return to his shop afterwards.

As a young man, Angelo Taglione hired a barrel organ complete with two monkeys from Carlo and Madeleine Duce. He pushed this from Carlo's yard on North Wing, down Church Bank to Peckover Street in Little Germany. On other

A typical tingalary with its monkeys and Italian attendants. For a few pence the crowd would be entertained with popular tunes of the day.

days he hired a Caddy's ice-cream cart. Whatever his takings, he handed over 10 per cent as the hire fee. After marrying Rosaria Donatelli at St Mary's Church in 1890 he settled down to more permanent work and raised four sons: Anthony was born in 1892, Nicholas in 1897, Cisino in 1899 and John in 1901. All four sons served in the Great War and survived, although John was disabled by his wounds. Cisino enlisted with the King's Own Yorkshire Light Infantry and in 1918 was serving as a translator in Italy.

Some Italian architects were involved in the design of buildings in Little Germany and the Italian Gothic style is still visible. Law Russell House in Vicar Lane is a good example. In addition, Bradford stone became a desirable building material and hundreds of tons were exported to Italy between 1830 and 1860.

In parallel with the Italians came an influx of German migrants who were to become some of the city's most successful merchants. An early pioneer was Jacob Behrens who arrived in Bradford from Hamburg in 1832. By 1845 the names Behrens, Mayer, Hertz and Schlesinger were established in Little Germany. By 1902, thirty-one out of sixty-three piece merchants were of German origin and the proportion of yarn merchants was even higher: twenty-one out of thirty-six.[5] These German merchants

The plain interior of the German Church which still stands on the corner of Great Horton Road and Chester Street.

built fine villas for themselves in Heidelberg Road, Bonn Street and Mannheim Road. The *Yorkshire Observer* goes on to describe the role played by these merchants:

> Their great forte was not a technical one. They knew very little about the manufacturing side of the industry, but they allied their powers as salesmen to the prowess of their Yorkshire colleagues as craftsmen and between them Bradford captured the markets of the world.

The German (Protestant) Church was established in 1882 and a building was consecrated in 1877 on the corner of Great Horton Road and Chester Street. A synagogue was built in 1880. In 1889 two Jewish congregations amalgamated.

During the first thirty years of the Bradford Chamber of Commerce over one quarter of its 200 subscribers were foreign merchants, the vast majority of these German. In 1894 Charles Semon became Lord Mayor of the City and Jacob Moser held this position in 1910–11.

Other famous Bradfordians of German descent include the composer Frederick Delius (1862–1934), the son of Julius Delius, a successful wool merchant who had moved from Bielefeld to Bradford with his wife Elise. Frederick was the fourth of fourteen children. It was a musical home and the composer later wrote, 'My father loved music intensely and used to tinker on the piano when he knew he was alone. He was a great concert-goer and he often had chamber music in his house.'

A postcard illustrating the self-portrait of William Rothenstein which hangs in Cartwright Hall Gallery.

The 'English' portrait artist Sir William Rothenstein was born in Bradford in 1872. Like Delius, Rothenstein was also the son of a Bradford wool merchant, Moritz Rothenstein, who came to England from Hanover in 1859. At the age of sixteen he studied at the Slade School in London after which he spent four years in Paris. He returned to England in 1893. Rothenstein later became professor of civic art at the University of Sheffield, principal of the Royal College of Art, a trustee of the Tate Gallery, and a member of the Royal Fine Art Commission.

Despite being a patriotic Englishman, Rothenstein's German name and accent made him unpopular in the Gloucestershire village where he lived during the Great War. Charles Masterman, the head of the government's War Propaganda Bureau, offered him a position as an official war artist, which Rothenstein quickly accepted.

Humbert Wolfe[6] was brought up in Bradford. After gaining a first at Oxford University he worked for the Civil Service. He began publishing poetry in the 1920s and his 'Requiem' (1927) on the Great War was highly acclaimed. On the death of Robert Bridges in 1930, Wolfe was one of the favourites to become Poet Laureate. During the Great War Wolfe wrote one of his most poignant poems, 'Requiem: The Soldier' (1916). It begins: 'Down some cold field in a world unspoken the young men are walking together, slim and tall.' We quickly realise that the young men he speaks of are already dead but, from beyond the grave, they are questioning 'What have they done with the lives we laid aside?'[7]

From the turn of the century there had been some growth in anti-German feeling at a national level and popular novels had to some extent fuelled this. For example, Erskine Childers' *The Riddle of the Sands* (1905) predicted a German invasion but the 'romantic' German spy, wearing lederhosen, was an unbelievable stereotype to Bradfordians: their view was exactly the contrary. Justices of the Peace, a Lord Lieutenant and school benefactors were the public face of Bradford's German citizens.

A postcard showing Esholt village. The reverse is shown below. Who were Clarence and Herbert?

meanwhile we are keeping everything going on at home in just the same way as far as is possible. We are all having to make sacrifices in one way or another, but we are not down hearted and will "stick it" to the bitter end, and make more sacrifices if necessary. We must and shall win. Well, must say good-bye for the present. The best of jolly good luck to you lad! From Yours sincerely

Herbert Shackleton.

Dear Clarence, I must apologize for being so late in wishing you A Happy New Year as we both do most heartily. It is our busy season and we are busier than we have ever been before. We are not sure of your address until we hear from you & so are too late to wish you a Merry Christmas, but hope you had one, and that you enjoy good health and are doing well every way. Thought you might like a p.c. of Esholt. I see it was printed in Germany but was imported before the war, so it wont make any difference. We shall have to boycott German goods after this as far as possible. The mills round here are all busy making khaki for soldiers uniforms, army blankets, etc. expect we shall be sending a new army, raised since the war (over a million at least) to the front in a month or two

This revealing message on the reverse of a 1915 postcard of Esholt village is a more usual view of all things German as seen by a Bradfordian. It reads:

Dear Clarence

I must apologise for being so late in wishing you A Happy New Year as we both do most heartily. It is our busy season and we are busier than we have ever been before. We are not sure of your address until we hear from you and so are too late to wish you A Merry Christmas, but hope you had one, and that you enjoy good health and are doing well every way.

   Thought you might like a p.c. of Esholt. I see it was printed in Germany but was imported before the war, so it won't make any difference. We shall have to boycott German goods after this as far as possible. The mills round here are all busy making khaki for soldiers uniforms, Army blankets etc. Expect we shall be sending a new army, raised since the war (over a million at least) to the front in a month or so. Meanwhile we are keeping everything going on at home in just the same way as far as is possible. We are all having to make sacrifices in one way or another but are not downhearted and will 'stick it' to the bitter end, and make more sacrifices if necessary. We must and shall win. Well, must say Goodbye for the present. The best of jolly good luck to you lad!

From yours sincerely, Herbert Shackleton

It is clear that the German population of Bradford made an exceptionally rich contribution to the commercial, cultural and civic life of the city during more than sixty years of expansion and development. They had become some of the city's most enlightened employers, prominent philanthropists and civic personalities. In 1913 the newly appointed parish priest of St Mary's Catholic Church was German-born Edwin Schreiber. Throughout the war he was regarded as an alien by the civic authorities despite the outstanding pastoral work which he undertook. When Canon Schreiber became ill in 1939 he returned to his home in Bavaria to recuperate.[8] The outbreak of war prevented his return to Bradford and he died in his homeland in 1944.

   However, when war was declared in August 1914 Germans became the enemy and, inevitably, attitudes changed and respected citizens became aliens overnight. The swimming baths complex in Morley Street/Great Horton Road, originally called the Kursaal, changed its name to become the more patriotic Windsor Halls comprising Kings and Queens Halls.

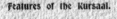

Features of the Kursaal.

THE KURSAAL comprises the King's Hall and the various baths, opened in 1905, and the Queen's Hall with the Saloon completed in 1914.

THE KING'S HALL contains the large swimming pond, which is emptied in Winter and covered with a spring floor for dancing, and the Hall, thus converted, is much resorted to for various public functions. Around the Hall are balconies and galleries. In premises leading from the Hall are various complete and up-to-date medicated, electric, Turkish, Russian and slipper baths, which are approached by entrances quite separated and shut off from the King's Hall.

The interior of the new QUEEN'S HALL comprises an area and a balcony in which there is accommodation for between 500 and 600 persons. There is a fully equipped stage and artiste retiring rooms and the Hall is adapted for use for concerts, public meetings, bazaars, banquets and other functions. The area is provided with a spring floor capable of being set to any degree of elasticity, and the balcony can be converted into a continuous promenade or may be utilised for banquets as well as the area. Leading from the area and the balcony there are cafés, smoke rooms and lounges. At the top of the building is a kitchen in which the latest electrical cooking appliances have been installed. The whole of the premises have been harmoniously decorated. An addition to the Queen's Hall is a SALOON which can also be utilised for various functions.

The souvenir programme marking the opening of the Kursaal, later to become the Windsor baths.

Maggie Newbery[9] recalls how quickly the uglier aspects of war appeared:

> Gangs of hooligans went and broke windows of shops owned by Germans. These shopkeepers were in the main good honest people who had served us well with their pork shops and delicatessens. Some had omitted to get naturalised and were taken away to internment camps. We had quite a lot of Germans in Bradford who had worked hard for the good of the city, but all came under suspicion and were looked upon as possible spies.

On 5 August 1914 the *Yorkshire Observer* reported on the departure of German reservists:

> During the weekend quite a number of young Germans residing in Bradford left the city in order to rejoin their regiments. Yesterday about 30 departed for London on the 2.15 p.m. train. They were seen off by friends and the German Pastor.

A German band played at the station, which was not popular. The paper went on to describe several other parties of departing Germans hoping to serve with the colours, 'if they are allowed to leave England'.

By 8 August the first man suspected of espionage was marched away, and by 10 August over twenty ethnic Germans had been taken to the new military prison at Bradford Moor Barracks. However, on 20 August the *Yorkshire Observer* reported on the departure from Forster Square station of four naturalised Germans who would serve as British Army officers: Muller, Hamlin, J. von Halle and F.N. Bernhardt. A party of dignitaries including the Lord Mayor, the Chief Constable and Colonel Hoffman saw them off. The first named of these officers, Captain Muller, was to die on the Marne on 28 July 1918. He was the son of Colonel G.H. Muller, who commanded the first Bradford Pals Regiment. Officers in the first Bradford Pals Regiment included the Hoffman brothers, sons of Frank Hoffman of Bradford.

The 1914 Aliens (Restrictions) Act was intended to prevent German spies infiltrating the state. It required the ethnic German population of Bradford to register with the authorities. Approximately 300 out of the estimated German population of 500 registered their names, addresses, ages and occupations. They were restricted in where they could travel and had to report regularly. Under the Act, the deportation of aliens was permitted.

In addition to these national provisions there were many instances of steps taken against aliens by local organisations. The Bradford Club's premises in Bank Street were originally built in 1865 by Thomas Williamson for the Union Club, which had been founded in 1857 by German immigrants and immediately attracted many of the principal merchants and manufacturers in the area. Its aim was to provide 'the advantages of a newsroom and an hotel with most of the comforts of a private residence for gentlemen of the town'. The club's newsroom had low armchairs, newspapers and periodicals.

The imposing doorway to the Bradford Club in Bank Street. An important meeting point for the merchants of Bradford, the club premises were close to the Wool Exchange.

The Union Club[10] held an Extraordinary Meeting on 4 September 1914 and resolved to affix the following to the notice board:

> that no subject of an Alien Country at war with England is eligible to use the Club either as a member or visitor.

At another Extraordinary Meeting in May 1915 the committee resolved that 'in response to a numerously signed requisition to the Committee, all Members who are of German or Austrian birth, although they may be naturalised British subjects, be requested to discontinue their use of the Club'.

On 29 November 1915 yet more action was proposed in the form of an Extraordinary Meeting to be held on 9 December at 5.30 p.m. for the purpose of considering:

> the future position of those members of the Club who are of German or Austrian birth and passing any resolution which may be deemed necessary.

This meeting was never held as the members affected voluntarily resigned. (It should be noted that the first President of the Club, whose portrait hung in the entrance, was Mr Sussman.) The club also took steps to ensure the welfare of its employees who volunteered for war service. At a previous Extraordinary Meeting held on 4 September 1914 it was resolved that a gratuity of £3 be given to each member of staff who volunteered for service at the Front, and in the case of the Head Waiter, an allowance of 10s per week be made to his wife, and 2s 6d per week be allowed to the father of the Junior Dining Room Waiter and that all the situations be kept open. On 16 November a Committee Meeting resolved that all members on active service remain members without payment of subscription until such time as they cease to be on active service.

An extract from the Suggestions Book of 26 May 1915 reveals that a member had taken offence at reports in the press. He suggested

> That the Club ceases to take in any publications controlled by the Harmsworth Press including The Times.

The Committee 'carefully considered the matter' but could not see their way to make the alteration suggested.

There were spasmodic outbreaks of anti-German feeling in many workplaces, along with acts of vandalism. The shop of a German pork butcher in Keighley had its windows broken and the *Yorkshire Observer* of 31 August reported more broken windows and a case of arson. This arose during a strike in a local engineering works, combined with drunkenness in a group of fervently patriotic Irish workers. This rioting was more widely targeted as the courthouse was attacked, as was the owner of the engineering works. No-one was injured but the riot leaders were punished harshly.

After the sinking of the *Lusitania* in April 1916, anti-German feeling entered a new phase. For example, women at Lister's Manningham Mills refused to work with German colleagues, who were promptly sacked. The expediency arising from a full order book outweighed the necessity for any kind of legal process.

The *Bradford Pioneer* (issued under the auspices of Bradford Independent Labour Party) reported on the anti-German actions of two city councillors: Alderman Fawcett and Alderman Johnson. These two men were said to believe that even naturalised Germans were traitors by definition: they had betrayed the country of their birth by leaving it. The Aldermen expressed their views with 'middle class eloquence' and the *Pioneer* reported that Fawcett had successfully secured the dismissal of three German-born council employees. The fervour with which Alderman Johnson went about his anti-German campaign was described by the *Pioneer* as making 'Prussianism look mild and harmless'. The Bradford Co-operative Society was persuaded to dismiss four pork butchers, and three workers were dismissed from the Council Sewage Department 'for being German'. It was clear that none of the sacked workers had much prospect of future employment.

The Socialists, through the *Bradford Pioneer*, were consistent in their defence of the rights of ethnic Germans in Bradford. Their vociferous spokesman was William Leach, an Independent Labour Party member. Under the headline 'What Germany has done for Bradford' he wrote:

> Germany's vilest militarism can be forgiven for it is a temporary aberration. I shall not hate Germans. I shall continue to like them, to respect them and to be glad I know so many of them. The German waiters, pork butchers, musicians, chemists, electricity experts, doctors, teachers and the like have served Bradford exceedingly well.[11]

As editor of the *Bradford Pioneer* Leach's voice was not widely heard, as distribution of the paper was limited. When the paper appealed to the readership for financial help to relieve the plight of needy individuals, the response was a measly £3 8s from only twenty-three readers.

Major injustices were matched by minor pettiness. German bands were banned from playing in public parks, German language classes were removed from schools and street names were changed. The Bradford Chamber of Commerce was more pragmatic in its appeal to common sense and humanity. For example, it defended the principle of its members selling off stocks of German and Austrian Christmas cards. After all, not selling them would cost good brass.

Around 139 German residents in Bradford escaped internment. Some anglicised their names (following the example of the royal family) and others kept a low profile for the duration of the war. Inevitably, but sadly, the harmonious relationship between ethnic Germans and ethnic Bradfordians became another casualty of war.

Notes

1   Census of Great Britain 1851, Population Tables, Vol. II Part 2
2   Census enumerators' manuscript returns for Bradford, 1851
3   Census of Ireland 1841, Table of Education
4   Frederick Taglione, *Bradford Italians – The True Story*, available in Bradford City Library
5   The *Yorkshire Observer*, special supplement to mark the centenary of Sir Jacob Behrens & Sons, December 1934
6   See P. Bagguley, *Harlequin in Whitehall – a Life of Humbert Wolfe, Poet and Civil Servant 1885–1940* (1997)
7   Humbert Wolfe, *Requiem: The Soldier* (1916):

> Down some cold field in a world outspoken
> the young men are walking together, slim and tall,
> and though they laugh to one another, silence is not broken;
> there is no sound however clear they call.
>
> They are speaking together of what they loved in vain here,
> but the air is too thin to carry the things they say.
> They were young and golden, but they came on pain here,
> and their youth is age now, their gold is grey.
>
> Yet their hearts are not changed, and they cry to one another,
> 'What have they done with the lives we laid aside?
> Are they young with our youth, gold with our gold, my brother?
> Do they smile in the face of death, because we died?'
>
> Down some cold field in a world uncharted
> the young seek each other with questioning eyes.
> They question each other, the young, the golden hearted,
> of the world that they were robbed of in their quiet paradise.

8   P. Grogan, *A History of St Mary's Roman Catholic Church, Bradford*, 1975
9   Maggie Newbery, *Reminiscences of a Bradford Mill Girl*, City of Bradford Metropolitan Council Libraries Division, 1980
10   C. Neville Packett, *The Bradford Club: A Brief History*, published by The Bradford Club, 1986. Copy held by Mechanics' Institute Library
11   *Bradford Daily Argus*, 4 April 1916

THREE

Bradford's Fighting Men

Gerry Beevers, Tricia Platts, Geoff Barker & Joyce Appleby

This chapter will concentrate on men who served with local Territorial Forces and those who volunteered for the New Army, although the 'regulars' will not be ignored. Citizens of Bradford fought in a surprisingly wide range of Army units during the war and it is useful to have a brief summary of how the Army was structured in order to understand why this was so. Before 1914 Britain's traditional armed strength lay in its navy while the Army was small in comparison to those of other European states. The British Army was divided into three main branches:

- The Regular Army of volunteer recruits: professional soldiers numbering some 247,500 fighting men
- The County Militias: a 'throwback' to a county style of life in rural Britain
- The Territorial Forces of part-time volunteer soldiers for service within the UK

By 1914 the soldiers of the militias had virtually all been absorbed into the National Reserve and were categorised according to their age (which was often in the range 40 to 55) and medical fitness. In 1914 the National Reserve was formed into Protection Companies, which were attached to Territorial Forces and were deployed in guarding railways and other vulnerable points in Britain. They were termed Supernumerary Companies in March 1915 but in July 1915 there was a trawl of these to identify men who were capable of marching ten miles carrying a rifle and 150 rounds of ammunition. The men were then divided among Service and Provisional Battalions and the Rifle Brigades of the Territorials. Some were sent to Egypt and India to replace Territorials who were moved to the Dardanelles and Middle East.

On the outbreak of war, all reservists who were surplus to the needs of regular battalions were posted to the Special Reserves (numbering about 64,000) which, in most regiments, was their Third Battalion, thus swelling the numbers in regular units.

The British Army had performed relatively poorly in the South African War and before 1914 and after a strategic rethink prompted by the growing threat of war in Europe, the Army planned an Expeditionary Force of six infantry divisions which would be capable of speedy deployment and mobility in a theatre of war. Secret talks with the French identified that it was most likely that Germany would attack France. In this case the BEF would become a small adjunct to the left flank of the mighty French army. It has been pointed out that 'the British force would be no bigger (if perhaps with greater promise) than the Belgian army'.[1]

Immediately before the declaration of war on 4 August the British government had become genuinely anxious about a German invasion and therefore two infantry divisions remained in England to protect the coast. Mobilisation of the other four divisions and transfer of men and equipment to France proceeded faultlessly and first encountered the enemy at Mons on 23 August 1914. The 4th Division crossed to France some days later in time to join the defence of Le Cateau and the 6th Division joined the Expeditionary Force in the advance to the Aisne. These six Divisions were joined by a seventh before the defence of Antwerp in October. This 7th Division was made up of regular battalions which had previously been deployed across the Empire and were ordered to return on the outbreak of war. All members of this combined force who saw action before 22 November 1914 derive their famous title from the Kaiser's Order of the Day:

> It is my Royal and Imperial Command that you concentrate your energies for the immediate present upon one single purpose and that is that you address all your skill and all the valour of my soldiers to exterminate first the treacherous English; walk over General French's contemptible little army!

Thus were born the Old Contemptibles and among them were many Bradford men. Their stories serve to illustrate what could happen. Lance Corporal Joseph Hill's home was at 239 Exeter Street, Otley Road, Bradford. For six years he had been a regular in the King's Own Royal Regiment which formed part of the BEF in August 1914. The story of his wounds and hospitalisation will be told in Chapter 4. Sergeant Major William Booth came from Idle and was a regular soldier with the King's Own Yorkshire Light Infantry (the KOYLIs). Within twenty-two days of the outbreak of war, Sergeant Major Booth was taken prisoner by the Germans, remaining in their hands until February 1918 when he was placed in internment in Holland. He told his story to the *Shipley Times and Express* in November 1918.

A regular with the KOYLIs, Sgt-Maj William Booth of Idle was held by the Germans from 26 August 1914 until February 1918 and suffered some extremely harsh conditions.

The 2nd Battalion of the KOYLIs had been in Dublin on 4 August 1914 but they were quickly moved to Bavay in France. On Saturday 22 August they moved up to Mons where Sergeant Major Booth was billeted in a brewery. His regiment formed part of the 13th Brigade with the King's Own Scottish Borderers, the East Surrey Regiment, and the Duke of Wellington's (West Riding) Regiment. The following morning the Brigade proceeded into action with the Dukes and KOYLIs acting as support to the KOSB and East Surreys in the front line. 2nd Lieutenant John Pepys became almost the first casualty when he was shot through the head and killed. Other men fell rapidly and it was quickly realised that the British troops were hopelessly outclassed in machinegun capability.

Sergeant Major Booth was involved in action continuously for the next four days. On Wednesday 26 August he and his company were captured by the enemy. Numbers were considerably depleted by the fighting and the total captured was only thirty-seven, consisting of thirty-four other ranks and two officers other than Sergeant Major Booth. However, when other prisoners were rounded up the total number rose to eighty-two (some of whom had been wounded) out of the force of 207 on the morning of the action.

The distinctive lapel badge of the KOYLI regiments with a white rose of Yorkshire in the centre.

Sergeant Major Booth's description of life in captivity is one of hardship and bad treatment. From the battlefield the men were taken first to a farmyard and then to a church in Le Cateau for their first night in captivity. The following day they were marched under escort to Mons where they entrained for Paderborn in Germany. Their captors provided no food and the prisoners were glad of the Belgian and French women who gave what they could. Booth reports one German soldier giving five prisoners a dry loaf of black bread to share which they found delicious, so hungry were they.

The prison camp at Paderborn amounted to an open, sandy enclosure where there were already several French prisoners as well as British, in total between 2,000 and 3,000 men. Booth's clothing was ragged and there were no replacements but this was almost the least of the difficulties. The prisoners lived outdoors. They slept on, or under, straw, had no soap or water and lived with filth, lice and vermin. The German captors put private soldiers to work. Non-commissioned officers regarded themselves as responsible for their men but, invoking the Hague Convention, exempted themselves from manual labour. The Germans reviled them for this.

In March 1916 the prisoners were moved to Minden where, for the first time, they slept on beds. After four months Sergeant Major Booth and the other warrant officers were moved to Soltan where they remained until 6 February 1918 when they were passed to the British Red Cross Society in Holland. Booth described their joy: 'Those sweet voices in the good old English language were veritable music.' Food now included sandwiches, sweet cakes, chocolate and tea! English magazines and newspapers completed the 'home from home' feeling of the grateful soldiers and helped restore them to health and strength in the months before repatriation. Sergeant Major Booth attributed some of his survival to his instinct to 'Be British' and was able to return home to marry and raise a family. Other prisoners could not share his determination and were mentally wrecked by the experience.

The British Territorial Forces closely followed the regular Army in terms of organisation, equipment and training. It was the intention that, in time of emergency, the Territorials would take over the home defence role. However, these men, who were under no obligation to serve overseas, when asked to do so, volunteered in large numbers and Bradford men were among them.

THE 1/6TH BATTALION, PRINCE OF WALES OWN WEST YORKSHIRE REGIMENT

Geoff Barker

History[2]

The 6th Battalion was formed in 1908 after the Army reformed following the Boer War. There had been various volunteer regiments in Bradford since 1859 (such as the West Riding Volunteer Rifle Co.) and they had all been based at Belle Vue Barracks, where a territorial regiment is based to this day. Nationally the territorials were often called the Saturday Afternoon Soldiers but locally they were referred to as the Bradford Rifles. They wore the Prince of Wales's plumes on their collars and the white horse of the House of Hanover on their caps. These can be clearly seen on the photograph of Arthur Skelly,[3] who joined them right at the start in 1908, aged eighteen.

Arthur Skelly, woolcomber, married man and 'Saturday Afternoon Soldier' at Belle Vue barracks, who served his country with the 1/6th West Yorkshire Regiment, the Bradford Rifles.

Background

The private soldiers in the Battalion were recruited at Belle Vue barracks in Manningham[4] from men often working in the local textile industries. Arthur Skelly, born in 1890 in Bradford, was the son of Michael, an Irish immigrant born in Cork. At the time of Arthur's birth Michael was a silk dyer's labourer living in Beamsley Street, adjacent to Listers Mill. When Arthur married in January 1911 his profession was given as woolcomber while his wife was noted as worsted weaver. Like most Bradfordians of his class Arthur would spend all his life in rented back-to-back housing, adjacent to a mill, without access to a bathroom or an inside lavatory. His family would summon a doctor only in an extreme emergency and he would leave school at ten, continuing as a 'half timer' until the age of twelve. As a result he hardly read books at all, had only the most basic knowledge of arithmetic and could write and speak his own language poorly.

In contrast, the Commanding Officer of the Battalion, Henry Wade, and his second-in-command Charles Edward Scott were solicitors in Henry's father's Bradford law firm of Wade, Bilbrough & Tetley at 8 Piccadilly. Both had been

BELLE VUE HOTEL,
MANNINGHAM LANE, BRADFORD.

HEADQUARTERS:

Bradford Command Legion of Frontiersmen.

The Belle Vue Hotel on Manningham Lane. Sadly neglected today, the hotel was the nearest hostelry to Belle Vue barracks.

educated privately at Bradford Grammar School in Manor Row, walking to school past the Belle Vue Hotel. Charles lived at Oak Leigh, which is now the Oakleigh Hotel, and Henry at the house next door, which was then called Oak Bank and is now the Park Hotel. While their homes were geographically quite near to Michael Skelly's in Beamsley Street, in reality they were a world away.

Scott and Wade had been instrumental in forming a group of old Bradfordians into 1 Coy, the 6th Battalion the West Yorkshire Regiment in 1900 with their depot at Belle Vue Barracks. They were incorporated into the Territorial Force in 1908. Drill and weapons training was undertaken within the barracks and surrounding countryside. Target practice was held on Baildon Moor and some of these targets can still be detected in the heather.

All the officers were 'professional men' living in comfortable homes and they had been well educated by the standards of the time. Nevertheless, unlike the regular

Traces of the targets used by the 1/6th Battalion for gunnery practice on Baildon Moor can still be found today.

battalions of the army, they met their men regularly at the weekly meetings at Belle Vue, went on the annual camps with them, knew them by name and were well aware of their social circumstances. The territorial service engendered a fierce loyalty in its men and fostered a family atmosphere. Given the horrors of the Great War many regular soldiers and most enlisted men left the Army immediately after the war ended, but Private Arthur Skelly stayed in the Territorial Army until he retired in 1938 as a company quartermaster sergeant major with the 1/6th Battalion.

Kitchener, on the other hand, was deeply suspicious of the relationship between officers and men in the territorials, feeling it lessened the necessary harsh standard of discipline in the Army as a whole.

Mobilisation
The Battalion was mobilised on 4 August 1914 and out of the 588 men on roll 575 reported for duty. As a result they were able to report 'Ready to move' before any other unit in the country. Having recruited to a high standard the extra men they needed and having purchased the necessary horses and mules, they left Bradford for East Yorkshire on 10 August. They were under active service training conditions at

The strength of support for the city's fighting men is evident in the crowds that gathered outside Forster Square station.

Selby, York, Redcar and finally in Lincolnshire from where they left for France on 15 April 1915. They had nearly all volunteered for overseas service and were desperately needed in France to replace the Regular Army which had by now been largely annihilated.

France 1915

With hindsight, the beginnings were comical. The transport section had no torches, could not speak French and their train left early before they could empty it of all their equipment. Harnessing the horses was a nightmare: it was of course raining hard. Finally every cart became hopelessly bogged down in the field where they were camping for the first night. In the meantime the infantry had marched off to their first night's billets. One of their officers had injured his knee but insisted on continuing the march. Entering the village of Le Sort he fell into a sewer hole up to his shoulders and the men had some difficulty pulling him out. They then made him a hot drink to cheer him up only for him to find, to his dismay, that someone had made it from water extracted from the same watercourse!

Billeting in an unknown village is a skilled affair requiring tact and language skills. At this time these had not been identified and the Battalion was strewn about Le Sort in some confusion. So many men had slept in a particular loft over one stable that in the early morning the loft floor collapsed and the men fell on to the horses below, fortunately without injury.

War

In late April 1915 the men began their baptism of fire in the trenches in a relatively quiet area at Fauquissart. At this time they learnt that weather and the conditions it produced in the trenches combined to be a significant enemy in themselves. Ninety years later as we sit in our centrally heated homes watching television we can hardly imagine what the men endured from the weather alone.

During 1915 in Flanders the 23rd Brigade evacuated 1,373 men to hospital in two months with trench foot. Trench foot was caused by standing up to the knees in water and mud for hours and could cost a man his leg from gangrene. Battle casualties during the same period were 576. At Fauquissart a dyke ran between the British and German lines and, taking no sides, it regularly flooded into both trench systems.

In May 1915 the Battalion moved to the Neuve Chapelle battlefield where they inhabited a huge cemetery of the unburied dead from the recent battle. They discovered that the British dead were equipped with the latest British Lee Enfield rifle, a model in advance of their own which they collected to re-equip themselves. At first HQ said they must give them back; they were for the new volunteer army being recruited by Kitchener and the Army Council, not for mere territorials. In the end they were allowed to keep the weapons they had recovered.

Later at Aubers Ridge they had their first casualties: eight dead and twenty-one wounded. They began to come to terms with the snipers, who killed if you were at all careless, with trench mortar shells which wobbled into the air while you watched and wondered where they might land, with artillery shelling which, if it were concentrated into a barrage, seemed unendurable, and with shrapnel which spattered its deadly shards everywhere. Finally there was the machinegun, which assisted the big guns in dominating the battlefield and made any attack a perilous venture.

Ypres

On 4 July the Battalion began their acquaintance with the ill-famed Ypres salient. Here they stayed until Christmas in a rising tide of water, gas and an everlasting rain of shells. Men took an hour to move 100 metres in the mud with Germans on the high ground constantly sniping at them. Sergeant Yates said, 'We started in exuberant health and spirits. At Christmas those who were left crawled out, broken in heart and almost in spirit.' The final German attack on 19 December included the discharge of gas from cylinders and shelling including gas shells. Thanks to new masks the attack was held but sixteen men were killed and eighty wounded.

Among many stories of heroism emerges the name of Samuel Meekosha, the son of a Polish father and English mother. The family moved to Bradford from Leeds in

Sam Meekosha of the 1/6th West Yokshire Regiment, the first Bradfordian to be awarded the Victoria Cross in the Great War for 'magnificent courage and determination'.

1893 and Sam's name has a special place of honour on Bradford's war memorial: the first, but not the last, Bradford recipient of the Victoria Cross.

Sam attended St Joseph's Roman Catholic School and on 11 February 1911 he enrolled in the 1/6th Battalion West Yorkshire Regiment as a territorial. Sam was twenty-two and a Corporal when on 19 November 1915, facing the Germans across the River Yser, he was with a small group of men in an isolated trench. Under heavy bombardment, six of his companions were killed and seven wounded. The citation in the *London Gazette*[5] read:

> When the senior NCOs had either been killed or wounded, Cpl Meekosha at once took command, sent a runner for assistance and, in spite of no less than ten more big shells falling within 20 yards of him, continued to dig out the wounded and buried men in full view of the enemy and at close range from the German trenches. By his promptness and magnificent courage and determination he saved at least four lives.

Sam Meekosha enlisted in the Second World War and survived. However, his unusual name led to so many people questioning him about his medal that he changed his surname to Ingham (taken from his mother's name, Cunningham) by Deed Poll in 1942. Sam died in Monmouthshire in 1950 and his VC medal was sold by Sotheby's in April 2001 for £101,000, more than double its estimate.

The Somme

The Battalion were in reserve until late in the afternoon of 1 July 1916. Many were killed simply reaching our front line and the Commanding Officer, Colonel Henry Wade, was wounded and invalided home. The attack was a disaster, with one in three of the attacking force a casualty. In total the British Army suffered 60,000 casualties. The other Bradford battalions contributed to this terrible loss and the black-rimmed pages in the local papers shocked the city.

The night of 1/2 July was like a scene from hell. The battalions located in Thiepval Wood came under constant shellfire, including gas, which pooled in the hollows where the wounded lay in their brown blankets. In two days the 6th

THE BOMBERS.

BACK ROW. — METCALFE, JONES, WILSON, HUDSON, FISHBURN, JEFFERSON, PRITCHARD, FOX, REECE.
3RD ROW.—PARKINSON, DUCKETT, COYNE, THISTLEWAITE, ROBINSON. ROOME.
2ND ROW.—CAWTHRA, L/CPL. ANDREWS, L/CPL. BUTTERFIELD, SERGT. MᶜIVOR, LT. H. A. JOWETT,
L/CPL. FOULDING, L/CPL. FOSTER, BROWN, HAIGH, BRADY.
1ST ROW.—SWITHENBANK, WATERWORTH, HANSON, WARD, BROWN, HALL, BANNISTER, MORRIS.
(All privates unless where otherwise stated).

The bombers of the 1/6th. Bernard Coyne is third from the left on the third row. He did not survive the first day of the Somme offensive.

Battalion had 264 casualties out of their nominal strength of 500. Among the casualties was bomber Bernard Coyne (see Chapter 2). Tempest[6] describes how each of the bombing parties was allocated six extra men.

On arrival at the German support line these parties will at once bomb and make blocks 100 yards up communication trenches towards the enemy. Special bombing parties will also be detailed within the second line. These consisted of one Lewis Gun, one NCO and six men carrying bombs and four bombers. On arrival at the support line these parties will at once push out about thirty yards and take up their positions, dig in and consolidate, after which they will dig back communication to German support line.

From all these groups of bombers it was almost inevitable that there would be few survivors.

On 13 July the Battalion moved to the Leipzig salient and took up positions in trenches at Authuille Wood on the 15th. On the 24th, shortly before they were due to be relieved, Major Scott and Captain Knowles were injured by shrapnel burst while making their rounds. Major Scott, Colonel Wade's friend and co-founder of the Battalion, died from his wounds later at Camiers Hospital near Boulogne. His wife's family placed a memorial window to him in St Chad's Church – where it can still be seen – and his name heads the war memorial inside St Barnabas' Church, Heaton. He is buried in grave 1.A.40 in Étaples Military Cemetery.

Winter 1916/17

The winter was spent in France in conditions of great hardship. Freezing conditions were so hard that the water in the trenches froze solid and a visiting senior officer from the Royal Engineers exclaimed 'but the men must freeze to death', and indeed some did. Today we would call it death from exposure.

Passchendaele

The Battalion took part in the attack on 9 October 1917 in conditions which staff HQ said would be 'slippery'. The reality was appalling. It took the infantry three hours to cover the 2,500m to their attack line. Men who fell into shell holes drowned and the attack failed. In two out of the four companies of the Battalion every second man was a casualty and it took two days to evacuate the wounded. While they waited they lay in the rain under the inevitable brown blankets. There followed another harsh winter in Flanders, when men wondered what the effect would be on the Western Front of the Russian Armistice following the Revolution in the East. How quickly would America's entry into the war have its effect?

1918

In April, having transferred his armies to the West, General Ludendorff began the series of offensives which so nearly won the war for Germany. The 6th Battalion, now much reinforced with eighteen-year-old conscripts from home, met the impact of the German advance in front of Ypres. By now all the gains of 1917, won at such grievous cost, had been lost, and General Haigh issued his 'backs to the wall' appeal to his men. And fight they did with great heroism. In the end the Battalion HQ was overrun and Colonel Winstance, the replacement CO, was killed. Although surrounded for twelve hours, companies did not surrender until their ammunition ran out. Many were killed and many of those taken prisoner were wounded and died in captivity. Captain Mossop the Adjutant died thus, as did Major Walmsley. RSM Barker was killed fighting hand-to-hand with his revolver as his company was overrun; he had served with the Battalion and its predecessors for twenty years. Twenty-two officers and 457 other ranks were casualties in this fighting but by their actions and those of other West Yorkshire members of the 146th Brigade, Ypres was saved and the German attack brought to a halt.

By 6 October 1918 the Battalion was again taking part in the final advances of the war from Cambrai to Valenciennes. The terms of the Armistice were read out to the men in the village of Evin Malmaison. Any history of the 6th Battalion from 1914 to 1918 is a history of several Battalions as men were constantly drafted in to replace those killed and wounded. By the end of the Somme battles of 1916 most of the original Territorials had gone. By the end of the war there had been 2,177 casualties, four times the average strength of the Battalion.

THE NEW ARMIES: KITCHENER'S MEN

Joyce Appleby

Field Marshal Earl Kitchener of Khartoum took over as Minister for War on 5 August 1914 and immediately ordered an expansion of the army. He was clearly of the view that the war would not be over by Christmas as so many journalists in England and Germany would have the public believe. Kitchener was unable to regard the Territorial Force with any seriousness and thus advocated the creation of a New Army of volunteers. Each man would enlist for three years or the duration of the war, whichever was the shorter, and would thus be a regular soldier but on a temporary basis.

On 11 August he called upon 100,000 men to enlist and the famous poster 'Your Country Needs You' appeared on the streets: the first of several such calls. Kitchener's initial target figure was achieved within two weeks. In Bradford young men formed their own Citizens' Army League and in two weeks in September 1,000 young men had joined the new 16th Battalion of the West Yorkshire Regiment. A further 1,000 came forward by February 1915 to form the 18th Battalion. Thus were formed the Bradford Pals.

There appears to be no shortage of volunteers at the Labour Exchange. Note the slogan 'Avenge Hartlepool'. Three German warships had caused considerable damage and loss of life during a forty-minute barrage beginning at 8.10 a.m. on 16 December 1914.

'Join together; Serve together' was certainly an attractive slogan and in Bradford the eager, innocent young volunteers responded with enthusiasm and a fine *esprit de corps*. Local people were also quick to support their boys with fundraising and gifts. However, the notion was fatally flawed and as casualty lists began to mount the names of young men from the same street, the same workplace and even the same family revealed the foolishness. The concentrated effect on the City of Bradford was reflected in many towns and cities across the country, especially where local Pals were attached to the 31st Division and were devastated by the attack at Serre on 1 July 1916.

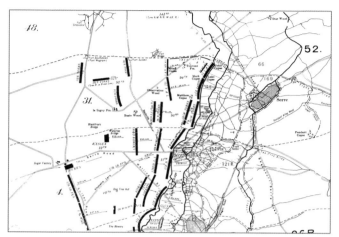

A trench map showing positions of the West Yorkshire regiments in 1916.

In the early days of recruitment physical requirements were quite strict and many were rejected on grounds of height and chest dimension. The War Office gradually relaxed the standard and 5ft 3in height and 34in chest became acceptable. Mr Wilf Leddy of Wibsey, a 93-year-old neighbour of the author, recalls his father being rejected by the examining doctor because of a varicose vein in his leg. The doctor considered him unable to march and he was therefore sent to the munitions factory at Crossgates, Leeds. Fortunately he survived an explosion at the factory which killed thirty-five of his fellow workers: a twice-lucky man!

The Pals suffered shortages of equipment of every kind. As Germany had been the only source of khaki dye, the 1st Pals marched to camp in Skipton wearing the dark blue serge uniforms of Post Office workers, which bore silver buttons bearing the Bradford coat of arms. A civic send-off complete with brass band was grand but there was little escape from the pouring rain which marred the eighteen-mile march. (Khaki uniforms were available in May 1915.)

A Bradford clerk, F. Rawnsley[7] kept a diary from which this list of 'Red Letter Days' is taken:

Sept 23rd 1914	Enlisted 16th Battalion West Yorks at Mechanics Institute
Jan 15th 1915	Marched to Skipton
May 20th	Marched to Ripon
Sept 23rd	Moved from Ripon to Fovant (between Shaftesbury and Salisbury, Wiltshire)
Dec 5th	Fovant to Egypt (entrained to Liverpool)
Dec 22nd	Arrived Port Said (after a very adventurous journey)
Jan 5th 1916	Moved to Kantara (on the banks of the Suez Canal)
Feb 29th	Left Point 60 (in the desert to prepare defences against the Turks)
March 1st	Sailed Port Said (SS *Minneapolis*, possibly the 29th.)

March 7th	Arrived Marseilles
April 20th	Went into trenches for first time
July 1st	BIG PUSH

1 July was the date of Private Rawnsley's final entry and the diary was returned with his personal effects to his home in Bradford. Although the time spent in Egypt was uneventful, it must have been quite an experience for the Pals, most of whom would never have been out of Yorkshire. The heat, constant battles with sand and lice combined with rationed drinking water would give them little inkling of what was in store for them in Europe.

A poem of the time by Ernest Osborne suggests the prevalent attitude of the civilian public towards the general capabilities of the Pals:

In England

Eh? What of the Pals, Oh, well!
Really – ahem!
You surely think they'd make soldiers of them?
Their training is poor, and discipline they lack,
And some of them – Well, they have their chests at the back.
For months now our Sixth[8] have been bearing the brunt,
But when do you think will our Pals see the Front?
No real soldiering there, but just a pretence.
They may do very well, say for Home Defence.
Such were the comments, often uttered with sneers,
But the Pals were not conscripts,
All volunteers.

Private Ernest Osborne[9] was himself a volunteer. Later promoted to Lance Corporal 1st Bradford Pals, he was posted to the Larkhill Training Camp on Salisbury Plain and, as his poem suggests, he was not over-impressed:

The Joys of Larkhill

There's an isolated, desolate spot I'd like to mention
Where all you hear is 'Stand at ease, Quick March, Slope Arms, Attention!'
It's miles away from anywhere, by Jove it is a rum 'un,
A man lived there for fifty years and never saw a woman.

There's only two lamps in the place, so tell it to your mother,
The postman carries number one and Robert has the other.
And if you want a jolly ride and do not care a jot,
You take a ride upon the car, the car they have not got.

There's lots of tiny little huts, all dotted here and there,
For those who have to live inside I've offered many a prayer.
There's mud up to the eyebrow, you get it in your ear,
But into it you've got to go, without a sign of fear.

There's soldiers living in the huts, it fills my heart with sorrow.
With tear-dimmed eyes they've said to me 'It's Larkhill Camp tomorrow!'
Inside the huts they say they've rats, as big as any goat,
Last night a soldier saw one trying on his overcoat.

Now when this war is over and we've captured Kaiser Billy,
To shoot him would be merciful and absolutely silly.
Just send him down to Larkhill Camp amongst the rats and clays
And I'll bet it won't be long before he drops and fades away.

Compared to what lay in store for Ernest later, Larkhill must have seemed like paradise. Like Fred Rawnsley, Ernest was posted to Egypt and his pay book, issued on departure and dated 04.12.1915, indicates they were on ship together. The next time we have news of Ernest is in a letter written on YMCA notepaper and dated 04.11.1916. It is addressed to Ernest's father and signed by 'Alec'. The letter informs father that Ernest has been wounded and his arm has been amputated. Despite his wounds, Alec reports Ernest to be well and in good spirits! Alec also mentions his courage and describes him as 'a brave lad'.

A further letter to Ernest's father is dated 08.11.1916 and was written on House of Commons notepaper by the ILP Member of Parliament for Bradford, F.W. Jowett. Beginning 'Dear Comrade' (and ending 'Yours fraternally') the letter is in response to enquiries regarding the possibility of travelling to visit wounded relations. Ernest's father is told that the cost of such journeys depended on the opinion of the Medical Officer in charge of the hospital. He had the power to grant free travel passes but only when the casualty was in a critical condition.

In spite of his injuries, Ernest made it home to Blighty and to Wakefield Road, Bradford, but many others were not so lucky. Private Leonard Crabtree (service number 16/609) was one of the many who lost his life on the first day of the Somme. He was twenty-six years old. Leonard had worked for the Bradford Dyers Association and played football for Bradford Old Boys. There is a fascinating collection[10] of postcards written by Leonard to his girlfriend, Holly Leach of Allerton, the first of which describes his time spent in training at Skipton, Grassington and Ripon in 1914–15. He also sent photographs, some of which show him wearing the Post Office blue uniform originally issued to the Pals.

Leonard and Holly were married in November 1915, and Leonard returned to the Battalion on 1 December. Holly never saw him again. Among the next group of postcards are some that were thrown from a train window in Marseilles (on the return journey from Egypt), one of which reads:

My Darling Holly. We are in France. I have received your parcel and letter when we landed in Marseilles. I am throwing this out of the window and trusting to luck that it reaches you. God Bless you Darling, Your faithful hubby, Leonard.
PS The parcel was grand and it is grand to be nearer home.

Another dated 10 March 1916 reads:

> Dear Holly, Arrived at billets. It feels very cold but it is grand: it feels like England. Best love, Leonard.

Holly's daughter writes:

> I found out after all these years that his name is on the Thiepval Memorial to the missing. Just one of the Bradford Pals but I just wish that mother could have known where his name was. He was my mother's first husband and when we can my husband and I visit Thiepval and lay a wreath for him. My mother never forgot him and she never forgave Earl Haig.

On 1 July 1916 the Pals 'went over the top' to face the fortified village of Serre, the uncut barbed wire and the German Maxim guns. Casualty numbers were horrendous. The 1st Pals had started the day with twenty-two officers and 675 men. Of the officers, eleven were dead and eleven wounded, one of whom died from his wounds on 5 July. Among other ranks the casualty rate was 75 per cent: 53 dead, 149 missing and 303 wounded. David Raw[11] points to the greater casualty figures in the 1st Pals being a result of their being the lead battalion. Not only would they be under enemy fire for longer but the wounded would also be left untended in no man's land for longer.

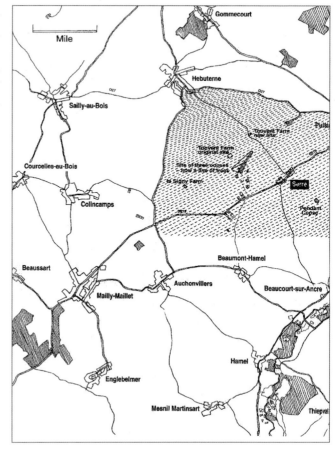

The area around the village of Serre where the Pals' battalions suffered severe losses causing disbelief in the streets of Bradford.

No6 Platoon. B. Co. Bradford Pals' Batt. 1914.

No. 6 Platoon of the 2nd Bradford Pals in Manningham Park before leaving for France. Photographers in Bradford were kept busy recording groups and individual soldiers. Many cannot be identified today.

The 18th Battalion (2nd Pals) had been involved in a disastrous trench raid on the night before the attack and their total casualties for the two days were, again, 100 per cent of officers (9 dead, 13 wounded), 118 other ranks killed and 375 wounded, some of whom died from their wounds. The ages of these men demonstrate the zeal of youth. Half of the dead were under twenty-two years of age and 20 per cent of the casualties were under age when they joined up, including Private H. Walker of Great Horton whose parents advertised for news of him in the *Bradford Daily Telegraph* in the summer of 1916.

On a national scale the casualty figures among Bradford Pals on 1 July 1916 seem small: many more were lost during the final 'push' in 1918. However, such is the nature of Pals' regiments that we are talking of whole streets, whole companies, whole sports and social clubs being decimated. On 1 July the local newspapers were mostly concerned with the Battle of Jutland and the full extent of the Somme tragedy did not become apparent for some days. Since 1914 the Defence of the Realm Act precluded detailed reporting and loved ones could only anxiously scan the columns of names and photographs of the dead. After the black-edged telegrams came the cruellest final stage: the return of the pathetic parcels of the deceased's possessions. These were usually unwashed and often indicated the depth of the tragedy with blood or bullet holes in the returned kit. At least one mother received a pigskin wallet penetrated by the shard of shrapnel which had killed her son. His great-grandchildren still preserve the relic, debating whether or not to send it to a regimental museum.

Once the full horror became apparent, the atmosphere in Bradford was one of shock, disbelief and almost overwhelming sorrow. Even those who had escaped personal bereavement could not fail to notice the drawn curtains in the front rooms of houses in every street. Such was the grief that some wondered if the mourning would last forever.

Private Harry Farr[12] first saw service in the Boer War and on the outbreak of war in August 1914 he joined the West Yorkshire Regiment. In May 1915 he was hospitalised for five months with such an uncontrollable shake that nurses wrote his letters home. He was returned to the Front but in April 1916 he reported sick again and spent two weeks at a Dressing Station. He reported sick again in July and September but on this latter occasion, because he did not appear to be wounded, he was instructed to return to the front line with a ration party. Harry Farr simply remained at the transport lines and said to the officer who found him 'I cannot stand it'. An escort was ordered to return him to the trenches but after a few hundred yards Harry Farr started to scream and struggle, protesting 'I am not fit to go to the trenches'. The Sergeant Major's reply was blunt: 'I'll blow your f*****g brains out if you don't go'.

Harry Farr was charged under Section 4.(7) of the Army Act (Misbehaving before the enemy in such a manner as to show cowardice). His court-martial lasted about twenty minutes and Harry Farr, despite the state of his nerves, conducted his own defence. The medical officer who had first treated him had been wounded and was not available but the verdict was issued with confidence despite the report from Harry's Company Captain whose report reads:

> I cannot say what has destroyed this man's nerves, but he has proved himself on many occasions incapable of keeping his head in action & likely to cause a panic. Apart from his behaviour under fire, his conduct and character are very good.[13]

Death by firing squad was carried out at 6 a.m. on 18 October 1916. Harry Farr's name is on the Memorial at Thiepval, Face 2A2, C&D.

On 5 September 1916 two men serving with the 2nd Bradford Pals were also executed. Herbert Crimmins and Arthur Wild were shot by members of their own company[14] which led to bitter resentment still remembered by an old Pal seventy years later. David Raw[15] describes how one of the firing party committed suicide in Cleckheaton years later and the officer in charge of the firing squad developed an alcohol problem. The feelings of the men were not helped by Major General R. Wanless O'Gowan's insensitivity when he declared, 'These men are best forgotten'. He was also observed kicking away the flowers placed on the men's graves by members of the firing squad.

The verdict of court-martials was always confirmed by the Commander in the field who, in this case, was General Haig. David Raw suggests that Haig ignored the recommendation for mercy to be shown in this case because of his preconceived doubts about the reliability of VIII Corps under Hunter Weston. His diary entry for 30 June 1916 reads, 'The only doubt I have is regarding VIII Corps which has no experience of fighting in France and has not carried out one successful raid'. At the end of the first day of the Somme he wrote, 'I am inclined to believe . . . that few of VIII Corps left their trenches . . . the VIII Corps needs looking after.' Crimmins and Wild received no such 'looking after', but then Haig probably did not mean it to be the caring kind of looking-after which shell-shock cases deserved.

In November 1916 the Pals Regiments were taken out of the Somme area after taking over the Hébuterne sector where their memorial is now placed. The reformed Pals served honourably throughout the rest of the war although they ceased to be a distinct group in February 1918. The few survivors of the original men and their reinforcements were merged with other units. The colours of the Bradford Pals still hang in Bradford Cathedral.

THE DERBY SCHEME

Gerry Beevers

In August 1914 Britain was the only European power which relied on a volunteer army and the Foreign Secretary, Sir Edward Grey, resisted the calls of politicians such as Winston Churchill to advocate a form of conscription. However, by May 1915 the demand for fighting men was outstripping the supply and the Prime Minister, H.H. Asquith, appointed Lord Edward Derby as Director General of Recruitment. Derby, an instinctive opponent of compulsory conscription, asked for men to register for service, safe in the knowledge that they would only be called when necessary. Furthermore, married men would not be called until the supply of single men was exhausted. By December 350,000 men had volunteered: far below

the number needed. The Derby Scheme was abandoned and in January 1916 the new Prime Minister, David Lloyd George, guided the Military Service Act through Parliament. This set out the terms for conscription.

Herbert Bolton[16] felt it was his duty to volunteer and on 11 December 1915 he took advantage of the Derby Scheme. As a married man he understood it would be some time before he was called. His wife Ethel and their two daughters, Hilda (born 1913) and Gladys (born 1915) lived in East Morton, and Herbert worked for the Bradford Dyers Association at the Stockbridge Works in Keighley.

Herbert was called up in May 1916 and sent for training in Ripon. He was attached to the 29th (Reserve) and later 84th (Training) Battalion, Northumberland Fusiliers (Tyneside Scottish). He

Herbert Bolton of East Morton, an employee of the Bradford Dyers Association, who signed up under the Derby Scheme.

Herbert Bolton's paybook, looking well-used and containing a record of wage payments made 'in the field'.

became Lance Corporal and then Corporal. In December 1916 he was transferred to the 18th Battalion Durham Light Infantry (Durham Pals) and immediately left for France where the Battalion was serving with the 93rd Brigade alongside the Leeds and Bradford Pals (15th, 16th and 18th West Yorkshires). The Brigade was billeted at Hébuterne on the Somme, and Herbert was involved in the 1917/18 battles at Rossignol Wood, Arras, Vimy Ridge, Hazebrouck, Bailleul and Ypres. On 12 September 1917 he was promoted to Lieutenant Sergeant in the field.

On the night of 28/29 June 1918 at La Becque, Herbert was wounded, evacuated and admitted to the 14th General Hospital at Wimereux. (Six months earlier, on 28 January 1918, the war poet John McCrae had died of pneumonia in the same hospital.)

The telegram received by Herbert's wife on 8 July 1918 reported that he had sustained 'gunshot wounds (severe)' to his right hand. Two weeks later he was transferred to Folkestone.

The telegram bearing the news of Herbert's wounds is still in the possession of his descendants. He lost the middle finger of his right hand.

On 27 July 1918 the *Keighley News* and *Bingley Chronicle* carried a full report:

Mrs Bolton of 41 Main Road, Morton, has received information that her husband, Sergeant Herbert Bolton, of the Durham Light Infantry, is in the Queens Canadian Military Hospital, Folkestone suffering from gunshot wounds in the right hand and a slight wound in the left leg. Sergeant Bolton is 28 years of age, married, and has two children. He joined the Army on 1 May 1916, and has been in France since December 1916.

After recovering from his injuries Herbert returned to his battalion in France. In England, after the armistice, he took up his duties as a Drill Instructor with his regiment at Barnard Castle, Durham, until his discharge on 25 September 1919. Herbert returned to his former employers at Stockbridge Works and he and his wife

Ethel went on to have twin daughters Iris and Lily, and a son Reginald. Herbert Bolton was a lifelong member of East Morton Primitive Methodist Chapel, where he served as deacon for many years. He died on 12 January 1970.

Notes

1 The websites www.1914–1918.net/regular, www.1914-1918.net/reserve, www.1914–1918.net/tf and www.1914–1918.net/pals contain detailed descriptions of the structure of the army and the deployment of forces during the opening months of the war

2 See Tempest, Capt. E.V., *The History of the Sixth Battalion West Yorkshire Regiment* Volume 1: 1/6 Battalion. Percy Lund Humphries & Co. Ltd, The Country Press, Bradford, 1921

3 Personal recollections of Arthur Skelly are reproduced with thanks to his family

4 Microfiche record of men volunteering and serving between 1914 and 1918, City of Bradford Reference Library

5 The *London Gazette*, January 1916

6 Tempest ibid. p. 144

7 Fred Rawnsley's diary is available in Bradford Industrial Museum. Of the 21 Rawnsley names recorded by the Commonwealth War Graves Commission there are two who most closely fit with the available details: F. Rawnsley 2736 1/7th West Yorkshire Regiment (Leeds Rifles) died 2 July 1916; Pte Herbert Vincent Rawnsley 16/1133 16th Battalion West Yorkshire Regiment (Bradford Pals) of Clayton, Bradford, died 1 July 1916. Both these men are recorded on the Thiepval Memorial, Pier and Face A2C and 2D and the latter is most likely to be Fred

8 6th Battalion, The Bradford Territorials, out from 14 April 1915

9 Papers belonging to Private Osborne are available in Bradford Industrial Museum

10 This collection is in the possession of Holly's daughter from her second marriage and the author is grateful for permission to publish these quotations from them

11 Raw, D., *Bradford Pals. A Comprehensive History of the 18th and 20th (Service) Battalions of the Prince of Wales Own West Yorkshire Regiment 1914–1918*, Pen and Sword, 2005

12 An account of Private Farr's court martial is available at National Archives: WO71/509

13 WO71/509 Ibid. Testimony from A. Wilson, Capt. OC A Coy, 1st West York. Regt

14 Accounts of the courts martial can be found in the National Archives: WO71/495 and 496

15 Ibid. p. 2

16 Papers belonging to Herbert Bolton are in the possession of his family and reproduced with thanks

FOUR

Soldiers' Stories

Gerry Beevers & Tricia Platts

Facts and figures can produce impressive statistics but it is in the ordinariness of volunteers, conscripts and their family members that we see the true price of war. The stories re-told here have been gleaned from local newspaper archives, from personal recollections of family members and from diaries and other records as yet unpublished. The intention is to add a personal face to the official records of the war, which will be of special interest to citizens of Bradford today.

Memories of war often focus on the bereaved and in Bradford there were thousands of these. Of those who returned from active service many were able to resume 'normal' lives among family and work colleagues. However, many others had great difficulty in readjusting. Experiences, memories, physical and mental illness had an effect for the remainder of their lives, which, in some cases, meant that life became a burden. For the Whitehead family the tragedy of losing two sons was too much for their mother. The firm of W. and J. Whitehead was based at Moorside Mills, Eccleshill (part of the building now houses the Bradford Industrial Museum). Geoffrey Nield Whitehead became a 2nd Lieutenant in the 11th Balloon Company of the Royal Flying Corps and was killed at Ypres on 15 October 1917. He was twenty-nine

Mrs Sarah Whitehead, former Lady Mayoress of the city, was doubly bereaved and reportedly unable to come to terms with her loss.

years old and left a widow living in Spofforth. His brother, Alfred Gordon Whitehead, reached the rank of Captain in the Royal Flying Corps (25th Squadron). He was killed on 29 January 1918. Their mother, Sarah, formerly Lady Mayoress of Bradford, died in December 1918, reportedly of grief.

An insight into the work of the balloonists is contained in the citation for the Distinguished Flying Cross awarded to Lieutenant William Stanley Eastaugh, a Bradfordian by adoption. In 1918 he was mentioned in the *London Gazette* in a tribute which also reflects the constant danger these young men faced:

> During recent operations this officer advanced his balloon over very difficult country, keeping up with the artillery and transmitting much valued information. His balloons were frequently burnt by hostile fire and on 1 September the balloon, hit by shellfire, dived about 1,000ft; Lieutenant Eastaugh, though subjected to heavy hostile fire, endeavoured to save the wreckage, setting a fine example of devotion to duty.

Lieutenant Eastaugh was awarded the DFC at Buckingham Palace in August 1919, four months before his twenty-ninth birthday. He served in the Second World War as a Squadron Leader in the RAF and died in Bradford in 1959.

Private Sam Jones of Undercliffe Road, Eccleshill, had enlisted as a Royal Marine after being educated at Eccleshill Baptist School. After training, Sam began service on board HMS *Monmouth*, an armoured cruiser built in 1901.

Right: Marine Sam Jones of Undercliffe Road, Eccleshill, who lost his life when HMS *Monmouth* went down at Coronel.

Below: HMS *Monmouth*, an old-design armoured cruiser whose armour plating proved ineffective against the weaponry of the German fleet.

Such was the pace of change in the navies of the world at this time that by 1914 the *Monmouth* was an obsolete design and she had been placed in the reserve. Her armour was deficient, her guns being too light in calibre and placed too near the waterline.

Nevertheless on the outbreak of hostilities, with the German China Squadron sinking our merchantmen in the Pacific and South Atlantic, she was included in Admiral Cradock's 5th Cruiser Squadron sent out to counter the German fleet. They met Admiral Von Spee's much more powerful ships off Coronel on 1 November 1914 and both the cruiser *Good Hope* and the *Monmouth* were sunk. Marine Sam Jones was drowned, as was Admiral Cradock and 1,500 sailors. It was the biggest British naval defeat for a hundred years. Six weeks later Mrs Jones, Sam's aunt, received his last letter telling her that he was quite well. In Shipley, Cecil Procter's parents mourned the loss of their son, a sailor serving on the *Good Hope*.

Sergeant Major William Booth's experiences with the British Expeditionary Force, his early capture and his life as a prisoner of the Germans is retold in Chapter 3. Lance Corporal Joseph Hill from Otley Road, Bradford, a regular in the King's

The Plymouth Memorial which bears the names of those lost at sea, including nineteen-year-old Sam Jones.

Own Royal Regiment which formed part of the original BEF, was wounded three times. During his second period of convalescence Hill was married in September 1915. His third wound was sustained during the Battle of the Somme in July 1916. A shell bursting on top of the trench occupied by his section had rendered Hill both deaf and dumb and he was invalided home to Greystones Hospital, Sheffield.

As he began to make a recovery, Joseph Hill asked his wife to bring their seven-week-old child to the hospital. Railway passes were granted by the hospital and, for the first time, Joseph Hill saw his daughter. Such was his joy that, within five minutes, he wrote on his notepad that he could hear what was being said. He then asked that they go for a walk in Sheffield during which time, hearing his wife comment that her sister's husband was leaving for the front, he exclaimed loudly, 'The war will be over by August.'

The headline in the *Shipley Times and Express* of 28 August 1916 ran: 'Joy That Cured: Bradford soldier's good fortune: Sight of baby restores speech'. The account ends with a long statement from Joseph Hill himself,

> She is the best baby in England. I should not like to lose her now, I have only seen her once, but I think the world of her. You wait until I get into civil life again and she starts calling for her daddy. She shall have anything she wants if I can possibly get it because it was her that brought back my speech and hearing, and I shall always think the world of her.

Not many stories had such a dramatic and happy ending. Eric Bosher was born in Micklethwaite and brought up at 10 Bridge Street, Crossflatts, and was employed by Messrs Longbottom & Farrar, Brass Founders in Keighley. He was a member of the Crossflatts Cricket Club and was described as one of the most promising young players in the district.

On 5 November 1914 he and his school friend were inspired by the recruiting campaign of the Seaforth Highlanders in Lister Park. They enlisted with the Seaforth's Ross Highland Territorial Force 4th Battalion within the 154th Brigade of the 51st Highland Division. After training they arrived at Prouville on 16 July 1916. They shared the village with the Indian Cavalry Corps.

Four days later they entrained for Mericourt and marched to Meult and the reserve trenches at Bazentin-le-Grand. They were destined to relieve the 1/4th Gordon Highlanders at High Wood on 21 July. The horseshoe of woods – Bernafey, Trones, High and Delville – were notorious as bloody deathtraps for both British and Germans.

Nineteen-year-old Eric Bosher of Crossflatts who was fatally wounded at High Wood in July 1916.

The barrage had lifted at 22.00 hours on 21 July and men from the 1st Queen's Royal West Kents and the 14th Royal Warwicks of the 5th Division made some progress until they met enfilading machine-gun fire from the east corner of High Wood. Two battalions of Eric's Brigade met very serious trouble from the same machineguns, as did battalions from the King's Own Scottish Borderers and the 15th Royal Warwicks. The troops, including Eric's division, found themselves back in their original position.

The trench, known as High Alley, had been improved and a second communications trench known as Thistle Alley had been started. These two trenches reduced the dominance of the Germans but, to quote the official reports, 'the position taken over by the 51st [Eric's Division] was very dangerous to traverse'. Although deprived of direct vision the Germans were using observation balloons. The 51st Division attacked High Wood again and it was after this attack that Eric received the wound which was to prove fatal. He was nineteen years old.

Eric's family always believed that he was acting as a despatch rider when he was shot in the head. However, the *Keighley News and Bingley Chronicle* carried an account of his death taken from the letter sent by Eric's Lieutenant to his family. It reads:

The site of the Casualty Clearing Station (CCS) near Dernancourt where the wounded Eric Bosher was taken. In winter time traces of the tented CCS can still be seen in the chalk. Beyond the field is the cemetery where Eric is buried.

I deeply regret to inform you that your son, Private E. Bosher has died of wounds received when marching out of the trenches with his company. A shell fell among them and your son was one among those struck. He was taken to hospital where he died four days later. While serving with this battalion he always showed himself a brave and hardy soldier and he died doing his duty. You have my sympathy and that of the other officers of the company in your great sorrow.

Procedures for dealing with the wounded in the field were clearly laid down and the first requirement was 'not to delay an attack to support the wounded'. The first treatment Eric received would have been the application of a dressing from his own pack. Stretcher-bearers would then have been called up to take him to a Regimental Aid Post. These were often sited in a captured bunker or in a reserve trench within the battle zone. From here, after very basic treatment Eric would be transferred to an Advanced Dressing Station. These can still be 'read' in the chalky downs of the Somme and appear as square areas with unmistakable disturbed chalk in the rusty earth.

From this makeshift place, at best under canvas and at worst under fire, Eric would have been taken back from the line possibly by narrow gauge railway or ambulance to a Main Dressing Station for 'comforts' and assessment. He would certainly have been taken to his final destination, the Casualty Clearing Station at Dernancourt, by some form of motorised transport.

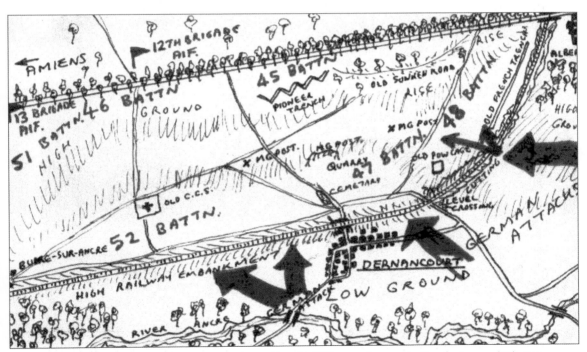

This hand-drawn contemporary map shows the old CCS, cemetery and other features which can still be traced today on the Albert–Amiens road.

Above, left: A simple wooden cross was erected whenever a soldier was buried on a battlefield. This one, photographed by the War Office shortly after his burial, marks the grave of Eric Bosher. *Above, right:* Later an official War Graves Commission stone was erected. Designed by Lutyens and with wording devised by Kipling, these stones are maintained to a very high standard.

The Casualty Clearing Stations were all based on railheads and developed in pairs so that when one was full, casualties could be routed to the other. Eric was mortally wounded and the best the Clearing Station could do was to make his final days comfortable. Others more fortunate would be sent to a major Base Hospital such as that in Étaples for routing back to the UK. Étaples, near the Channel Ports, was itself by no means safe and was bombed with significant casualties.

The evacuation system, part of which Eric passed through, was totally overloaded during the Somme battles. The system had been planned to deal with 25,000 total casualties but in fact 30,000 arrived in the first twenty-four hours. Many men who should have survived 'to fight another day' died, and perhaps Eric was one of these.

The communal cemetery at Dernancourt is a quiet place which took the first dead from the Casualty Clearing Station – it was augmented by a military cemetery. Eric's present grave is visited regularly by his cousin's son and he has a photograph inserted, quite illegally, in the book of the dead at the cemetery.

Private William Firth of Eccleshill was more fortunate than Eric Bosher. Private Firth was in the 2nd Yorkshire Regiment which came to grips with the enemy at a village called Glenvelt, near Ypres. The brigade at that time was 20,000 strong, but they were opposed by a force of 75,000. In January 1915 the *Shipley Times and Express* interviewed Private Firth who told the story graphically:

We could hear the Germans coming over the hill in front all night long, and next morning they began to shell our trenches. They must have known the range to a yard, for after the first few shots they plumped them among us. They bombarded us for a week, and when they thought they had thinned us down they sent their infantry forward to attack. Their big guns are marvels and terribly accurate. One shot buried seven of our men alive. If they wished to knock a building down they could do so in a few shots. The village where we were was razed to the ground, and even the road had disappeared.

For four days men and officers lived on turnips which they pulled up from an adjoining field under cover of darkness. One man found a large tin of jam, so they were able to spread some on turnip slices to 'enrich' their diet. Enemy planes flew overhead, and this enabled the enemy to keep the men pinned down for three weeks along a five-mile front without reinforcements. The Germans gradually encroached until they were on three sides, at which point Private Firth and his comrades were given the order to withdraw. The retreat was over open fields and the scene was described in the words of Private Firth:

Their Maxim guns were trained on to those fields, and many a brave fellow met his death while crossing. The sights I saw are too horrible to talk about. We had to run about 3,000 yards, and till then I never knew I was a sprinter. Some men left their rifles in the trenches, and others threw off their knapsacks, for it was a race for life. The roll was called after this retirement, and of 1,300 men only 300 were left.

The surviving men dug in for the night but the scene was repeated the following morning. Private Firth describes the pleas of the wounded:

One of the most distressing things in this retirement was to hear our own wounded men begging of us not to leave them. But they had to be left, or we should have perished with them.

The arrival of reinforcements enabled the enemy to be driven back beyond the original line. British troops now occupied German trenches and Private Firth and his comrades were ordered to march back all day and all night for seven days rest.

He then saw action near Armentières where each turn in the trenches lasted only three days. British tactics (to hold fire until the Germans came up to the wire) were so effective that the Germans fell back. Ironically, Private Firth escaped all this without injury but one day, while carrying rations towards the lines he was shot by a sniper:

About two miles in our rear was an old mill and this place was used for the unloading of the transport. A party of eight was sent to carry the rations from the mill to the trenches, and both going and coming snipers were at work to end our career. A shot from one of the snipers went through my left forearm and came out just above my elbow.

Private Firth (and his tin of bully beef) made it back to the lines where he was bandaged up and sent off to hospital.

Firth claimed that the snipers were behind the British trenches and posed as Belgian farmers. During the day, in an attempt to glean information, they sometimes came to the trenches and offered coffee to drink and then at night they took pot shots. Two of them were caught in the act. On being searched valuable information was found on them and they were shot. Another anecdote illustrates just how close the two enemy lines were:

> When I left the trenches the Germans were in other trenches only 70 yards away. We could distinctly hear them singing and talking when the wind blew in our direction, and their gramophone entertained both friend and foe alike. . . . The Germans used our shells at night, and by the light thus made they threw hand grenades into our trenches by means of spring-boards.

After the field hospital at Geluveld (which Private Firth describes as having been bombed several times) he was moved to Southampton, Edinburgh and then to his home in Bradford. Losses had been enormous and Private Firth must have felt amazed to be still alive:

> If I had been told before I set off for the front about the sights I should see I could not have believed it. We lost all our officers except the one engaged in transport duty, and out of 14 men who chummed together there is only me and another left.

Private Firth's life was probably saved by the band of men who dodged shells and gunfire to rescue wounded men from the battlefield. Fred Beanland, a stretcher-bearer with the West Yorkshire Regiment, was one of these. He kept a diary for his mother between December 1916 (when he left Hartlepool for Calais) and January 1919, when he returned home. It is clear from the diary that Fred was a man of Christian faith: he often 'Praises God' for narrow escapes and lightness of wounds. Fred describes his work in terse and graphic phrases as the following excerpts show:

9 January 1917
We was flooded out with rain . . . a bombing instructor had his hand blown off.

19 January 1917
Marched with full pack 10 miles to Montrelet and arrived 2.45pm and it was teeming down with rain all the time and we billeted in a pigsty.

5 March 1917
My first time under shell fire.

28 March 1917
Private Henderson of the Dorset Regiment was shot for desertion.

29 April 1917
Two of the West Riding stretcher-bearers was killed by a shell dropping in the entrance of dug out.

7 June 1917
The earth around us shook as the British had blown the 2 biggest mines since the war began and we was about 3 mls from them, and immediately after the explosion a terrible bombardment started and the R.I.R.s captured 17,000 prisoners and I myself saw over 3,000 come in and they seemed frightened to death.

10 June 1917
I had a wonderful escape – a 9.2 shell dropped 2 yards from out dug out sending part of the sides on top of me and Praise God it only gave me a little shock.

14 August 1917
We could see a British Tommy in a shell hole bleeding to death so 3 of us S.B.s out of 10 volunteered to get him and we managed to get him in but a German sniper kept his gun on us all the while and wounded my S.B. mate, F. Parton. About 12 o'clock an officer asked us to try and get a sergeant out of a shell hole who had got fast and was sinking in the sludge and he thought he was bringing important news . . . about 20 yards from the spot the sniper shot me in the right calf. I crept ½ mile . . . and then a S.B. chum carried me on his back under shell fire to aid post . . . Praise God it was a nice Blighty and that brought me out safe.

19 August 1917
I arrived safe at Morton Banks War Hospital, Keighley on Sunday morning praising God for allowing me to be brought so near home.

Morton Banks Hospital near Keighley was the war hospital which treated Fred Beanland, a stretcher-bearer with the West Yorkshire Regiment.

24 December 1917
Left Étaples in cattle trucks 8.15am arrived at Gillicourt 11.30pm Xmas Eve.

12 January 1918
We was shelled very heavily and I fell into a trench and got fast over knee deep in mud and had a great struggle to get out.

9 February 1918
I visited a French cemetery which had been shelled very heavily . . . British, French and German dead lay side by side and there was also a cremating place with bodies of French Generals waiting for cremation.

21 March 1918
Orders came that the enemy had broken our lines so we had to go to dig trenches straightaway and try to hold him back. Artillery and Infantry were fleeing for their lives, tanks went into action and we managed to hold him back for a time.

27 March 1918
Fritz again broke through on our left and after an awful fight we was forced to retreat about 2,000 yards . . . . About 3pm shells and bullets were dropping all around and one shot passed right through my coat, cardigan and shirt sleeve . . . but just later I got wounded in the left thigh by a bullet passing through. The enemy that day wiped out our lads in hundreds . . . but Praise God he watched me through it all. I had to walk with the help of a comrade and a stick about 14 miles to nearest dressing station . . . taken in motor lorries to casualty clearing station . . . we had to sleep outside in the cold.

29 April 1918
Left hospital for 10 days leave.

8 June 1918
Arrived Boulogne 4.30pm this being my third time entering France . . . left Étaples 4.30pm in cattle trucks.

22 August 1918
The enemy made a terrible gas attack on us and I had many narrow escapes of being hit.

23 August 1918
Three quarters of our company went away gassed . . . and I was very slightly gassed but did not get away.

4 October 1918
I was called out and found two of our cooks killed by a shell that had been buried in the ground and the heat of the fire exploded it.

12 October 1918
The enemy was retreating and we met him in Corbanham [*sic*] . . . . and then began some terrible street fighting. Enemy machineguns were firing down the street . . . upon us while I was attending the wounded and he was even hitting the stretcher and put a bullet right through my pack which I was using for a pillow. Praise God he again brought me safely through.

10 November 1918
Sunday . . . we moved forward . . . about 6 miles from Mons.

11 November 1918
We was paraded and at 11.05am our Commander read to us that hostilities had ceased.

7 December 1918
We started having Education in the Army to get us ready for going back.

19 January 1919
I was warned to get ready to proceed home to be demobilised.

24 January 1919
We set sail for England 2pm and we landed at Tilbury Docks midnight up the Thames river. There we was given a good feed and then left by train for Clipston arriving Saturday Jan 25th. We then handed all our arms in and signed all sorts of discharge forms and I was a free man again at 1pm and I caught a train for home at 2pm and arrived in Bradford at 6pm. I praise and thank God for a safe return.

Thus ends the war service of another ordinary man who, despite extraordinary experiences, and seemingly without rancour or regret about his months abroad, simply praises God and returns to civilian life. Fred Beanland's daughter, Audrey Dooley, has his tin box complete with bullet hole and containing the bullet from his experience on 12 October and, most precious of all, the diary which records two years of her father's life.

The tin box which saved Fred Beanland's life on 12 October 1918.

William Heaton was born in Bradford in 1883 and, on leaving school, was employed in the woollen industry as a warehouseman. As soon as war was declared he enlisted with the 16th West Yorkshire Regiment, the 1st Bradford Pals. On the first day of the Battle of the Somme in 1916 he was wounded and picked up by the Germans. He was cared for by German medics in a convent and was later to say that this care saved his life. On recovery, he was taken to a prisoner of war camp in Silesia and was put to work in a colliery for around two and a half years. When repatriated he was emaciated and in very poor physical shape but he eventually recovered his health and survived into his sixties. William's wife, Elizabeth, kept their two sons by volunteering for war work and her story is told in Chapter 11.

Reginald James (Rex) and David Percival Dixon lived at 40 Arncliffe Terrace with their mother, four sisters and their brother Charlie. Charlie was serving in the police force in Bradford and remained in the city for the duration of the war. The family had moved to Bradford from the village of Wray near Lancaster in about 1905. Their father had died in 1898 leaving ten children and, after the three eldest were married, it became essential that work was found for these younger children. Bradford became their temporary home.

Lance Corporal David Percival Dixon of 40 Arncliffe Terrace. An early volunteer in the 1st Bradford Pals, Percy survived until 22 October 1918 when he was posted as 'missing'.

So it was that, at the outbreak of war, Percy became one of the first thousand young men to volunteer for the 16th Battalion and became a Bradford Pal. His name appeared in the *Bradford Weekly Telegraph* on 6 November 1914 under the banner headline 'First Complete Roll Call – A Credit to the City'. Two friends enlisted at the same time: Raymond Smith of 184 St Stephen's Road died on the first day of the Somme and is commemorated on the Thiepval Memorial, and William Lassey of Waverley Avenue was killed by a sniper in May 1916.

Percy Dixon remained with the Pals until February 1918 when he was transferred to the 1/8th (Leeds Rifles) Battalion. On 20 October Percy's company was involved in the crossing of the River Selle. They were involved in some skirmishes and on 22 October pushed on beyond a factory building for some 200 yards. The war diary records:

B Company suffered heavily from shellfire and still more machinegun opposition . . . . casualties for the day were 2 officers wounded, 12 O.R. killed, 74 wounded and 11 missing . . . the bulk of the casualties were from B.

Lance Corporal Dixon's body was never found and he is commemorated on the memorial at Vis-en-Artois.

Rex Dixon fared rather better, surviving both the First and Second World Wars. In July 1914, a month after his eighteenth birthday, he completed his evening courses in draughtsmanship, mathematics and workshop practice at Bradford Technical College. On 4 August Rex enlisted in the Royal Navy. After initial training he was assigned to HMS *Benbow*, an Iron Duke Class Dreadnought Battleship. The ship was only completed in September 1914 and in November it joined 4th Battle Squadron Grand Fleet.

Benbow was the Squadron flagship until June 1916. During the Battle of Jutland in 1916 *Benbow* fired forty 13.5in rounds and received no damage. However, being a self-confessed nosey young man, Rex came up on deck during the barrage to see what was going on. A shell exploded in his face and he only saved his sight by covering his eyes with his hands. He was burned by cordite, for which he received treatment but which left him with a permanently red nose. Rex became a Petty Officer and eventually Ship's Artificer. During the Second World War he served with the British Military Mission in the Mediterranean.

As a young boy Rex had heard about Baden Powell's new organisation and wrote to him enquiring how he could enrol as a scout. He received a hand-written letter from Baden Powell welcoming him to the 'Scout brotherhood' and informing him about the local association. Rex joined the scouts in August 1908 at the YMCA in Bradford, virtually making him a founder member. From 1910 until 1914 he was with the St Stephen's Church Troop. Rex carried this interest into the Navy and while serving with the Grand Fleet he became secretary of the Old Scouts. (He eventually met Lord Baden Powell in the Bahamas on 14 February 1930.)

A family member finds Lance Corporal Dixon's name on the memorial wall at Vis-en-Artois.

HMS *Benbow* on which Reg Dixon served. She is pictured with other early Dreadnoughts.

A rare photograph of the crew of HMS *Benbow* in 1914. One of these faces will be Reg Dixon.

Scouting remained one of Rex's great interests and he was actively involved for the rest of his life as Deep Sea Scout, Rover Leader, Group Scout Master, founder and organiser of the BP Guild in Plymouth and a member of the BP Guild and Trefoil Guild, London Branch.

As the conflict wore on Mrs Dixon returned to her home area. All her 'Bradford' children were by then either living away from the city or, in Charlie's case, had married. Her granddaughter, Dorothy Platts (née Dixon), aged ninety-five, recalls her sitting in her rocking chair at the fireside quietly singing 'Keep the Home Fires Burning'. When news of Percy reached her, the singing ceased.

Horace James Cannon was born in 1895, the son of an army sergeant. He attended St Bede's Grammar School but left home at the age of fourteen to join the Rootes Group in Coventry where he received training as a car mechanic. In September 1914 Horace enlisted with the 16th Battalion West Yorkshire Regiment as a Bradford Pal.

While training with his regiment at Skipton in the early months of 1915 he volunteered for the Royal Flying Corps and became an aircraft mechanic, serving in France and England. He was later promoted to Flight Sergeant. While stationed at Spittalgate Airfield near Grantham an incident occurred which resulted in Horace being decorated for bravery. On 26 January 1918 a plane crash-landed at the aerodrome and Horace, with Flight Sergeant Warne, rescued the pilot from the burning plane. The pilot did not survive but Horace became the only Bradfordian to be awarded the Albert Medal for Bravery. Having retired from the RAF in 1918 Horace served with the Home Guard in the Second World War but was better known in Bradford for his car dealership and repair shop on Manningham Lane.

A photograph of a group of Royal Flying Corps men taken in Bradford. Is Horace James Cannon among them?

A story involving Germans was reported from Bingley Magistrates' Court. PC Brawn had been patrolling at Crossflatts in the very early hours one Friday morning when he came across two men asleep on the footpath behind a wall. He roused them and asked them several questions, but they refused to speak. He put his hand on one of them who struck out at him. The police constable defended himself with his truncheon.

The two men then ran off up Morton Lane with the policeman in pursuit. When he caught up with them he explained that he was a police officer and asked who they were, where they were from and where they were going. One of

The footpath next to the main road at Crossflatts where two escaping German prisoners were recaptured.

the men replied that they were Dutch sailors. They had been on a ship in the Channel when it was either mined or torpedoed. They were picked up by another vessel and landed at Liverpool. They were now making their way to Scarborough where there were fishing boats on which they could obtain a passage back to Holland. One of the men also said, 'If you will show us the way to the railway station I will give you some money.' The police officer duly took them to the station: the police station at Bingley.

At first the men gave their names as Jaun Servaas and Adolph Herandof but on appearing in front of Police Superintendent Slack they gave their real names as Carl Reitz (37), a sergeant-major in the German Army and Ernst Hyl (23), a sailor. They had been prisoners at Handforth Camp in North Cheshire. The court arranged for them to be returned there, along with a third escapee who had been found in Otley. The Magistrate, Mr J.H. Robinson, congratulated the police officer for apprehending the two men and commended the police for their vigilance. Constant lookouts needed to be kept in wartime when there were strangers wondering abroad at night, and he was very pleased indeed that these men should have been caught in his division.

Lt Evelyn Lintott, ex-Bradford City player and the first professional footballer to receive a commission.

Evelyn H. Lintott was signed by Bradford City Football Club in November 1908 from Queen's Park Rangers. The fee was £1,000. He played for England seven times in all and in 1912 he transferred from Bradford City to Leeds. While in Bradford he taught at a school in Dudley Hill and lived at 13 Cornwall Place, Manningham. With his brother, the *Bradford Daily Telegraph* reporter F.S. Lintott, he edited the magazine of the Football Players' Association, of which he was president.

Evelyn enlisted with the 15th Battalion West Yorkshire Regiment (Leeds Pals) on 14 September 1914. Three months later he was commissioned as a lieutenant and thus became the first professional footballer to gain a commission. He was killed in action on the first day of the Battle of the Somme aged thirty-three, and is commemorated on the Thiepval Memorial.

Private D. Spink, reporting the death, said 'Lt. Lintott killed by machinegun at 3 p.m. in the advance. He was struck in the chest.' More details were published in a letter to the *Yorkshire Post*:

Lt. Lintott's end was particularly gallant. Tragically, he was killed leading his platoon of the 15th West Yorkshire Regiment, Leeds Pals, over the top. He led his men with great dash and when hit the first time declined to take the count. Instead, he drew his revolver and called for further effort. Again he was hit but struggled on but a third shot finally bowled him over.

The telegram which announced the wounding and also the death of Lintott in July 1916.

Evelyn Lintott's personal effects were sent to his mother in Surrey and were listed as: three books, two bank pass books, one cheque book, one advance book, two notebooks, photograph case and photographs, photographs and postcards and £78 to be distributed among his family.

Finally, a heartwarming story from Harry Drake who had been a teacher before enlisting with the 16th West Yorkshire Regiment, the 1st Bradford Pals. He had a working knowledge of French, which proved useful as a billeting officer. He describes the beginning of an unusual wartime friendship:

We were coming out of the line to a small village called Famechon in the winter of 1916/17. The billeting party of one officer and five more 'other ranks' arrived at the village, and set out in parties to find the possibilities of the place. I knocked at the door of one cottage that stood in the corner of a small field, and an old woman came to the door.

Wrinkled, tousle-haired, toothless and bent, the old lady had all the appearance of a witch. She offered her son's straw bed on condition it was not for an officer and Harry Drake went on his way. His billeting party found accommodation for all and Harry decided to take the old woman's offered bed for himself. As soon as she was able, and in between pinches of snuff, she quizzed Harry closely to find out as much as she could. His life story obviously met with approval as she adopted the 'tu' rather than the more formal 'vous'. Harry called the old woman 'ma mère' which she seemed to like.

On the second evening the old woman noticed Harry shiver slightly as he sat by the stove. She immediately ordered him to bed and, amid protestations, Harry had to obey. Soon afterwards she climbed the stairs with a large bowl of hot milk, which he was ordered to drink. He slept that night bathed in perspiration and woke to find the Medical Officer standing over him, feeling his pulse. An orderly was sent with tablets and for several days the old woman plied Harry with hot milk and watchfulness.

On the last of the company's 'rest' days, the Medical Officer explained that Harry had been very close to a case of pneumonia. If he had not had a bed and a 'nurse' he would have been sent to the field ambulance. Harry knew of a man who had died of pneumonia in the field ambulance and tried to find a way to show his gratitude to the old woman who had saved him from a similar fate:

> She took my great rough hand in both of hers, and with a look of inestimable charm that her wrinkles could not efface she looked up into my face and smiled. 'My boy,' she said, 'thou art such another as the son I had, but whom the good God thought fit to take from me. Thou art of his form and almost of his face. Thou art of his age, too. Sometimes I have prayed that the Blessed Virgin might send him back to me, but that thou knowest is impossible. She sent thee to me when thou hadst most need of a mother, and for these last few days I have been with a son of my own again. Talk not to me of repayment. I will tell thee what thou mayst do for me. Buy no more than quatre sous' worth of snuff, for a pinch is good for the head.'

The Bradford Roll of Honour, drawn up in 1922 when the war memorial was unveiled, bears the names of 37,000 Bradford men. The 1911 census had recorded the population of Bradford as 288,458. This figure would obviously have risen by 1914 but the total number of men between the ages of eighteen and thirty (being the ages of the vast majority of those who served) cannot have been much more than 55,000, and thus the Roll of Honour represents a high proportion of the men of the city, a handful of whom are remembered here.

FIVE

The War Service of J.B. Priestley

Alison Cullingford

I spent nearly five years in the infantry, was three times a casualty, and saw the flower of my generation mown down among the barbed wire. All the best fellows, as we used to say, 'went West'. *(Letter to a Returning Serviceman)*

Bradford-born author, essayist, journalist and playwright J.B. Priestley served in the British Army between 1914 and 1919. I have based this chapter on his powerful and moving description of this time in his 1962 memoir *Margin Released* and other published and unpublished writings. The account in *Margin Released* begins with Priestley's re-reading of his letters home from the army and rediscovery of a few surviving possessions:

Right: J.B. Priestley's officer's commission.
Below, left: D of W's shoulder-tab and military medal miniatures.
Below, centre: A collection of J.B. Priestley's archive army items: a shoulder-tab, military medal miniatures, his commission, army-issue red wallet for documents, field service pocket book (1914), field message book.

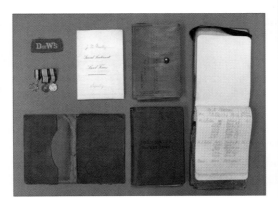

A regimental shoulder-badge, not in metal but khaki cloth, and the fragile remains of one of the old ten-shilling notes, which looks as if it had been half-eaten by a rat, and probably was. There is a Field Service Pocket Book, not well-thumbed, for, like the book on penguins lent to the little American girl, it tried to tell me more than I wished to know. There is a Field Message Book, which starts hopefully at one end with the names and numbers of men in no. 5 Platoon and even more hopefully at the other end with pencilled verses beginning 'I stand forever in the shadow of your hair . . .'.   (*Margin Released*)

Priestley's army experiences were not unusual, but, unlike so many others who had similar experiences, he was not only fortunate enough to survive them but had the talent to bear witness to and express his feelings about them. W.J.P. Aggett, in his history of the Devonshire Regiment, considers that Priestley's account of the Armistice in *Margin Released* 'distills with dazzling clarity and precision the hundreds of descriptions of others less articulate one has heard over the years'.

GROWING UP IN BRADFORD

John Priestley was born in Bradford at 34 Mannheim Road on 13 September 1894. His family knew him as 'Jack' or 'Jacky'; he adopted the middle name 'Boynton' later. In August 1914, he was nineteen. He still lived with his family, which in 1904 had moved a few streets to 5 Saltburn Place. His father, Jonathan, was a schoolmaster. His mother, Emma, died when he was very young, but he got on well with his stepmother, Amy. Jack's sister, Winnie, was the other family member.

Jack had been educated at Belle Vue School. He had found school life boring and restrictive so had left at sixteen, taking a job in the wool trade as a junior clerk with Helm & Co. in the Swan Arcade. Later, Jack came to realise that there had been romance in the wool trade, with its links all over the world, but at the time he found this job very dull and put little effort into it, lingering over errands and secretly reading poetry at his desk. Jack's ambition was to be a writer and he spent much of his limited spare time pouring out stories and verse. Already he had been published, reviewing plays and concerts for the local Labour Party journal *The Bradford Pioneer* and even contributing an article to a national magazine, *London Opinion*, about the new music craze, ragtime. He also enjoyed walking on the moors, music both classical and modern, theatre and music hall.

WAR: AUGUST 1914

In August 1914, at the outbreak of war, Jack was alone at Saltburn Place. The rest of the family were away 'at the seaside'. He had already been on holiday that year, walking in a Europe soon to change forever, in Holland, Belgium and along the Rhine. Bradford then was cosmopolitan: the woolmen travelled all over Europe and many Germans had settled in the town, so there was nothing unusual about Jack's holiday. The previous night, he had gone with a friend to the annual fair at Manningham Tide and talked about the international situation. Thinking back to those August days, he recalled the heat and the 'newsboys . . . running and shouting every day and all day'.   (*Margin Released*)

Jack made up his mind to volunteer. In *Margin Released* he tried to explain this decision:

> The usual explanations were no good. I was not hot with patriotic feeling; I did not believe that Britain was in any real danger. I was sorry for 'gallant little Belgium' but did not feel she was waiting for me to rescue her. The legend of Kitchener, who pointed at us from every hoarding, had never captured me. I was not under any pressure from public opinion, which had not got to work on young men as early as that; the white feathers came later. I was not carried to the recruiting office in a herd rush of chums, nobody thinking, everybody half-plastered; I went alone.

His friends joined later, when the 'Bradford Pals' were formed. So why did he join? It was a challenge:

> There was a move I had to make. I went at a signal from the unknown . . . There came, out of the unclouded blue of that summer, a challenge . . . to what we felt was our untested manhood. Other men, who had not lived as easily as we had, had drilled and marched and borne arms – couldn't we?

However, Jack waited until the family returned before enlisting. We are not told their response. On 7 September 1914, he joined the Duke of Wellington's West Riding Regiment. This regiment was formed in 1881 from the old 33rd and 76th Regiments of Foot and was popularly known as the 'The Havercake Lads' or 'The Dirty Dukes'. Since the start of the war this regiment, like most others, had raised very quickly a large number of new battalions when it became clear the old regular army would not be adequate to fight this war. Jack found himself in No. 8 Platoon, B Company of the 10th (Service) Battalion. As 'Service' denotes, this battalion was formed as part of K3 (Kitchener's Third Army).

Jack was something of a dandy: he reported to the regimental depot in Gibbet Lane, Halifax, wearing a 'newish sports coat and flannel trousers'. He recalled that the regular sergeant, 'noting sardonically' his outfit, set him to removing congealed fat from cooking pots, a foretaste of the life to come.

For a week or so, he commuted from home by tram, but on 23 September 1914 he and a thousand others took the 4.30 a.m. train from Halifax to Farnham in Surrey. Here they joined the 23rd Division.

SOUTHERN ENGLAND 1914–15

Priestley is at pains in *Margin Released* to emphasise that Great War soldiers were far from being the brave but half-trained amateurs of popular belief: he had had 'months and months of severe intensive training', often for ten hours a day, before being sent to the Front. The first year of his army life was to be spent in various camps around the south of England.

The first camp was at Frensham, 5 miles south of Farnham. The camp was huge, holding 10,000 men. Jack shared a bell tent with eleven others. The work was hard:

they might rise at 5.30 a.m. and drill all day or go on long route marches or practise moving silently at night. The camp was overcrowded and conditions were difficult. Pay took many weeks to come through. So the occasional treat, like a bath at Lady Napier's house or a delicious sixpenny tea at a farmhouse, was worth recording. Jack's family sent him parcels of cake, tobacco and toffee, plus books he requested, such as Conan Doyle's *White Company* or a French grammar. There were few opportunities for him to continue his writing, but he read what he could and played draughts or chess.

Jack seems to have made friends easily with the men who volunteered when he did and also with those from the old militia, many of whom were Irish and tended to be stubborn, resist the establishment and never volunteer for extra work. He came to identify with these grim characters as his initial enthusiasm waned, or was knocked out of him by the hard conditions. The men received little information about what was happening or where or when they were to be sent to the Front, so rumours abounded. During this first year, Jack often told his family that they might be going out in a fortnight or a month, and possible destinations included the Dardanelles, Egypt or India.

Another problem was the lack of equipment. Jack received a khaki uniform when he enlisted, but had to swap it for a 'convict-style' blue serge outfit, with a little forage cap. The dye ran out of these caps in the rain, which made the men look ridiculous. Still something of a dandy, however, Jack supplemented this uniform with a larger forage cap he'd picked up from somewhere, a long black overcoat and an odd scarf, which puzzled the girls at home when he returned on Christmas leave:

Ah knew you'd joined up, Jack – but – Ah mean to say – what are you in?

(*Margin Released*)

They eventually received khaki uniforms again in February.

A very wet autumn meant that the camp was soon extremely unpleasant, knee-deep in mud. Not surprisingly, Jack and all his tent-mates fell ill; convalescence was hard in the cramped conditions, where there was no way to keep warm and dry.

At last they were moved indoors for winter at Oudenarde Barracks in Aldershot at the end of November 1914. They spent a week at nearby Camberley for fieldwork, which included musketry and timed trench digging at night.

In February 1915, the Division moved again, in what Jack called a 'Great March' to Folkestone, covering 20 miles a day, sleeping in schools and other public buildings, and carrying rifle, ammunition and all their other kit with them. The column was a mile and a quarter long, the bands played and people waved and cheered: Jack seems to have relished this experience. Kitchener inspected them along the way: Jack was ambivalent about him, able to admire his creation of the new armies but finding him in person a frightening, unreal figure, with 'rather bloated purplish face and glaring but somehow jellied eyes'.

Folkestone was a jolly interlude, which felt like a holiday: Jack was billeted in a private house, a welcome opportunity to sleep in a bed and have proper meals again. He was allocated officers' mess fatigue (washing up and kitchen work), hard work

Lance-Corporal J.B. Priestley in uniform.

but Jack enjoyed the characters he met behind the scenes and it was a change from endless drill. In April, Jack was promoted to lance corporal.

In May 1915, the Division moved outdoors again, to another giant camp at Bramshott in Hampshire, this time crowded with huts instead of tents. Mud was not a problem: conditions were hot, dusty and stifling, with tar dripping from the roofs of the huts. However, the food was better and the men had a good recreation room and cinema shows (although the film tended to break before the end).

Throughout the summer, Jack's letters show that he was becoming frustrated at 'fooling around'. In one letter he reports that the men were becoming 'thoroughly dissatisfied at being kept so long training & training month after month' and that possible disturbances were being prevented by much stricter discipline.

FRANCE 1915–16

All at once, after a year of waiting, change came swiftly: in late August 1915 the 23rd Division were sent to the Front, sailing through the night to Boulogne after a hurried last leave spent mainly on crowded trains. They had a hot, dusty march to the Front, sleeping in rat-infested barns. In his first letter home, Jack likened the experience to a dream, and this feeling of unreality was to recur for him throughout the war. His division relieved 8th Division (composed of units of the regular army) in Bois Grenier-Laventie-Fleurbaix, which was then quiet, with front lines far apart, and sandbags instead of trenches in some places.

They were soon moved towards Neuve Chapelle, in preparation for the big offensive: the Battle of Loos, which began on 25 September. Jack, understandably, would never forget waiting to climb the scaling ladders, so laden with full kit, extra cartridges and bombs that he could barely move. Above him, shells passed like

> invisible express trains. . . . Once up the ladders and out of the trench, I felt a cat would not live five minutes. But the luck was in – I had a lucky war – and because the attack on our right had not gained sufficient ground we were never thrown into the assault, stayed where we were and saw the scaling ladders taken away.
>
> (*Margin Released*)

The weather turned arctic as autumn wore on and winter arrived with rain, sleet and snow. There were no more large offensives that winter, just raids. But these could also prove deadly:

> the barbed wire entanglements, which the artillery said had been cut there, proved to be still intact; and there we were, trapped, no longer in darkness, but in the sinister illumination of star shells and pistol lights, asking to be machine-gunned out of this world, as many were.   (*Margin Released*)

Jack and a companion were able to save one of these men, dragging him back badly wounded.

Jack found the conditions even worse than the dangers: the mud, the lice and the lack of hot food (they were fed on bully beef and biscuits). The bitter cold and wet could not be kept out even by long rubber boots, fur jackets, mackintosh capes, three pairs of socks or rubbing the feet with whale-oil, as Jack reported in a letter to Winnie. The nights were as bright as day and seemed very long: sleep was difficult. Jack became angry that during so-called rest times, the men had to dig and carry out other difficult and tiring tasks. The worst of all these tasks (Jack said) was carrying coils of barbed wire up communication trenches, knee-deep in water, under shellfire; a task that made powerful men weep. *Margin Released* gives a sense of the strange nightmare of this winter. One unforgettable image Priestley conjures up is of a line of reserve trenches running right through a village cemetery, full of large French graves and the 'pathetic' small wooden crosses of British soldiers' graves, bullets ricocheting off the stones.

The worst horror of all was the constant noise. Jack explained that one became used to some sounds (sniping, machine-gun, grenades) but never the cannonading

> drumming hell into your ears, no matter whether it was their guns or yours, began to wear you down, making you feel that flesh and blood had no place in this factory of destruction . . . as time wore on I was more and more a chap who wondered what the hell he was doing there and how the hell he could get out of it – a mouse in a giant mincing machine.   (*Margin Released*)

Looking back, Priestley felt that he had been temporarily brave but became less so as the war went on. He had been well trained and was tired of waiting to get to the Front, but this initial enthusiasm was very soon driven away. As he later remarked to his good friend and biographer Diana Collins, 'I spent the first year [of the war] trying to be a hero and the rest of the time trying to stay alive'. (*Time and the Priestleys*)

The physical hardships were exacerbated by endless petty rules and restrictions, which he resented having to impose on the men and which made him consider reverting to the ranks. His only comfort was tobacco, sent in parcels from home, which temporarily drove away hunger and lack of sleep.

In November 1915, Jack escaped briefly: he was sent to replace a clerk at 3rd Corps HQ who had been hospitalised. Though safe and dry in a wooden hut, he disliked the 'Kafkaesque' bureaucracy and more pointless bullying. A shock awaited him on his return to B Company: his best friend in the Battalion, Irvine Ellis, who had joined when he did, had been killed.

Soon after his return to the Front, Jack was slightly wounded in the hand by a rifle grenade. He was sent to hospital and then to convalesce at Le Tréport. Again he felt isolated, without money or post, and was almost relieved to return. He was sustained by the great solidarity he developed with the men, both the grim old soldiers and those who had joined when he did. Priestley was seen to have potential as an officer, but he refused to apply for a commission out of loyalty to these men.

During this terrible winter, all his other close friends in B Company were killed. Jack was filled with anger and bitterness towards the 'cavalry captains, back in the chateaux' for this, which rings out in *Margin Released*, written almost fifty years later:

> They tell me Passchendaele in '17 was worse still – I was never there, thank God – and now I believe the Army ought to have turned on Haig and his friends and sent them home. Even without the negotiated peace we ought to have had in 1916, we could have saved half a million British lives if we had handed the whole mess over to a few men from Imperial Chemicals, Lever Brothers or Lyons & Co.'

Modern authors have tried to counter the conventional criticisms of these commanders by emphasising that the technologies were driving men into trenches and causing stalemate, plus the problems of poor communication. Jack understood these problems: his point was that the British officers handled these problems badly. He noticed and pointed out in his letters home that the French soldiers in particular had better food and conditions, and were allowed to rest between their times at the Front. He felt that the British men were ordered into pointless activity for the sake of giving them something to do, in case they might mutiny.

In March 1916 the Division was sent south, to relieve the 17th French Division on Carency-Souchez front. Although the distance was not great, the journey was difficult: Jack was one of an advance party which became hopelessly lost and had to sell non-essential kit to survive.

The place they reached was ghastly:

> This was a very sinister sector into which we crept now, half-blinded by the last
> snowstorms of the winter. Names there enjoyed a grim notoriety – Notre Dame
> de Lorette, Souchez, Vimy Ridge and the Labyrinth.   (*Margin Released*)

The 'Labyrinth' was their destination: a maze of 'great hills half blown away with
enormous shells; villages absolutely razed to the ground; old trenches full of heads,
legs and arms; bloodstained clothing & old equipment.' (Unpublished letter, 14
March 1916)

The British trenches were very close to the Germans, who were on higher ground
and so their varied artillery dominated. Jack had found rifle grenades very unnerving
since he was wounded, but most feared were the *minenwerfers* (big trench mortars),
which were noisy, short-range and unpredictable.

Although clearly at a disadvantage, the British were ordered to 'hot it up',
illustrating Jack's belief that those in charge did not understand what they were
doing. The results were terrible, a pointless waste of life:

> Outside any plan of campaign, without any battle being fought, any honours
> being won, we went through the mincer. It was not long before our own B
> Company, with a nominal fighting strength of 270, had been reduced to a grim
> and weary seventy. Two hundred men had gone somehow and somewhere, with
> nothing to show for it.   (*Margin Released*)

One June morning, Jack was in a small dugout sorting the platoon's rations (bread,
meat, tea, sugar, tinned milk), when he heard a rushing sound; he knew it to be a
trench mortar, but could not get away in time and 'the world blew up'. The mortar
had landed only two or three yards from Jack, but the dugout seems to have
protected him. Jack could not remember what happened next, how he was found
and dug out, or any hospitals in France; he came round in North Evington hospital
near Leicester with his parents at his bedside. He had suffered minor injuries, was
partially deafened for a time and developed a high temperature, which took some
weeks of bed rest to come down. But he knew that he had been very lucky.

BLIGHTY: 1916–17

Jack was sent to convalesce at Hambleton Hall in Rutland, travelling in the bizarre
costume of the convalescent: sky-blue coat and pants, white shirt and scarlet tie. The
country house proved to be a delightful and absurd place, with comic butlers,
amiable doctors, motherly nurses and pretty VAD girls. Jack played the piano, badly
but with enthusiasm, and soon set up a little concert party of the convalescent men.

They were not particularly talented, but provided fun, so they were soon invited
to other convalescent homes.

Reporting to the regimental depot in Halifax in the autumn, Jack was still not
considered to be fit, so was sent to another convalescent camp at Ripon. Conditions
here were poor and very brutal. Priestley felt that the army was still relying on

A convalescents' concert party at Hambleton Hall, 1916.

punishments designed to subdue the press-ganged or violent men of past eras but which were not suitable for the respectable decent volunteers of this war. Fortunately, after a few miserable weeks, though still not yet fit, he was moved to a larger and better camp near Alnwick. However, Ripon had been the last straw: Jack had had enough of the terrible conditions, unfairness and brutality the men had to endure, and he changed his mind about applying for a commission. Officers faced danger too but at least led more comfortable lives. Once he was passed fit he was temporarily attached to the 3rd Battalion on Tyneside, waiting to be sent for officer training.

Jack later looked back on 1917 as a 'dead time': he was not dodging the war, but he had long lost all his original enthusiasm to be a good soldier. He had little heart for anything and spent much of his time drinking beer. He had to be careful not to make a mistake and lose his chance for a commission, but Alnwick was a large camp; it was easy to dodge parades and fatigues, and Jack took full advantage: he and a group of fellow skivers would join the full parade, march neatly round the corner out of sight, then disappear for the rest of the day.

At last, Jack was sent to the 16th Officer Cadet Battalion, whose camp was at Kinmel, near Rhyl in North Wales.

Here he was able to regain a sense of purpose. The cadets were worked hard but Jack enjoyed this time, despite noticing how out of date the training was. He passed his exam and was commissioned to the Devon Regiment:

Out of the allowance we were given we bought greatcoats and British warms, tunics and Sam Browne belts. We were officers free for ever from cookhouse fatigues and carrying coils of barbed wire. . . . After a few days swagger at home I arrived at [the Regiment's] headquarters and barracks at Devonport as new and shy and glossy as a bridegroom.   (*Margin Released*)

The Battalion was not needed in France, so Jack remained at Devonport until the end of summer 1918, leaving only to take a few courses at camps in Cornwall. This was a pleasant life, in comfortable barracks and with good food. Jack found another way to avoid the hated parades: in charge of funeral parties, he took the band to the station, saw the coffin off and spent the rest of the day in the cinema, music hall or strolling.

RETURN TO FRANCE: 1918

Jack and two Devonport friends were among six subalterns ordered to France to join the 16th (Royal Devon Yeomanry) Battalion of the Devons. They sailed to Boulogne on a ship full of American soldiers, with a ragtime band on the top deck. The Battalion, which had had over 200 casualties earlier in September, was far below strength. It was attached to 231 Brigade and attacking towards Ronsoy, near Peronne. His two friends were killed within days and Second Lieutenant Priestley was soon rapidly out of action. One evening, Jack was in a railway cutting on to which gas shells were dropped. He wore his mask and made sure the men wore theirs. However, it later became apparent that Jack had inhaled gas, because during the attack next morning, 18 September, he became ill and got lost in the mist. The effects were worsened by the many tots of rum taken as he waited to attack just before dawn. Soon he could not see the battle at all, though he could hear it. He came across a young German, only a schoolboy, so waved his revolver at him and pointed him towards the British lines. Jack stumbled around for a while, unable to breathe, and eventually rested in a shell hole, where he was found by stretcher-bearers.

He was taken to base hospital, then to the Medical Board Base Depot near Rouen to await the decision of the Medical Board. While waiting, the officers spent their time censoring letters, paying troops and drinking a great deal of Guinness. Jack later described this time in his short story 'The Town Major of Miraucourt'. The Board eventually decided that Jack, a 'wheezy parcel', as he says in the story, was unfit for active service, downgrading him to 'B2'. He was still fit enough for other work, so he was sent to the Labour Corps Depot, where fortunately his interest in theatre and music soon found him a niche in supplying entertainers: conjurors, comedians and female impersonators.

ARMISTICE AND AFTER: NOVEMBER 1918-19

The genuine Armistice took us by surprise after so many false reports, and we had to hurry to get drunk enough to go shouting and reeling round the town. I can remember trying to work myself up into the right Bacchanalian mood, trying to ignore the creeping shadows, the mysterious rising tide of regret and sadness, which I think all but the simplest men suffer from on these occasions.   (*Margin Released*)

A souvenir photograph of German PoW warrant officers and senior NCOs, 1919.

Despite the Armistice, Jack's war was far from over. He was sent to report for duty at a prisoner of war camp near Calais, presumably because he knew some German from his wool trade experiences. He reported that the PoWs were well fed and treated, but that the psychological effect of imprisonment made them cowed and pitiful, although they were far more afraid of their own sergeants than of the British. The sergeants awed Jack too, describing them as 'iron men with Iron Crosses, Kaiser moustaches, terrible rasping words of command'.

But at Christmas he burst in on them in sentimental reverie around a very small tree. At once they all leapt up and clicked their heels. For Jack this summed up the German character. It is interesting that his accounts of the war express no hostility towards the German soldiers.

The POWs were then ordered to move up to the Lille-Roubaix-Toucoing area to carry out salvage work. The major and the lieutenant senior to Jack were away, so it befell that Jack was in charge of the move of 600–700 Germans and 80 British troops, the most responsible job he had ever had. Transport and rations were chaotic, but Jack enjoyed the challenge. He had developed loyalty to his POWs as he had to his Platoon companions. The following incident shows how much Jack was prepared to risk for his loyalty. While still in temporary charge, he was ordered to move the men to a canvas camp area in a shell-holed waterlogged area in early December, he protested that this would be dangerous (many of the men were sick) and refused to do it. He was threatened with court-martial, but, after he found a

PoW company football team, 1919.

better place for the camp and promised the men would improve it without help or funds, he won: consent was given and the men worked hard and built a cosy camp.

Despite such successes in organising his men and defeating the 'red tabs', Jack felt trapped: he did not want a 'cushy billet', like some: 'There was a rumour, before I left, that it was taking three full colonels to run a laundry in Lille.' He wanted to get on with his interrupted life. As a casualty three times, Jack had some priority. The Major, who did not like him, quickly forwarded his applications for demobilisation and at last he was sent back to England.

The journey back was a nightmare. Jack was the only officer on the Lille–Boulogne train, which was crammed with men, often drunk, who had had more than enough of the army. The train was badly delayed and discipline about to crack. Jack was able to control the situation by asking some of the more sensible of the NCOs to keep things calm. Then the men had to be marched from train to camp. Again, he told them that if they formed some sort of column and kept together, everything would go more smoothly. But on arrival at the camp, a 'little fuss-pot of an adjutant' began to shout 'Left, right!' at them. The men laughed and shouted at him and he hurriedly left, having interfered and stirred up a situation he could not manage. This incident for Jack summed up the problem he had with the army, which treated the men like rabble rather than the decent citizens they were, and threw them into attacks not for good reasons but because it was the thing to do.

RETURN TO BRADFORD: 1919

> After the war I could not have remained in or near Bradford, never considered
> doing so.   (*Margin Released*)

At last, in the spring of 1919, Jack returned to civilian life. But, back in Bradford,
everything had changed. Most of his friends had joined the Bradford Pals battalion
of the West Yorkshire Regiment, which had suffered extremely heavy losses, notably
on 1 July 1916: the first day of the battle of the Somme. Jack knew he had been
lucky to survive, but could not settle back to life when so many were lost:

> Sometimes I feel like an old man, for I seem to know intimately more dead men
> than living ones. To think about an old playing field is to see a crowd of ghosts.
> (*The Lost Generation*)

Priestley himself had changed, of course. The war had shown him the class system,
which had not impinged on his Bradford boyhood:

> Call this class prejudice if you like . . . I went into that war without any such
> prejudice, free of any class feeling. No doubt I came out of it with a chip on my
> shoulder; a big heavy chip, probably some friend's thigh-bone. (*Margin Released*)

He also resented the time he had lost and was keen to make up for it. The drifting
of his pre-war years was over. He received a very small ex-officer's grant to go to
Cambridge University, where he studied modern
history and political science, supplementing the
meagre income with writing and coaching.

In 1921 he married Pat, a pre-war friend who
had written to him during the war and visited
him in hospital. Jack did well at his studies,
completing his degree in two years, but found
academia no more congenial than the army, and
took the bold step of moving his family to
London to write freelance.

Jack began his writing career proper with
journalism and essay writing, but soon branched
out into novels, especially the great success *The
Good Companions*, and then drama. He began to
consider social issues more deeply as the 1920s
turned into the '30s, and in particular the results
of the war: the loss of so many good men and the
treatment of those who had returned.

J.B. Priestley in the early 1920s, wearing an academic
gown over his officer's uniform.

THE REUNION: 1933

On 28 October 1933, Jack returned to Bradford for the Battalion reunion dinner, in the Market Tavern Hotel. This was the first such dinner arranged by the Battalion's Old Comrades' Association and Jack had not seen the Battalion since he was wounded in June 1916. While he had convalesced and then become an officer, they had been at the Somme and Passchendaele, and spent the last year of the war fighting in Italy. Jack's famous account of the reunion was published in *English Journey*. The room was crowded and hot, the atmosphere uproarious. Jack thought about the bonds that had formed between these men and their great affection for good leaders such as the Major, known as 'Daddy', and what a pity it was that such bonds were formed only in war and could not be directed towards peaceful aims.

We have seen Jack's war through his eyes: it is pleasant to report that the Battalion thought highly of him, as is shown by this in 'The Iron Duke', the Regiment's journal, in 1934:

> Nobody then realised that all the time [Priestley] was sitting with his old comrades he was making mental notes of what was taking place so that he might incorporate them in a chapter in a book he was writing. . . . Mr Priestley's modesty forbade him mentioning his own part in making the dinner such a success, but none of those present will forget the entertaining speech he delivered, the dozens of autographs he gave and the manner in which he wound up the proceedings by playing 'Auld Lang Syne' and 'God save the King'.

The dinner stirred Jack's growing social conscience. Some men were so poor they could not afford to attend the reunion, so Jack and some of the others had arranged for free tickets to be supplied; however, these men had still been unable to attend as they had no suitable clothes. Jack was furious: these men had 'fought for a world that did not want them . . . had come back to exchange their uniforms for rags'.

JACK THE WRITER

During Jack's army service, it had been very difficult for him to do any sustained writing, though he continued to experiment with verse: his *Field Message Book* contains verses pencilled during this time. He did publish one book during the war, at his own expense, a collection of poems: *A Chapman of Rhymes* (Moring, 1918). Later he found this work embarrassing and attempted to suppress it, so very few copies survive. These poems are totally unlike any of Priestley's later writings, lacking the precise, detailed and evocative style of his later career. I find these poems moving not because of their content, but because they illustrate that Jack did not expect to return from the war: these could easily have been his only literary memorial. Yet he survived: his literary career spanned six decades and included successful novels, essays, plays, history, journalism and much more.

Yet Jack did not, perhaps could not, write directly about his experience in the trenches until *Margin Released*. He produced no novel or play set on the battlefield. As he explained in the memoir, when he left the army and started his career he did not want to look back to that which was lost, but to get on with his interrupted life. Later, he considered other writers had already produced better works than he could have done. A deeper reason lay in the very nature of his writing talent. Priestley came to believe that some writers, such as Hemingway, 'found in war, however much they hated it, the deeper reality we all look for'. He was not of this class. He could not reconcile the tragedy and brutality of war with the comic, almost farcical aspects of army life.

Jack believed that England would have been very different had the finest men not all been killed in the war. Those that remained, like himself, were the 'runts', not up to the standard of the dead. Jack returned to this painful idea several times in his writings, one example being *Benighted*, a 1927 tale about two groups of people marooned by a storm in a very strange house in the wilds of Wales. Although marketed later as a thriller, it is also a dark and thoughtful philosophical exploration. Nothing has gone right for the character Penderel since the war: he has been jilted, swindled, tried and failed to become a writer. He feels that all the best men, like his brother, were killed, imagines how different things would be if 'you could bring 'em all back, fellows like Jim, hundreds and hundreds and thousands of 'em'. Now he has 'nothing to do, no aim of any kind, very few real friends'. Bitter, disillusioned, shell-shocked, he knows that he cannot excuse his failures because of the war, but that does not help him:

> I know this disillusionment or cynicism or bitterness or whatever it is, is the new cant, an attitude, weakness trying to disguise itself. And that makes it worse for me. I say I ought to be able to win through, and then I ask myself 'Win through to what?'

Penderel is fictional, he should not be seen as a portrait of Jack, but nevertheless the feelings and problems Jack gives him in this book are ones Jack himself and millions of other Front-line veterans and other survivors were tackling in their own ways:

> Suddenly that old feeling had returned. . . . A grey tide, engulfing all colour and shape of things that had been or were to be, rushed across his mind, sweeping the life out of everything and leaving him all hollow inside. Once again he sat benumbed in a shadow show. Yet as ever – and this was the cruel stroke – there was something left, left to see that all the lights were being quenched, left to cry out with a tiny crazed voice in the grey wastes. . . . It wasn't panic or despair, he told himself, that made so many fellows commit suicide; it was this recurring mood, draining the colour out of life and stuffing one's mouth with ashes. One crashing bullet, and there wasn't even anything left to remember what had come and gone, to cry in the mind's dark hollow; life could then cheat as it liked, for it did not matter; you had won the last poor trick.

Jack drew on his experiences of war in his *Postscripts*, the famous Second World War radio broadcasts. His understanding of the meaning of war added depth to these moving talks and helped him bond with listeners who had had similar experiences.

Later, he was instrumental in founding the anti-nuclear movement, emphasising his experience of how fighting starts, and how disastrous this could be in a world with nuclear weapons:

> Everybody who was in the trenches will remember how, one night when all was quiet, some young ass of a sentry would fire a few quick rounds at nothing, just to warm his hands. So a German sentry would loose off a few rounds. Then more English, more Germans. The machineguns would join in. Then the light artillery and the trench mortars on both sides. Then the heavy artillery would be called in, until finally the night would be a daft inferno. That is war. (*The Lost Generation*)

It is also significant that two of Jack's most admired and popular works, the novels *Bright Day* and *Lost Empires*, cover the period around the war and are full of his views about the period and the causes of the war. *Bright Day* (1946) is the story of a writer looking back at pre-war Bradford and the effects of the war and changing society on a golden family. *Lost Empires* (1965) is a young artist's life helping his magician uncle in a 1913–14 music hall. This book was written after *Margin Released* and echoes the memoir in many interesting ways. Young Richard, the artist, joins the army at the outbreak of war, like Jack, not out of any great patriotism but because he sees it as a challenge and is dissatisfied with his life. His Uncle Nick tries to persuade him not to volunteer: he sees all too clearly that 'we're in for the biggest bloody massacre of all time. And you can't even wait for them to fetch you'. Although the cynicism and intelligence are typical of Uncle Nick's character, it is easy to see this as the Priestley of the 1960s talking to his younger self, the 'chump' who had rushed to join the infantry. Richard's experiences of the great army camps in the south-east of England are Jack's, down to the leaking dye of his forage cap, but Priestley leaves Richard reunited happily with Nancy at one of the English camps and the novel does not follow his army career to France.

Priestley was far too subtle a writer to portray pre-war Bradford or England as perfect, indeed the music hall life he portrays in *Lost Empires* is brutal and sordid, and the downfall of the Allington family in *Bright Day* is not caused by the war. But both works are pervaded by a sense of loss, of time passing and of the power of reminiscence, reflecting his view that the war was:

> A great jagged crack in the looking glass. After that your mind could not escape from the idea of a world that ended in 1914 and another one that began about 1919, with a wilderness of smoke and fury, outside sensible time, lying between them.
> (*Margin Released*)

Acknowledgements

For permission to quote from Priestley's published and unpublished works, thanks to the Priestley Estate.

For permission to quote from W.J.P. Aggett, thanks to the Trustees of the Regimental Association of the Devonshire and Dorset Regiment.

For permission to quote from *The Iron Duke*, thanks to the Duke of Wellington's West Riding Regiment.

SIX

Bradford's Textile Industry 1914–18

Mike Woods & Tricia Platts

On Wednesday 5 August 1914 the Council of Bradford Chamber of Commerce[1] was hastily convened 'under the sense of the deep gravity of the situation and of the particularly trying position with which the traders of Bradford were suddenly confronted'.

The members agreed that the position required fortitude, calm, courage and determination in order that they might stand by and assist each other. Members would be required to unite in doing their utmost to find employment for the work people so that the city and trade might emerge from their difficulties with as little loss and damage as possible.

During the nineteenth century the textile industry had transformed Bradford from a small rural town into a rich and famous city. The mechanisation of the industry meant jobs became plentiful and thousands were drawn to the city. Lack of regulation caused housing to grow haphazardly, producing squalid, unhealthy, overcrowded living conditions. Cholera, typhoid and anthrax (also called wool-sorters disease) were prevalent. However, companies were aware of the need to improve the health of their workers and their families and steps were taken to improve the environment within which people lived and worked.

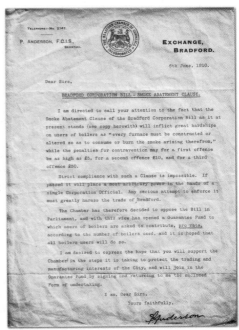

A 1910 letter from the Chamber of Commerce urging members to oppose the introduction of smoke abatement. To enforce it would 'greatly harass the trade of Bradford'.

In 1847 Bradford became a municipal borough and elected its first local government representatives. A start was made on improving conditions for the citizenry, an early priority being the provision of clean drinking water and the building of underground sewers. Street lighting, public baths, the building of a public hospital and regular rubbish collections enabled citizens to live healthier lives and provision of recreational spaces, public libraries and public transport were all signs of a prosperous community.

By the middle of the nineteenth century Bradford's wealth and civic pride was reflected in fine buildings such as the Town Hall, Wool Exchange and St George's Hall. In 1897 the town became the City of Bradford, otherwise known as 'Worstedopolis'. The foundation stone of the Bradford Exchange was laid by Lord Palmerston in 1864 and the building became the heart of an international market place:

> On a busy market day a visitor to the Bradford Exchange will rub shoulders with men who have first-hand knowledge of almost every market in the world. It is doubtful whether any other industry has produced so many first class linguists; men who are accustomed to travel to far-off lands to sell the products of Bradford's spindles and looms.[2]

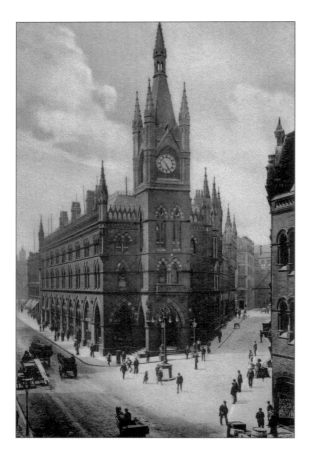

The 'Venetian Gothic' style of Bradford Wool Exchange (built 1857) symbolised the wealth and importance of the textile trade in the city.

The detail on this picture of Ivegate reveals much about conditions in the city: shops windows with the latest fashions and the busy hum of people going about their business.

The arrival of the first steam engine in 1798 had revolutionised all the processes involved in the production of cloth which previously had been done by hand. The first steam-powered spinning mill opened in Bradford in 1800 and within twenty years thirty-nine more were operating. An estimated 14,000 handloom weavers were working in West Yorkshire in 1838, but within ten years almost all had been either driven out of business or into the mills to operate the new power looms. The mechanisation of wool combing took a little longer but, in time, the Lister Nip Comb took the chore out of even this process. The arrival of the railway in the early part of the century enabled goods to move in and out of the city and the boom years were born.

Bradford's specialism was worsted, a lightweight cloth made of long-staple combed wool yarn. Supplies of wool from all over Britain and from abroad were being processed in thirty-eight worsted mills in 1841 and Bradford quickly established itself as the world's leading producer. The business was reported upon in the *Wool Record* dating from 1909, and other journals included *Journal of the Textile Institute*, *The Textile Institute & Industry*, *Textile Month*, *Wool Science Review*, *Textile Horizon*.[3]

The industry also spawned the first specialist college courses from about 1850. Bradford College now houses an extensive and important archive which records worsted manufacture in the city. There are samples of cloth used by teaching staff as illustrations between 1850 and 1910, student design workbooks and large bound volumes of pattern books from many of the leading manufacturers. Among these are the 'America' series of Salvador Dali printed textile designs. The archive is now with the Confederation of British Wool Textiles and is housed in Salt's Mill.

To support the textiles boom, a proliferation of small, mutually dependent firms sprang up ranging from the supply of steel pins, spindles and flyers to printing, banking, insurance and the transport industry. It was not always plain sailing. The Chamber of Commerce record books and local press reports contain interesting accounts of skirmishes between firms. For example, in December 1915 Messrs Baron faced a shortage of weft and were unable to fulfil an order for 19,500 yards of khaki at 3s 4½d per yard for Mitchell & Priestley for finishing. Mitchell & Priestley's sued Messrs Baron for the sum of £760. In 1916 the Chamber of Commerce tried to prevent Burberry adopting 'gabardine' as a trademark.

Relationships between workers and bosses were not always harmonious and, almost by accident, Bradford became a political pioneer. In the 1890s there was a long and bitter strike over pay cuts at Lister's Mill.

Out of this dispute, at a conference of trade unionists in 1893, was born the Independent Labour Party which was a forerunner of the modern Labour Party. In education Bradford pioneered school meals (a movement in which Margaret MacMillan played a leading role), health care, swimming baths and nurseries. It was a Bradford MP and worsted manufacturer, W.E. Forster, who in 1870 pioneered the first Act of Parliament which was to give every child in Britain a free education.

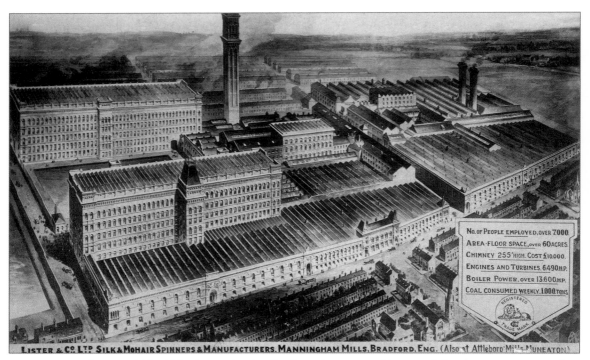

No. of People Employed, over 7,000.
Area Floor Space, over 60 Acres.
Chimney 255' high. Cost £10,000.
Engines and Turbines, 6,490 H.P.
Boiler Power, over 13,600 H.P.
Coal Consumed Weekly, 1,000 Tons.

Lister & Co. Ltd Silk & Mohair Spinners & Manufacturers. Manningham Mills, Bradford, Eng. (Also at Attleboro' Mills, Nuneaton)

A view of Lister's Mill which also carries details of employees, machinery and the vast area it occupied.

As the population of the city increased throughout Victorian times, semi-suburban housing areas developed beyond the city centre and the emerging middle classes moved out to Bradford Moor, Great Horton, Heaton and Allerton. Horse-drawn buses provided transport and, from 1882, were joined by electric trams. The trolleybuses introduced in 1911 were the first to be seen on England's streets. Surrounding villages became absorbed by the city, including Baildon where, in 1915, the street listings give the trades of residents: warp dresser, worsted spinner, textile designer, stock weightman, top and noil merchant, spinners manager. These people represent the increasingly prosperous face of the city.

However, even by 1914 'Worstedopolis' was showing signs of decline. During the 1890s a worldwide depression had brought falling prices and profits while foreign competition became intense. Tariff barriers imposed in North America hit Bradford hard. The powerful congressman William McKinley had introduced a trade act in 1890 which imposed a 50 per cent tax on imports. He saw this as a tool to 'keep up the wages of the American worker as well as the profits of key new businesses, until the US could compete on a global basis'. In 1914 the Foreign and Colonial Trade Committee of Bradford Chamber of Commerce reported tariff barriers in Austro-Hungary, Chile, France, Italy, Russia, Switzerland and Turkey.

Fashions were also changing. Worsted was a hardwearing, sensible cloth but softer fabrics were becoming popular. Bradford manufacturers were quick to develop new fabrics and threads and marketed them across the world.

Competitors in French factories and even Huddersfield were also producing finer men's suitings, flannels and sportswear. As Bradford had been first into the market, its factories were suffering from ageing machinery and it took time for some manufacturers to realise the changes in business practices which might be necessary. For example, it was realised that the 'new' manufacturing countries were willing to import Bradford yarns from which they could weave their own styles. A report from the Black Dyke

Manufacturers were quick to highlight the range of cloths supplied.

Mills showed that in the period 1880 to 1904 worsted exports were virtually static yet the export of yarns was up by 33 per cent and graded raw fibre, tops and noils increased by 50 per cent.

Bradford tried to exploit the principle of 'Imperial Preference' where countries of the Empire were expected to give first choice to English suppliers and tariffs did not exist. European markets were also targeted, including the German-speaking world. German citizens came to Bradford in large numbers as part of this strategy, and substantial sums were invested in German companies. An excellent relationship with Germany was thus established and the area of Bradford known as Little Germany became a distinctive area of the city.

Mill owners gradually became less autocratic and more benevolent. Titus Salt had already moved out of the city to Saltaire and a smaller model development was established by H.W. Ripley of the Bowling dyeing company at Ripleyville in 1863. It was intended that workers would purchase their houses but this proved unpopular. The houses were put into a trust, which existed until the second half of the twentieth century.

Other manufacturers, on a more modest scale, encouraged social and recreational clubs, excursions and a more supportive, conciliatory atmosphere. However, works outings and football competitions did not always meet with the approval of the workforce and a stronger political awareness developed. A widespread interest in trade unions and, ultimately, the Labour Party, reflected a sharpening of relationships. There was also a faltering of investment and research into the industry.

Some mill owners, in addition to providing employment, had also given the city outstanding facilities (such as Manningham Park and Cartwright Hall Gallery), some fine houses and energetic civic leadership. Great names such as Lister, Salt, Forster,

Ripleyville has now been demolished; the area was not as attractive as Sir Titus Salt's village.

Ambler, Roberts and Willey are still remembered today. However, wealth also left the city, being spent on large country estates, horse breeding or growing orchids.

John Foster (Black Dyke Mills) bought Hornby Castle in 1861, Samuel Lister bought Swinton Castle in 1891, Joseph Dawson purchased the Nun Appleton Estate and Francis Willey bought Blyth Hall in Nottinghamshire. Towards the end of the nineteenth century it was becoming apparent that the next generation who inherited businesses from their fathers and grandfathers was less inclined to stay in the textile industry.

John Foster was co-founder of Black Dyke Mills at Queensbury.

While the thrusting Victorian entrepreneurs might have earned their retirement, their sons and heirs were not following their earlier, wealth-creating example. The profits of the forefathers was spent on public school and university educations, and thus was born a new breed of young man seeking a different lifestyle. Careers in the armed services, the professions, politics or the simple, but expensive, pursuit of leisure led to a distancing from the family roots of the worsted industry. Examples are numerous and include Hugh Ripley, son of H.W. Ripley, who went into the army. Matthew Thompson's son Reginald, educated at Uppingham and Cambridge, became a gentleman of leisure. Percy Holden Illingworth, son of Henry, also a Cambridge man, became well known as a rugby player and big game hunter before successfully turning to a career in politics. Alfred Hutton, son of an Eccleshill manufacturer, followed a similar route into politics.

Increasing demands on production were widely reported and as early as December 1888 the *Bradford Observer* reported:

> One weaver will now mind two looms handling as much as 11,000 to 12,000 ends for practically less wages than were once paid for minding two looms with a matter of 800 ends each.

The *Observer* also noted that the machines per worker were being increased so that in mohair spinning, one operative per frame had become one operative per six frames. At Garnett's in Apperley Bridge[4] automatic looms were installed in 1913 so that 'skilled people were less needed'.

Women were very much part of the workforce. When the men left for war they moved into slightly higher managerial roles.

On 31 December 1914 the *Yorkshire Observer* printed its annual report on the city's textile business under the headline 'Huge Orders for Army Cloth'. The article explains perfectly the decline and revival of textiles:

There has been no more wonderful and eventful year than that which is just drawing to a close in the whole history of the woollen industry. In January production costs were rising, raw materials costing more and demand for finished articles was declining after the exceptionally mild winter of 1913 in England and on the continent. By February the margin of profit had reached vanishing point. Even on the outbreak of war the outlook was gloomy. Production had been cut by half and mill closures seemed probable.

But then it was announced that the Army was to raise one million men with another million to follow. The orders for khaki and blankets were enough to set all the machinery running again at the highest possible pitch of pressure.

Never before in the whole history of the woollen industry has there been such wonderful activity as during the past three months . . . the heyday of prosperity.[5]

In the summer months there had been substantial demands from the Textile Workers' Union for out-of-work pay but those days were now gone. The paper warned that large contracts would go a-begging if manufacturers could not meet the time limits attached to government orders. The *Observer*[6] had previously listed tenders for clothing which had been put out by the Bradford Battalion in October:

Greatcoats	Messrs Wright Burrows & Co., Huddersfield
Jackets and trousers	Mr David Murie, Bradford; Mr R. Mettrick, Guiseley;
	Miller, Rayner & Haysom Ltd, London;
	Messrs George Brown & Son, Bradford
Puttees	Messrs Fox & Todd, Bradford
Regulation army caps	Brown Muff & Co., Bradford

The newspaper went on, with great pride,

> The whole of the serge for the jackets and trousers is Bradford made, and the lustre lining and other linings are from Bradford houses. The puttees are made in Bradford. The buttons, a great source of difficulty, have been specially made to a Government pattern by a Bradford firm.

The volunteers were all measured for their uniforms and it was found that only about 120 men were below the 'standard height', which was given as 5ft 6in. The 'average' height of the Battalion was found to be 5ft 8½in. Speed was critical and the newspaper reported that it was expected to clothe the entire Battalion in ten to fourteen days! However, from this point onwards it was extremely rare to find any newspaper references to clothing the troops: such information became restricted as possibly prejudicial to the war effort.

In 1919 the Chamber of Commerce was able to report on the ever increasing call upon the industry for uniforms and underclothing for all the allied armies as the chief wool textile centres in France (Roubaix, Tourcoing and Lille) had been under German occupation since early in the war.[7] The same publication listed the orders placed by the Army Contracts Department between 4 August 1914 and 31 December 1916 which included:

87,566,000yds khaki for tunics, trousers and great coats
105,105,000yds flannel for shirts
10,729yds Barathea, Bedford cord and whipcord
21,175,000 blankets
10,000,000 woollen and flannel vests
63,565,000 pairs worsted socks
8,382000 pairs of woollen gloves
20,950,000 pairs of woollen drawers
13,326,000 wool cap comforters

In addition to military orders, it was essential that a substantial export trade in civilian wear and domestic requirements for the home market be maintained. All this was achieved despite approximately 50,000 men from the Bradford district being involved in military service.[8]

134   *LISTER'S MAGAZINE.*

In this issue we publish the sixth instalment of our survey of the firm, which brings our narrative up to the present time. Our aim throughout this brief outline is to convey to the reader some idea of the romance which is bound up with the story of the firm's rise to fame.

The outbreak of war in 1914 immediately dislocated the smooth running wheels of industry. Large numbers of employees joined the forces within a short space of time and later no less than 1200 enlisted, whilst many others left to be munition workers. Vast quantities of material necessary for war purposes were manufactured by the firm and all possible assistance was given to the Bradford National Munitions Factory from 1915—18.

From the time when Lord Masham had ceased to take an active part in affairs, Mr. Wm. Watson and Mr. Reixach had stood side by side in control. In consequence of the death of Mr. Reixach in 1915 Mr. W. Watson became Chairman and Managing Director. In 1919 Mr. W. H. Watson became joint managing director with his father and also Vice-chairman.

In May, 1918, the King and Queen paid an official visit to the Mills, where they were accorded an enthusiastic reception. They inspected the various processes of manufacture, including the weaving of shell cloth, immense quantities of which were then being supplied to the Government. The tour concluded with an inspection of a fine display of finished goods.

Another acquisition to the already enormous concern was the purchase in 1920 of Priestgate Mills, Darlington, owned by Messrs. Henry Pease & Co., Ltd. Over 600 employees are engaged in spinning and combing at these works. 1919 and 1920 were years of vast trade expansion following the end of the Great War, and Lister & Co. shared to the full in the great " boom." Inevitably came the world wide " slump " from the effects of which the textile industry is only now beginning to recover.

In 1925 by the death of Mr. W. Watson, Chairman and Managing Director, the Company lost one of its stalwart pioneers, for Mr. Watson and his family have been associated with Lord Masham and the firm from the very earliest days. Mr. W. H. Watson succeeded his father as Chairman and Managing Director of the Company.

Reference should be made here to a post-war development which has taken place not only at Lister & Co., but in many of the

LISTER'S MAGAZINE.   135

Mr. W. H. WATSON.
Chairman and Managing Director of Lister & Co., Ltd.

The sixth volume of *Lister's Magazine* summarised the period of the Great War, including the visit of the king and queen in May 1918.

The West Yorkshire Archives hold the annual reports of the Chamber of Commerce, which provide detailed accounts of wartime business activity in the city. Significantly, membership of the Chamber increased dramatically: from 601 in 1913 to 1,035 in 1919. Does this represent a realisation that the fierce independence of Yorkshire business people in peacetime might not withstand the demands of wartime? The pragmatic response was to present a coordinated voice in the face of waves of government regulations, overseas debt and general uncertainty. The Chamber continued to be dominated by the textile business, 80 per cent of members being directly involved or in closely related businesses.

The Chamber of Commerce recognised that wartime regulations would be a necessary evil but this did not prevent members opposing issues that could be harmful to business. For example they successfully opposed a government-introduced ban on the use of timber for the construction of packing cases. Worsted consignments continued to be packed in wooden crates. They also opposed the formation of a National Dyestuff Company and petitioned for War Risk Insurance to be handled by local brokers. The issue of war indemnity arose early in the war when the German cruiser *Emden* captured and sank several merchant vessels in the Indian Ocean. The BP oil installation in Madras was shelled and, for a time, all shipping was suspended with adverse effects on trade, and insurance rates never recovered.

It is clear from Chamber of Commerce records that the Bradford business community wielded considerable influence with government and it was to Bradford that the War Department[9] turned for the chairmanship of its advisory council on the supply of wool for military purposes. In 1916 Mr Albert Illingworth MP, a former President of Bradford Chamber of Commerce, was asked to advise on all matters relating to the purchase and distribution of the wool clip (the raw wool produced from the annual clipping of sheep).

At the beginning of the war the trade in raw wool from Australia and New Zealand had continued much as before but in August and September the Professor of Economics at Leeds University and a retired civil servant submitted a memorandum to the government which suggested that control of wool supply would be necessary under wartime conditions. It was not until early in 1916 that the government faced up to the likelihood of a prolonged war and moved rapidly to set up the Wool Control Board.

In June 1916, the Army Council announced its intention to buy the whole of the British wool clip. There were three objectives. First, it was imperative that adequate supplies of wool for military purposes were secured. Second, it was necessary to prevent wool from reaching enemy countries and third, it was essential to ensure supplies of wool after the war for the restoration of the textile industry. Before the end of 1916 it was announced that the whole of the Australian and New Zealand wool clips for the 1916/17 season would be bought. The South African clip was also included some time later. Many merchants in the trade were taken by surprise but when one Bradford merchant stood up in a London meeting to protest he was greeted by a roar of 'No!' and the wisdom of the Control Board was quickly recognised.[10]

In December 1916 the Army Council ordered that wool from Australasia should only be sold to the Director of Army Contracts. The government paid a price 55 per cent above the rate paid in June 1914 on the understanding that any wool not required by the military would be offered within the trade. Purchase and distribution of wool was under the direction of Lt-Col F.V. Willey (later Lord Barnby).

A Wool Control Board under Charles Sykes (Director of Wool Textile Production) was established and the Great Northern Victoria Hotel in Bradford was commandeered to become the headquarters of the organisation. J.A. Harrison describes how the Wool Control Board 'was largely made up as it went along'. He had answered an advertisement placed by Sir Frederick Aykroyd in 1916 for 'someone who knows something about wool and who has a sense of fairness'. Those involved, including Sir George Garnett, Isaac Smith, Henry Whitehead, Sir Harry Shackleton and Sir William Bulmer 'had to grope their way to steer wool to the most important uses. They had no previous plan or experience to guide them.'[11]

The Victoria Hotel opposite the Great Northern Railway station (now the Interchange) became the headquarters of the Wool Control Board.

Government wool purchase provisions were extended to cover the 1919–20 season by which time the bill had reached a staggering £200 million. Wool sales started again in London in April 1919 and in 1921 BAWRA (the British–Australian Wool Realisation Association) was formed to dispose of surplus wartime stocks. By May 1924, when it was wound up, BAWRA had disposed of 2,908,151 bales of raw wool.

Throughout this time the Bradford Chamber of Commerce continued to protect the interests of its members, many of whom, before Control, had been enjoying the rewards of government demand. For example, in March 1917 the Chamber passed a resolution concerning differential rates which were being paid to manufacturers for what were perceived to be the same products. The War Office (Contracts Department) responded with a long and detailed letter of 21 March 1917:

> With reference to the resolution, I am to remind your Council that a difference in the prices paid to manufacturers need not in itself constitute an anomaly, since the object of the Department is, as far as it is possible, to secure that the price paid yields approximately the same rate of profit to the various manufacturers engaged on the order.

In the present circumstances, it is frequently necessary, in order to secure the full production required by the Allied Armies, to place orders with manufacturers whose plant or organisation is not so well adapted to the particular cloth as that of manufacturers who specialise in that cloth and are normally able to meet the needs of the Department, and this may clearly result, owing to unavoidable difference in the cost of production, in differences in the actual prices paid for the cloth.

Any alternative scheme under which the price paid was based on the cost of production of the most expensive producer could, obviously, not be justified in present circumstances.

A constant worry for manufacturers was foreign debt. In addition to the collapse of the European market, businesses in Bradford were also unable to find settlement from European firms of outstanding debts. To alleviate the cash-flow problem the Chamber of Commerce pressed for a one-month moratorium from the banks, from 6 August to 11 September. This was extended to 3 October but it was resolved by the Chamber that the termination of this would be disastrous. Government assistance was called for:

That the Council of the Chamber of Commerce recommends the government to provide amounts whereby the export houses requiring monies from Germany, Austria and Russia should receive assistance either by way of advances or by way of guarantee of their debts on the basis of 75 per cent or less (as may be required) of the total amount outstanding.

Finally, 50 per cent was agreed upon but the debate about interest on the extended loans continued. Not until 1919, under Article 296 of the Treaty of Paris, were these debts finally settled and then it was 'at the pre-war rate of exchange'.

	Total amount of property belonging to persons resident in the UK	Debts due to persons in the UK from persons resident in:
Germany	£42,692,626	£54,906,238
Austria and Hungary	£17,554,678	£15,115,163
Bulgaria	£377,593	£1,205,481
Turkey	£4,189,283	£4,781,516

These are national figures, but the size of the manufacturing trade conducted from Bradford would suggest that a significant proportion of this debt was to Bradford businesses and individuals.

Bradford businesses exerted every effort throughout the war to keep as much machinery operating as possible but the cash-flow problem brought enormous

TELEGRAPHIC ADDRESS "DYERS" BRADFORD.
TELEPHONE Nº 3800 (10 LINES)

THE BRADFORD DYERS' ASSOCIATION, LIMITED.

39, WELL STREET,

BRADFORD.

REGISTERED
A/I.

The red logo of the Bradford Dyers' Association was familiar in Bradford until the 1970s.

pressures. Shortages of materials and labour had to be faced and, for the people of Bradford to see their own men parading for the new Pals regiments in Post Office blue uniforms, was particularly galling.

The Bradford Dyers' Association was registered on 3 December 1898 and comprised about 90 per cent of the Bradford piece dyeing trade. The number of

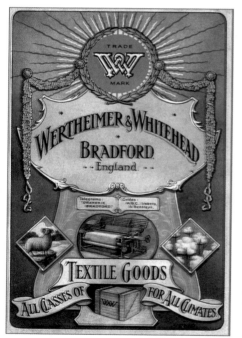

The quality of the artwork on this poster from the Anglo-German company of Wertheimer & Whitehead is exceptional. Wool and cotton were their raw materials.

people employed by the Association in 1898 was about 7,500, and the goods treated – silk, mohair, wool as well as cottons – were in use in almost every household in the UK, besides being shipped to all parts of the world.

The fact of the matter was that by 1914, 80 per cent of dyestuffs used in British manufacturing was produced by German companies, either in Germany or in factories owned by German companies, particularly those at Ellesmere Port (Meister, Lucius and Brunning) and at the Mersey Chemical Works. The Patents Act of 1917 had made it possible for German companies to take out patents to protect their interests in Britain, but no reciprocal measure was adopted for British companies in Germany. German companies were also able to obtain industrial alcohol free of duty. Relationships had been close in Bradford but would clearly come under strain.

Britain's consumption of alcohol in the dyeing process amounted to 20,000 tons per year, of which 18,000 tons (representing a value of about £2m) was imported from Germany. Simple dyes such as aniline oil and sulphur black were home-produced but for 80 per cent of the dyes used, including khaki, Britain was dependent on Germany.

On 27 October 1914 the Chamber of Commerce sent the following letter to the government:

That in view of the great dependence upon Germany for supplies of dye wares and the consequent domination by that country of the whole of the textile and certain other industries, this Chamber urges respectfully upon His Majesty's Government the vital necessity for furnishing such support as is essential to the establishment and effectual continuance of the manufacture of aniline dyes on an adequate scale in this country.

This was a paradoxical situation. William Perkin had invented the coal tar industry, particularly the aniline dye process, in the previous century but, despite the efforts of the Prince Regent, this British industry had gradually been taken from us. The government's response was to propose a National Dyestuffs Co.[12] in which the government would hold a major share.

In the early years of the war, labour shortages were quickly felt as men volunteered for the forces in large numbers. In 1916, 21 per cent of the spindles in Bradford factories were closed because of labour shortages. Forward-looking mills had started de-skilling even before war began but such was the need for skilled employees that the Chamber of Commerce successfully had many jobs reclassified as 'reserved occupations'. In May 1916 the Chamber petitioned for the school leaving age to be reduced from 14 to 13. Women were gradually employed in a wider range of jobs within the mills and some manufacturers were reported as being amazed that 'women could be just as diligent as men'. The unions described the use of women workers as 'dilution', and immediately war ended they put a stop to it.

The shortage of coal was a further problem which the Chamber of Commerce tried to solve. Traditionally, many companies had rented mill premises and facilities, including power supplies. Coal shortages meant that the owners of the mills were unable to supply power and companies could not operate their machinery. Despite this, mill owners continued to charge full rent and the Chamber of Commerce was unable to break the deadlock.

One success story of the war years was the discovery by a Bradford doctor of the cause of anthrax, the wool-sorters disease.

Frederick William Eurich (of German birth) had been appointed head of a bacteriological laboratory at the City's Technical College and, in 1917, he eventually traced the disease to specks of blood on the wool of diseased sheep.

A Bradford wool sorter of unusually large physique. A high proportion of these men suffered from anthrax, the 'wool-sorters' disease'.

Dr F.W. Eurich determined the cause of 'wool-sorters' disease', and devised the necessary precautions to be taken.

He instituted rigorous cleaning of wools at mills throughout Bradford and suggested that all dangerous wools from abroad be imported through a single port, Liverpool. On his retirement in 1937, Eurich was awarded the Gold Medal of the Bradford Textiles Institute in recognition of his work, which saved many hundreds of lives in the woollen industry.

By 1917 the Chamber of Commerce had begun planning for the employment of wounded soldiers, the re-integration of men returning from the war and especially the placement of officers. While managerial positions at first seemed obviously appropriate, there were some concerns that not all officers, especially those promoted in the field, were gentlemen.

In 1917, Dudley H. Illingworth, Director General of the Chamber of Commerce, visited the Western Front to review motor ambulances and hospital units donated by Bradford. His report, addressed to John H. Robinson Esq. JP, President of the Chamber, was printed in full in the *Annual Report*. Illingworth's comments display an intelligent man, sensitive to the devastation and human cost of war while retaining his vision as a textile man:

The sacrifice that France has been compelled to make in this war literally passes comprehension, and no section of the community has suffered more than the textile trade, and especially the worsted trade. At its very best it must be a bitter and long struggle for those gallant and industrious people to re-establish their industries and, whatever sacrifices Great Britain may be called upon to make – and these must be supreme – the sympathy of the Yorkshire Industries must, I feel sure, always go out to those in Europe who have paid such a bitter price to provide a battleground for the world struggle.

The generous contribution of the City of Bradford to the war effort was acknowledged by the French Ambassador, Paul Cambon:

In the contributions to the British Empire Fund for the sick and wounded soldiers of France, there are indications of the special sympathy of certain localities and industries. Among these stands out the West Riding of Yorkshire represented by the donations from Members of the Bradford Chamber of Commerce, amounting to a grand total of £12,738 16s 6d. It is, therefore, all the greater pleasure for me to beg you on my behalf to thank every one of your members who has contributed to this fund.

The 1918 *Annual Report* of the Bradford Chamber of Commerce reads:

> In looking back upon the history of four years of terrible warfare, the City of Bradford, and the textile trade that is in its centre, may justly claim credit for the honourable part it has played during a period of national peril.
>
> Not only have the millions of fighting men been better clothed in wool garments than any preceding armies, but Bradford holds a high place among the great industrial centres with regard to enlistments in His Majesty's Forces, investments in war loans and War Savings Certificates, war work of all descriptions, in generous support of deserving institutions, and its care of the dependents of men who went to fight their country's battles.

Notes

1   Minutes of the Bradford Chamber of Commerce West Yorkshire Archives, Bradford
2   *The Centenary Book of Bradford*, *Yorkshire Observer*, 1947
3   Copies of these journals can be found in the *Bradford Textile Archive* housed at Bradford College
4   Dobson, E.P., *The Garnett Story 1831–1962*, William Sessions, York, 1962
5   *Yorkshire Observer*, 31 December 1914
6   *Yorkshire Observer*, 23 October 1914, p. 9
7   *The Commercial Yearbook of the Bradford Chamber of Commerce* (Incorporated) first issue 1919
8   Ibid.
9   *Bradford Chamber of Commerce Centenary 1851–1951*, published by the Chamber of Commerce, 1951 and available at Bradford Industrial Museum
10 Harrison, J.A., 'Two Wool Controls' in *The Journal of the Bradford Textile Society*, 1962–3
11 Ibid.
12 In 1926 NDC joined with Brunner Mond, Nobel Explosives and United Alkali to form ICI Dyestuffs.

SEVEN

Manufacturing Industries

Geoff Barker, Mike Woods & Gerry Beevers

In 1903 Orville and Wilbur Wright made the first flight by powered aircraft. At the time this had little impact in Europe but when Blériot flew across the Channel in 1909 Britain woke up to the fact that the sea was no longer an obstacle to its enemies and that it had better take a much closer interest in aviation matters.

In 1911 Britain still had only about a dozen aircraft in service compared with France's 200. The Chief of the General Staff considered 'military aircraft were a useless and expensive fad'! Even the First Sea Lord estimated naval requirements for aircraft at no more than two planes. Fortunately, other officers took a different view and believed that air observation would be crucial in any future conflict.

By the time war broke out in August 1914, there were four squadrons of aircraft in service with the Royal Flying Corps, comprising Henri Farman pushers, Blériot tractor aircraft (pushers had the engine and propeller behind the pilot, Tractors had these in front), Farnborough-designed BE2s and BE8s, and Avro 504s: a total of forty-four aircraft in all.

The Royal Flying Corps[1] (RFC) was founded on 13 April 1912 and was intended to encompass all military flying. The Royal Navy, however, was reluctant to see a part of its potential handed to the army and formed, without seeking permission from the War Office, its own Royal Naval Air Service (RNAS). Such was the influence of senior naval staff in political circles that this decision went unchallenged and the RNAS was officially recognised on 1 July 1914. By August 1914 the RNAS had more machines than the RFC and also had bases around the coast from Aberdeenshire to Anglesey. Brigadier-General Sir David Henderson KCB, DSO, commanded the Royal Flying Corps and on the continent were mustered some 105 officers, 63 aeroplanes and 95 vehicles. Coastal reconnaissance, some bombing of German shipping (not entirely successful) and support of ground troops were the chief tasks. By early 1918 the RNAS had grown to 67,000 officers, 2,949 aircraft, 103 airships and 126 coastal stations.[2]

Meanwhile the RFC had also been growing and at the end of August 1914 three of its aircraft saw action when they forced a German Taube aircraft to land. One of the British planes also landed and its officers chased the German crew into nearby woods. The German plane was torched before the British crew made a safe take-off. A few days later, Lieutenant L.A. Strange dropped a bomb on a German truck near

Mons, thus achieving the first bombing raid of the war. In September, an RFC reconnaissance report to Sir John French was passed to the French military under General Joffre. He was able to order a counter-attack, which succeeded in halting the German advance towards Paris. Joffre paid credit to the airmen:

> The British Flying Corps played a prominent, in fact a vital part, in watching and following this all-important movement [of German troops]. Thanks to the aviators I was kept accurately and constantly informed of Kluck's movements and to the RFC owe the certainty which enabled me to make plans in good time.[3]

The two services remained independent for a large part of the war but competition for aircraft, together with dissatisfaction with Britain's overall air effort following German bomber attacks on London, led to the decision to create a unified Royal Air Force (RAF) in 1918.

From the beginning the Royal Navy Air Service usually had better aircraft than the Army's Royal Flying Corps as the Admiralty considered itself to be more experienced in managing technology than the War Office. In the main, the RFC had planes designed and built at Farnborough, a government establishment. The RNAS used private manufacturers and designers who seemed more flexible in interpreting the suggestions and demands of RNAS officers. Given the early success of air reconnaissance and the rate of attrition from losses in action and accidents, it was quickly realised that production would have to be significantly increased – and this is where Bradford enters the story.[4]

In June 1915 Mr P.J. Pybus of the Bradford company Phoenix Dynamo[5] was invited to the Admiralty to meet Commander Randall (Captain of Aircraft at the Admiralty) in order to discuss the building of aircraft at the Phoenix Dynamo Works. Pybus was taken to Rochester to view aircraft in manufacture at Shorts' Works. At this stage there was no guarantee of firm orders or any government contract but the seeds were sown in the mind of Mr Pybus.

On his return to Bradford, Pybus attended a magic lantern show at Eastbrook Hall and while there had a discussion with Leonard Pratt of the furniture manufacturer, Christopher Pratt. By this time Christopher Pratts was a well-established Bradford furniture manufacturing company. Their cabinet-making business had begun in Brummits Yard, off Darley Street, in 1845. They formed a private limited company in 1913 and opened showrooms in North Parade, an establishment that will still be remembered by Bradfordians today.

Years of experience in working with wood, particularly cabinet making to a very high standard, made the firm ideally placed to adapt to the production of airframes. Most aircraft of the time were constructed of timber ribs with a covering, usually of linen, to the fuselage and wings, thus achieving as light a structure as possible. To accommodate this new production process, Pratts purchased property bounded by Rawson Street, Infirmary Street and Simes Street and adapted the premises for workshops and a garage. Premises were also rented at the rear of Parkinson, Clark & Co. in Rawson Road and at the old artillery barracks in Hallfield Road. The manufacture and assembly of aircraft could now begin.

The Phoenix Dynamo Works at Thornbury increased dramatically in size to produce munitions for the war effort. Note the 'WD' on the vehicles – this denoted War Department transport.

A Maurice Farman Longhorn of the type built in Bradford.

Phoenix Dynamo Manufacturing Co. Ltd in their Trafalgar Works, Thornbury, were already constructing the Maurice Farman Longhorn S7, designed by Maurice Farman of Billancourt-sur-Seine, Paris. This aircraft was generally used for training, although some undertook reconnaissance work in France. A model of the Longhorn S7 can still be seen in the Shuttleworth Collection in Bedfordshire.

Women assembling wings and fuselages in the Pratt workshops off Rawson Street with, on the left, Christopher Pratt junior and his foreman Jim Pickard.

So scarce were drawings for the S7 that draftsmen from Phoenix Dynamo had to take measurements from an aircraft being produced by Brush Electrical in Loughborough. Working drawings were produced by Mr Leonard Brown, E. Wigglesworth and L. Barradell[6] of the Bradford company.[7] These were then distributed to Christopher Pratts and manufacture could begin. The company's existing manpower, with expertise in cabinet making, was now added to by women. Their job was to cover the airframes with fabric and apply the 'dope' (a varnish). Up to the end of 1916 proprietary dopes were used for all fabric parts, producing an overall clear varnish finish which would provide the strength and rigidity to support the aircraft in flight. This demand for new skills brought about a change in the gender balance of the workforce at Pratts. In 1914 the company employed 105, of whom only 10 were women. By 1919 staff numbers totalled 245 and included 69 women. In fact, the proportion of women workers had risen even more sharply in 1915 but, as airframes in production became heavier, too heavy for women to handle, their number declined somewhat.

Some sources suggest that for early test flights, the early seaplanes produced in Bradford were disassembled and taken in crates to Yeadon Tarn. Once reassembled, they were launched from the Tarn. Present-day dinghy sailors should not confuse these Great War machines with the planes which take off and land above their heads at Leeds Bradford Airport today: the early seaplanes were midgets by comparison and Yeadon Sailing Club would have been quite safe! In time, the larger planes were taken to Brough on Humberside for trials and stowage on board rudimentary carriers.

As well as an expanding workforce and the development of new skills, additional materials were required on an unprecedented scale. Of these, the one most difficult to obtain in quantity was flax. As the *Yorkshire Observer Budget*[8] reported:

> The revival of the flax industry is at present a matter of very urgent importance, since it is a factor determining the number of aeroplanes turned out. We have in Yorkshire 3,000 acres under flax this year. At present Mr A.G. Ruston (Agriculture Department, Leeds University) is engaged as Adjutant of a large camp at Bramham where 250 scouts are camped under military conditions, and go out either using their bicycles or in large military lorries to the flax fields, in some cases eight or nine miles away at Towton.

Flax was the 'raw material' of linen, the covering for the wings, each one of which required one acre of flax to be grown. A skilled picker took one week to harvest an acre of flax and, of course, skilled adult workers were in short supply. The answer to the problem was Boy Scouts who, along with those acting as auxiliaries at the War Hospital, provided an important labour reserve. The Scout Association was shocked to be asked how the boys were paid: 'It was all voluntary effort. Of course they were not paid!'

Scouts harvesting flax at Bramham.

On 24 June 1915 the Admiralty informed Phoenix Dynamo that a brand new aircraft, the Short 184 Seaplane, was at the Isle of Grain and available for measurement. Once again, the Chief Draughtsman travelled to Sheerness to make accurate production drawings. The Short Type 184 was truly state-of-the-art in 1915. It was only in March 1910 that a plane had taken off from water under the control of Monsieur Henri Fabre, yet another French pioneer. The Short design came two years later in 1912 and was so successful that it was still in service outside the UK in 1933. Between 1915 and 1917 sixty-two of these seaplanes were built in Bradford and the histories of some of them can be traced through the Fleet Air Arm Museum at Yeovilton. These stories bear witness to a period of aviation when every flight was a serious risk and outstanding courage was an essential part of the job description.

A Short Type 184 Seaplane pictured on the Humber near Brough in East Yorkshire.

The history of Short Type 184 Seaplane Number 8372 is very special.[9] Aircraft No. 8372 left Phoenix Dynamo works and was delivered and accepted by the Royal Naval Air Service at Felixstowe on 23 April 1916. She was packed into crates on 14 May 1916 and sailed for Port Said on 12 June, arriving in Egypt in July.

At this point the newly created warship, HMS *Ben-My-Chree*, enters the picture. Before the war the *Ben-My-Chree* (meaning 'Woman of my Heart') had been an Isle of Man ferry working the route between Liverpool and Douglas. With a service

The rudimentary aircraft hangar added to the deck of HMS *Ben-My-Chree* can be seen clearly. There is also a davit for lowering the planes down to the water for take-off.

speed of 24.5 knots she was the fastest cross-channel steamer in 1914[10] when she was commissioned as a seaplane carrier. A large hangar was fitted to the after part of her superstructure which was able to accommodate four aircraft. A flying-off platform was added over the forecastle, although this was rarely used.

After commissioning on 2 January 1915, the *Ben-My-Chree* spent some time in home waters, at one point attempting unsuccessfully to launch an aircraft to intercept a Zeppelin over the North Sea. She sailed for the Mediterranean shortly afterwards, arriving there on 12 June 1915 and taking part in the Gallipoli Campaign.

On 12 August 1915 HMS *Ben-My-Chree* made history when a Short seaplane armed with a Whitehead Torpedo was launched from its hangar. Under the command of Flight Commander C.H.K. Edmonds RN, the plane attacked and torpedoed a Turkish steamer of 5,000 tons in the Sea of Marmara. This was the first ever sinking of a vessel from the air. Five days later, Commander Edmonds torpedoed another steamer, which caught fire and was completely gutted. A fellow pilot, Flight Lieutenant G.B. Dacre, was forced to land on the water with engine trouble. Taxiing towards a Turkish tugboat, he fired a torpedo while on the water.

A Felixstowe F3 in assembly. The detail of the wooden framework can be seen as well as the construction of the nose and wings.

Relieved of the weight of the torpedo, the plane was then able to take off and return to the *Ben-My-Chree*.

With the evacuation of the Dardanelles the *Ben-My-Chree* was transferred to operations in the Red Sea area, joining the seaplane carriers *Anne* and *Raven 2*, which thus became the first carrier taskforce. Throughout this time the carriers were using the Short 184 seaplanes and on 18 July 1916 the Bradford-built 8372 joined the taskforce. The record shows that the plane was flown by Squadron Leader A.J. Nightingale and Lieutenant P.M. Woodland, RNVR. These two officers were to be taken prisoners of war by the Turks on 2 December 1916 when their plane was shot down over Ramleh while bombing Turkish positions.

The *Ben-My-Chree* continued to mount very effective operations. For example the carrier bombed the garrison at Jiddah (in what is now Saudi Arabia) with her 12-pounders while her seaplanes carried out constant bombing raids until the garrison surrendered. The *Ben-My-Chree* was eventually sunk on 8 January 1917 after being fired on by Turkish shore batteries.

The last planes to be produced at Phoenix Dynamo were the three flying boats, the Felixstowe F3 and F5, and the P5 Cork. The production of seaplanes in such an unlikely inland city was honoured with a royal visit from King George V and Queen Mary in May 1918. Lord Cromer's letter of thanks for the visit was, fittingly, addressed to Mr P.J. Pybus:

Buckingham Palace
1 June 1918

Dear Sir,

I am commanded by the King and Queen to assure you of the pleasure it afforded Their Majesties being able to pay a visit to Thornbury yesterday, and to see your Works.

The various activities the King and Queen observed in progress are of special importance and utility to the Country at the present time, and Their Majesties were naturally immensely interested in all that they saw.

In thanking you for the arrangements you were good enough to make in connection with yesterday's Programme, I am to add that the King and Queen were greatly pleased at the loyal and enthusiastic welcome given them by your workers.

Believe me,
Yours faithfully,
Cromer

P.J. Pybus Esq., CBE
Managing Director
The Phoenix Dynamo Company Ltd, Thornbury

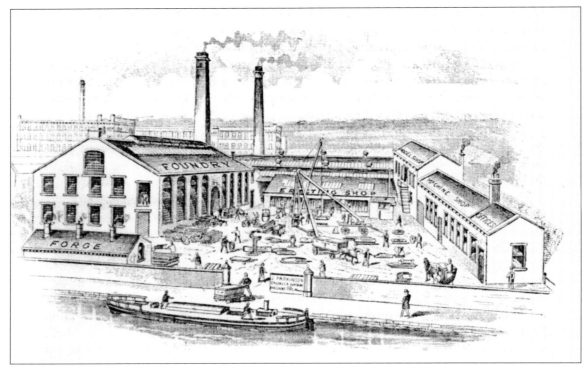

A detailed drawing of Parkinson's Works in Shipley.

The City of Bradford had several other manufacturing strengths in 1914, although tracing the history of Crofts Engineering and J. Parkinson & Son has proved tricky. Crofts were based at the Empire Works, Thornbury, had eight subsidiaries and 4,000 employees operating 35 acres of plant. They were world leaders in gear trains for industry and were taken over by Renolds, a Manchester company based in Wythenshawe, which is still in existence. Enquiries to their Head Office made little progress in the hunt for the history of the old firm other than a recommendation to look in the Manchester City Archives. Some documents about Parkinsons and Crofts were available from there and have helped piece together the story of this very successful Bradford engineering company.

J. Parkinson & Son was founded in 1893 and sold sewing machines. Joseph Parkinson's shop was in the Exchange in the town centre although he moved to better premises near the early Mechanics' Institute building, opposite the Town Hall. Realising the potential of sewing machines in the era of extravagant ladies' fashions, he decided to manufacture his own machines. Unfortunately this business failed but it provided him with knowledge of the milling process. Parkinson found that a milling machine, which was necessary to refine the crude castings of the time, could be made 'in house'. Bill Allen, the chief designer for Parkinson's, had worked for a manufacturer of milling machines in America. He 'remembered' some of the designs on which he had worked in the States and used them to produce a milling machine in Bradford. This machine helped solve the problem of drilling fine holes around a metal ring: a technique required in order to produce Temple Rings. Parkinson went on to develop and patent a better ring.

His next invention was designed in response to the new fad of home-milled flour. In 1880 he invented an improved wood-turning lathe and, in so doing, realised the need for a new vice for holding wood samples. His newly patented device, the 'Perfect Vice' created and held the market.

All this progress was made at the Chester Street premises and eventually, in 1893, the company moved to new premises which had the advantages of good rail and canal links. This was the site of the Prince of Wales Foundry on Cromwell Road, in the wharf area of Shipley.

The canal enabled deliveries of materials and transport of products. With the judicious acquisition of the nearby Gateland Joinery and Building Co., the foundry site was expanded to cover 3,320 square yards.

Joseph Parkinson, now helped by his entrepreneurial son Ernest, branched into the cycle business and produced the machine tools which enabled others to make the cycles. By 1909 they had mastered high-speed steel and gear cutting technology. Within a few years came the war and an unexpected order.

On 9 May 1915 the British attack on Aubers Ridge failed and General Sir John French blamed the failure on a lack of shells for the British 18-pounder guns. Shells were being produced by Cammell Laird & Co. Ltd of Sheffield and their Chief Engineer realised the importance of securing good quality lathes for the improved manufacture of shells. In August 1915 he placed an order with J. Parkinson & Son of Bradford for a massive order of 251 lathes for delivery within eight months. The lathes were to be suitable for the rough finishing of the shell bodies.

This lathe for turning 11-in shell bodies was one of hundreds produced by Parkinsons in Shipley.

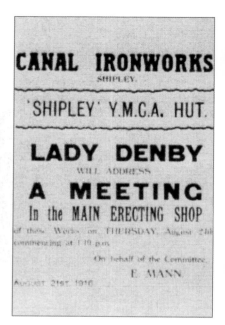

CANAL IRONWORKS
SHIPLEY.

'SHIPLEY' Y.M.C.A. HUT.

LADY DENBY
WILL ADDRESS

A MEETING
In the MAIN ERECTING SHOP
of these Works on THURSDAY, August 24th
commencing at 1.30 p.m.

On behalf of the Committee.
E. MANN

August 21st, 1916.

Above: A newspaper photograph of Lady Denby at Parkinsons in 1916. *Right:* The announcement of Lady Denby's visit. Such visits provoked mild excitement in both the workforce and the community.

Parkinson's workshops were continually redesigned to accommodate changing machinery, and contemporary illustrations show the erecting shop to be lined with lathes in 1916. By 1917 their place had been taken by milling machines.

The workshops were also the venue for large meetings of workers, for example when Lady Denby visited on the occasion of a new YMCA hut being opened in Shipley.

At this time Lloyd George's Ministry of Munitions had calculated a shortfall of 14,000 skilled workers. Parkinson's probably made full use of the rules of dilution (i.e. the employment of low-skilled workers including women) in order to meet this order. There was already a significant number of women employed in textile manufacture in Bradford and it may be that the extra labour came from domestic servants and the pool of labour which lay beyond the city boundary. In this photograph of workers at the meeting addressed by Lady Denby, which was held in the milling shop, the female workers are seated on the left-hand side and the male workers on the right.

The mass meeting of workers. Women and children are to the left and the men to the right. Above can be seen some of the lathes produced in the factory.

The Scott guncar produced in 1915 was an attempt to make machine-guns more mobile on the battefield.

The agreement of the unions to allow dilution was, of course, only for the duration of the war. When men returned to their normal occupations more restrictive practices would resume; that is, no women allowed.

Army Order 480, dated 12 November 1914 and sanctioned in February 1915,[11] approved the addition to each Army Division of a motor machine-gun battery. This was designated to be a unit of the Royal Field Artillery and was known as the Motor Machine Gun Service (MMGS). Scotts of Bradford produced the earliest motorcycles used. Alfred Scott had exhibited one of his cycles with machine-gun attached at Olympia in 1912, and this proved to be the prototype upon which the War Office developed the MMGS.

Men were found from the volunteers, or by special enlistment of men known to be actively interested in motorcycles, such as cycle club members.[12] By October 1915 the corps had around 3,000 men, each battery of which had eighteen cycle/sidecar combinations, carrying six Vickers machine-guns with ammunition and spare equipment, eight motorcycles without sidecars, two or three wagons or cars and a sidecar combination for the commanding officer. The men wore leather gaiters, goggles, gauntlets and waterproofs (no crash helmet) and their cap badge was similar to the Machine Gun Corps but with MMG lettering.

In 1914 production at Scotts went over entirely to the production of these cycles but the War Office soon realised that the machine was too lightweight for the task required of it. As the photographs show, the concept of a machine-gun on a motorbike produced an inefficient fighting machine.

The rider had to dismount in order to fire and his pillion had to provide the extra rounds of ammunition while using his weight to stabilise the machine under the recoil from the machine-gun. The Scott cycle was superseded by Matchless, Zenith, Enfield

The pillion rider is feeding a magazine through the machine-gun while using his weight to stabilise the motorcycle.

and Clyno machines, which were more robust. By May 1916, most of the motorcycle batteries had been withdrawn and from late 1916, many men of the Motor Machine Gun Service transferred to the Heavy Section of the Machine Gun Corps, which was later to be known as the Tank Corps.

By 1916, brothers Benjamin and William Jowett had produced the first forty-eight of their motor cars. The original had an 815cc flat twin water-cooled engine, a three-speed gearbox and tiller steering, which was converted to wheel steering in 1914. Production was halted during the war and, on moving to an enlarged site at Idle, Jowetts concentrated on making components for various other manufacturers working on war contracts. Car production began again in 1920 and led eventually to famous names such as the Jowett Javelin, Jowett Bradford van and Jowett Jupiter. The company which was founded in 1901 with capital of £90 in premises in Church Street producing largely motorcycles was to become a household name for reliability and style in motoring.

Today, the City of Bradford has cinema complexes, retail parks, supermarkets and hotels on the sites of industries which played a crucial part in equipping the nation for war in 1914. Thornbury, Idle and the canalside area of Shipley are transformed from the days when thousands of manual workers were employed in the war effort and are cleaner, more pleasant places as a result. Some readers will be surprised that an inland city could produce seaplanes and that motorcycles could carry battlefield weapons but the ingenuity of local manufacturers enabled Bradford to play a hugely important role in the war effort.

Notes

1   See www.rafmuseum.com for details of the development of the flying services in the Great War
2   Ibid. RAF Museum figures
3   Ibid. RAF Museum time-line of flight 1914
4   Cairns, J.K., *Ordered by the Admiralty: Built in Bradford*, Historical notes on the collection of aircraft blueprints at Bradford Industrial Museum, June 1995
5   Phoenix Dynamo was also involved in the production of shells, producing well over one million during the war years: a drop in the ocean of 170,385,295 used by British forces! See *Statistics of the Effort of the British Empire in the Great War*, quoted by Robinson, P., *The Great War*, May 2005
6   Ibid. Cairns
7   190 drawings of the Maurice Farman S7 Longhorn are deposited in Bradford Industrial Museum
8   *The Yorkshire Observer Budget*, Saturday 17 August 1915
9   With thanks to the Fleet Air Arm Museum, Yeovilton
10 Le Fleming, H.M., *Warships of World War 1*, Ian Allan Ltd, p. 210
11 See www.1914-1918.net/mmg
12 Ibid. 1914-1918.net The Coventry offices of the enthusiasts' magazine *Motor Cycle* was listed as a recruiting office for the MMGS.

EIGHT

Low Moor Explosion

Tricia Platts

The outbreak of war in August 1914 caught British forces unprepared. Since the end of the Boer War the army had been used mainly for policing the Empire and, despite its experiences in South Africa, the army's fighting methods remained rooted in the nineteenth century. Great faith was placed in the bayonet and the shrapnel shell. It quickly became apparent that German forces were considerably better equipped. Machine-guns and high explosive shells were their stock in trade and caused heavy British casualties in the opening skirmishes and battles. In May 1915 Sir John French was quoted in the press when frustrated by the lack of armaments and was roundly criticised in the highest quarters. On 14 July 1915 Sir Douglas Haig wrote,

> He [the King] criticises French's dealings with the Press, The Times, Repington, Lord Northcliffe, etc. All most unsoldier-like and he had lost confidence in Field-Marshal French.

A cabinet reshuffle in May 1915 saw the creation of a separate ministry for organising and controlling wartime supplies and in June 1915 David Lloyd George was appointed the first Minister of Munitions. This newly formed government department was to become the largest the country had ever seen and reached into every industry.

The Ministry of Munitions of War (which continued until April 1921) established government control over armaments production and ensured that the demand for shells and other weapons was efficiently met. The Ministry also organised the development of new weapons including tanks and encouraged the mass employment of women. Before the outbreak of war, Britain consumed 20,000 tons of steel annually, of which 18,000 tons came from Germany. About 80 per cent of artificial dyes (including the khaki dye used for British uniforms) were also made in Germany.[1] The British government took control of all previously German-owned companies immediately after the war began. By 1918 the government was buying 98 per cent of all steel produced and the number of munitions factories had risen from 4 to 218. Low Moor Chemical Co., Bradford, became Factory No. 182 and was renamed Low Moor Munitions Co. Ltd.

The stamps on this postcard of Low Moor are franked July 1914. The scene clearly shows the proximity of houses, the church and industrial plants.

The company was situated in an industrialised area about 4 miles south of the city centre and was surrounded by residential housing. Adjoining the factory site were the Bradford Corporation Gas Works, Low Moor Iron Works Co. and Sharps Dye Works. All these were served by a rail link and there would be some shared technologies, for example the by-products plant at the iron works would be capable of extracting phenol from the coal tars produced by the coke ovens.

The Low Moor Iron Co. was formed in 1790 on a site with abundant coal and rich supplies of iron ore. The pair of Napoleonic cannon now housed at Bradford Industrial Museum was manufactured at the works in 1794. For many years they stood at the entrance to the works and were an important local landmark. During the Crimean War (1854–6) the company smelted iron for guns, mortars and cannonballs. This level of manufacture caused a substantial increase in the population of the area, although living conditions in such a polluted atmosphere cannot have been pleasant.

The Low Moor Chemical Co. became affiliated to the Bradford Dyers' Association and in 1898 began producing a dyestuff to be used in carpet manufacture. In addition to its yellow colour, this picric acid also had explosive properties and in September 1898 the factory was issued with a licence to produce explosives in the name of Messrs James and M.S. Sharp & Co. The capacity of the factory increased rapidly until it became one of the major producers of picric acid in the country. However, the juxtaposition of blast furnaces, gas works, coke ovens and an explosives manufactory was to have disastrous consequences for the people of Low Moor.

Peter Woulfe (1727–1803), a chemist of British and Irish origin, discovered picric acid in 1771 and, because of its taste, he took its name from the Greek pikros meaning 'bitter'. It was used to dye silk and wool and is made from mixing phenol with sulphuric and nitric acids. The sulphur content produced a yellow dye, and during the Great War munitions workers were called 'canaries' because their skin was stained yellow through working with the picric.

Physical effects on workers were evident. In addition to the yellowing of skin, teeth, nails, eyeballs and hair, other symptoms included irritation inside the nose, mouth and throat and a constant bitter taste in the mouth. Sometimes this would cause nausea and vomiting. While these effects would be seen on an almost daily basis, other more extreme symptoms would probably also have been experienced. These might include conjunctivitis, irritation of the middle ear, eczema, menstrual irregularities, and more severe poisoning leading to spasms, digestive problems and even kidney trouble.

The explosive characteristics of picric acid were discovered early. In 1885, experiments were conducted at Lydd in Kent and picric acid was adopted as an explosive material and renamed lyddite in 1888. It was the first compound that was suitable for placement in shells. However, lyddite frequently misfired (since it is difficult to detonate, especially if wet) and it produced very black smoke, which made observation difficult on the battlefield. From 1916 it began to be replaced by TNT (which the Germans had used since 1902).

Only under certain conditions is the explosive property of picric acid evident. It exists as a dry crystalline substance and if large quantities are kept in suitable containers with a large surface area it remains stable, although its surface may burn slowly. If it is in a confined space or concentrated in a small volume where pressure can increase, it will explode. Anhydrous picric acid is similar to TNT. It usually needs a 'booster' such as a primer to create the explosion but, if efficiently detonated, it is one of the most powerful explosives, especially if its density has been increased by melting or pressing.

As a strong acid, picric attacks common metals creating explosive salts, which are shock-sensitive to varying degrees. For example, lead picrate detonates violently but picric acid does not react with tin and aluminium. This has implications for the storage and transportation of the substance of which the management at Low Moor Chemical Factory was well aware. The need for good ventilation in the factory was recognised and, in the most sensitive areas, floors had a rubber covering and protective clothing was worn. There was also a water sprinkler system fed from a large tank. However, the familiarity which breeds complacency coupled with the pressures of maximising production inevitably led to some cutting of corners although, after the explosion, the sprinkler system was found to be full.

The licence to produce picric acid had been issued in 1898 at a time when it was considered a manageable fire hazard. (Should a fire develop it could easily be extinguished with water.) There appear to have been no restrictions on the quantities of picric which could be held in any one building. As demands on production increased, extensions to the licence were readily approved and the number of drying sheds, each holding 2,000lb, rose to seventeen with two sifting and packing sheds to hold 10,000lb. These totals were often exceeded if onward transportation was delayed or analysis by government inspectors was held up. Weekend working to meet the demands of war resulted in larger than usual quantities building up prior to transportation on Mondays.

Accounts contained in the Health and Safety Executive's Low Moor Explosion[2] file and in reports of the coroner's proceedings describe Monday 21 August 1916 as a lovely summer's day. Between 2 and 2.30 p.m. James Broughton, a labourer, was moving eleven drums of picric acid from the drying shed to the sifting and packing shed on a horse-drawn, rubber wheeled, low-level bogie. The picric acid was in old carbolic acid (phenol) drums, each containing up to 200lb and weighing about 240lb in total. The drums were tin-plated and lined with wood. Crucially, however, the drums had no protective wooden bands or spars which would prevent the tin-plate coming into contact with hard ground or stone benches. As it was a fine summer's day with no wind, the protective covers (which were mandatory under the Explosives Act and protected the contents from hot clinker, dust, ash and grit as well as rainwater) were absent. Not even the tarpaulin used in wet or windy weather was thrown across the drums.

This extremely rare contemporary photograph of the explosion was taken on 21 August 1916. It is a powerful and dramatic image.

Outside the door of the sifting and packing shed there was an 18-inch high wooden platform on to which the drums could be unloaded from the bogie, thus avoiding contact with the Yorkshire stone setts which formed the roadway. Inside the building the floor was probably covered with rubber mats to prevent abrasion of the tin-plated drums, and the brick walls were probably match-boarded. (Some years earlier, in 1900, there had been an explosion at Messrs L.B. Holliday & Co., Huddersfield, caused when iron picrate had formed on the iron hoop of a wooden barrel. It detonated when the hoop struck a brick wall.)

At about 2.27 p.m., as he turned to the bogie to remove another drum, James Broughton heard a sizzling sound. On turning around he saw that the there was some fused acid just inside the top of the first drum. This suddenly burst into flames with such violence that he was knocked to the ground. A few yards away was Frank Beverley, a chargehand. He turned to his mates then ran up the road, only to turn back in order to activate the sprinklers and raise the alarm. Later he could not say if any water came out: three weeks earlier when there had been a smaller fire (successfully extinguished) he knew that the water only trickled out of the sprinklers.

Twenty yards away in the laboratory was fifteen-year-old Fred Stobart, a trainee chemist. Through the window he saw huge flames coming out of the lower packing house. He escaped through adjoining offices and joined a crowd of men leaving the factory through the top gate. A.E. Charlesworth, an engineer sitting in another office, was apparently unaware of the flames or any alarm. A few minutes later he was blown through the window but those few minutes were enough for the majority of the 200-strong workforce to flee.

Flames were also seen by Percy Nudds in his confectionery shop at the corner of Cleckheaton Road. Percy Nudds lived into the late 1970s. He produced two typewritten histories of Low Moor which he sold for 30p each on behalf of Cancer Research, and he also recorded his memories of the munitions disaster. There was no doubt in the minds of any of these observers that an explosion was inevitable.

It came at 2.45 p.m. It must have been huge as Bradfordians visiting Pateley Bridge that day reported hearing it[3] and those enjoying the sunshine in gardens and parks across Bradford were in no doubt that 'summat was up'. An eyewitness to this first explosion described the lower packing house being blown into the air, scattering debris over a wide area. A large piece of metal landed over a mile away and houses and open ground were hit by bricks, wood, iron pipes and other unrecognisable objects. A cloud of acrid orange smoke spurted into the air and the sulphurous smell was yet another memory recalled for years to come.

Station Officer Sugden and his men from Odsal Fire Station were already on their way when burning debris fell around them. It is assumed that the Chemical Works fire team were already doing what they could but none of them survived to give a report. The Works Manager, John Majerus, was seen at around 2.30 p.m. with the foreman William Asquith directing fire fighting at the lower storage shed. He was seen again about three hours later crawling on his hands and knees in the debris, having miraculously survived a series of explosions. He was taken home but succumbed the following day to the effects of shock and smoke inhalation.

The newly acquired mechanised fire engine named 'Hayhurst' is shown flanked by two of the horses it replaced.

The firemen from Odsal were soon joined by the team from the Central Fire Station on Nelson Street, Bradford. Chief Officer Scott arrived with eighteen men in the brand new motorised fire engine named 'Hayhurst', the first of its type in Yorkshire.

Chief Officer Scott, accompanied by a specially hired driver, Tom Cousens, had only recently travelled by train to London to take delivery of it. It had solid rubber tyres and they must have had an uncomfortable time driving it all the way back to Nelson Street.

Scott and driver Cousens assessed the scene and agreed that saving lives inside the factory was the priority. However, before all the men had even dismounted there was another huge explosion which blew some of them off the engine. Within thirty minutes of the alarm being

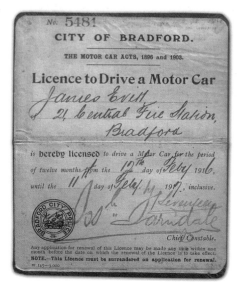

James Evitt's driving licence, which enabled him to drive 'Hayhurst'. His address is given as Central Fire Station.

A fireman standing tall in his uniform.

The signal-box was completely destroyed minutes after the signalman had sent out his message and then run for his life.

raised in the Nelson Street Station at 2.33 p.m., six of Scott's firemen were dead and the remainder injured. Scott was himself badly burned and had broken bones but survived. The 'Hayhurst' lay in ruins. Firemen also arrived from Brighouse but there was little which could be done to avoid the inexorable.

Members of the Railway Company Fire Brigade were also hard at work. About 30 carriages and wagons were destroyed and about 100 seriously damaged. One fireman was killed when gas canisters under a wagon exploded. The signalman, having reported the accident by telephone, set the lights to red and left his box, thereby saving his own life.

A scene of devastation in the gas works adjoining the chemical factory.

After the first explosion the adjoining dyeworks of Messrs J. and M.S. Sharp caught fire. The walls and roof facing the munitions site were demolished by the blast but, remarkably, only one fatality occurred there despite the site being almost completely gutted. One of the gasholders belonging to the Corporation Gas Works was hit by flying debris after the second explosion. The gasometer detonated with an almighty bang and was further destroyed by a fierce fire. A piece of the gasometer, approximately 10ft square, narrowly missed Mrs Wilson as she walked past Holy Trinity vicarage.[4]

Around twenty-two explosions, large and small, occurred until about 9.30 p.m. in the evening and sporadic fires burned for almost thirty-six hours. Surprisingly, within the Chemical Works compound itself, the major damage was from blasts, rather than widespread fire. Fred Stobart later described how each explosion threw up a huge cloud of black smoke rising to a great height then flame bursting from the top.[5] The walls of many buildings remained standing and were demolished later when the site was cleared.

As windows shattered and the explosions continued, residents of Low Moor could only abandon their homes and make for the fields. Percy Nudds described people coming from Wesley Place, many of whom were injured by flying debris. Many slept out in Judy Woods and on the hillsides around. Not only people got away. Harry Seed of Storr Hill, Wyke, reported seeing 'dogs galore running away in all directions'. Some were found as far away as Wakefield, Huddersfield and Halifax. Herbert Smith, a sixteen-year-old working at Champion & Lord, Shearbridge Mills wrote an account of the day and described damage done to his sister Minnie's house in Wyke: 'There was a gap in the wall, ceiling was down, laths and plaster all over the house, a terrible mess and no mistake.' Minnie's husband Fred went back to defend their home as people were 'going about looting'. Herbert Smith also reports that women and children were herded into Judy Woods 'but had nothing to eat until 8.30 at night'.

Fred Stobart described the explosive blasts causing such a vacuum of air that, in the houses around the site, windows shattered as they were sucked outwards. Roof slates were also dislodged in large numbers and the ten or so houses on East View Terrace had their doors blown off and chimneystacks badly damaged. Mrs Graves, who lived in one of these houses and was ten years old at the time of the explosion, could point to marks on a sideboard which had been caused by glass from the windows being blown into the room.[6]

The Bradford City Surveyor reported that about fifty houses were so seriously damaged as to require rebuilding, but a further 2,000 other homes were also affected.[7] Raw Nook School was extensively damaged and was only reopened in January 1917 after the roof, floors and window frames were replaced and furniture renovated. Hill Top School could not be used and, along with children from Raw Nook, pupils were redirected to Low Moor Central School. Pupils from the New Works Girls' School (Miss Briggs' School) spent a week at Grange Road Camp

Despite sustaining damage, New Works School was briefly used as a mortuary after the explosion.

School before being accommodated at Carr Lane Infants' School. A claim for damage to property was also submitted by Hightown Council School, 2¾ miles away.

However, so many families had to leave their homes that school attendance was disrupted for some months afterwards. Children were also reported as suffering long-term effects. In April 1917 the headmistress wrote in the logbook 'pupils are still nervous from explosion shock' and on 15 May 1917 the medical inspector at Raw Nook School noted:

> An unusual number of children with enlarged tonsils evidently the result of exposure after two explosions.[8]

Considering the severe and wide-scale damage caused, the death toll from the Low Moor explosion was remarkably low. The Health and Safety Executive gives a total of thirty-eight dead. Injured workers were ferried to the Infirmary in, or on, any forms of transport to hand, ranging from handcarts and bicycles to vans and horse-drawn carts. Three deaths occurred in the Infirmary and two in St Luke's. The Coroner's Office also reported the death of the only female fatality. Mrs Martha Briggs of Kellett Buildings, Wyke, suffered 'from a fit of apoplexy brought on by shock resulting from the explosion'.[9] There were some remarkable escapes. Arthur Charlesworth was blown through his office window and survived. Edmund Clack, a chemist, was pinned down by a beam but the debris under which he lay buried all night probably saved his life.

As a munitions production plant, the Low Moor works was guarded by members of the Lincolnshire Regiment. Four soldiers are listed as casualties. Private William Gray (54) of Norton Gainsborough was knocked out. Private John Jinnery (56) of Lincoln, Corporal James Rothwell (45) and Corporal William Smith (34) sustained other injuries. Police Constable William Gridcombe (42) was injured and acting Police Sergeant Harold Reveley (35) suffered fatal injuries.

The firemen's memorial pictured today in its new setting at the fire service headquarters at Birkenshaw.

Gold medals were struck for all the firemen serving that day and for the families of the dead. Five men, including Chief Officer Scott, were awarded the BEM and OBE. A civic funeral was held for the dead and, despite the lack of press coverage, the people of Bradford had very quickly learned the extent of the disaster and thousands of mourners lined the streets. In 1924, a memorial was unveiled at the site of the graves in Scholemoor Cemetery. In 2003 the statue and the surrounding stonework was renovated and the memorial relocated to Fire Service Headquarters in Birkenshaw. Those who lost their lives were Joseph Binns, Eli Buckley, Fred Normington, Knighton Pridmore, Edgar Shaw and Charles Sugden.

The absence of detailed reports in the press was inevitable in wartime and local people could only speculate as to the causes of the explosion. A favourite theory was sabotage and suspicion fell on the Belgian workers at the plant. During the early stages of the war Belgians had been subjected to very harsh treatment by the invading forces. Reprisals against civilians were not uncommon and in Britain there was considerable sympathy for 'plucky little Belgium'. It is estimated that half a million Belgian citizens were welcomed to England and many of them were provided with employment in cities and towns across the country. On the day of the explosion several of the thirty Belgian employees at Low Moor were absent from work but they were all able to give perfectly satisfactory reasons for their absence.

For many years there had been a strong German presence in the dyeing and chemical industries in Bradford, and German saboteurs or even Zeppelins were also suspected. Again, no evidence was ever found and the coroner could only conclude that the accident had indeed been exactly that. The *Leeds Mercury* in 1924 concluded:

> The most careful enquiries failed to reveal the slightest foundation for these suspicions. The works had always been under military guard and were protected by barbed wire entanglements and plain-clothes detectives were continuously on duty.

The Low Moor munitions factory never again produced picric acid. This must have initially caused supply difficulties as the factory had been built up to be one of the most productive in the country. The shortfall would no doubt have been made up elsewhere but the Ministry of Munitions was also switching the focus to the production of TNT as an equally effective and more stable alternative. The loss of the Low Moor factory was felt much more strongly at a local level. Workers were without employment and homes had been devastated. Families squeezed in with relatives and friends or moved away. On 11 September 1916 the logbook at Low Moor Church of England School states:

> During the week it has been ascertained that many of the children have definitely left the district. Many others are away from home until the houses are restored. The attendance is still very poor.

With the New Year came more accidents and disruption. The school logbook reads:

> February 19th. The school re-opened this morning with only ten children present. Another explosion . . . has caused many people to leave the district again. Then last night the gasworks near here took fire and the people in the houses were ordered out for a time.

> February 26th. A few more children made an appearance today, some for the first time since last July. Still only 40 present.

By the end of the summer term there is a more optimistic note:

July 19th. The following is a copy of the Diocesan Inspector's Report: 'The work of the school has been happily resumed after the disturbances of last summer. The children are still a little nervous, but did very well in the examination. The repetition was excellent.'

The year 1916 was extremely difficult for the City of Bradford. The deafening noises, smoke, fire and destruction which ordinary people experienced on 21 August was short lived and very localised compared to conditions on the Western Front. The colossal loss of life at the Battle of the Somme in July was only just dawning on the citizenry when the Low Moor explosion compounded the sense of a city on a war footing. Few realised there were to be two more years of loss and destruction.

The fire appliance AK 3081 pictured outside Nelson Street fire station in 1917. This replaced AK 1142 ('Hayhurst') which was destroyed in the Low Moor Explosion.

Notes

1   Trusts in British Industry 1914–1921, J. Morgan Rees MA, Univ Aberystwyth, 1922
2   Health and Safety Executive Report No. 379/1916
3   Account by the Low Moor Foster Society, 1972
4   Recollections of her son, Mr A. Wilson, recorded by John Nicoll Nov–Dec 1972
5   Interviewed by John Nicoll, Nov–Dec 1984
6   Ibid.
7   Report of the City Surveyor, September 1916
8   Jackson, John C., The Low Moor Explosion, published by Raw Nook First School
9   Letter from Coroner's Office, Bradford, to Major Cooper-Key, HM Inspector of Explosives 20.09.1916

NINE

Military Hospitals &
Convalescent Homes

Patricia Featherstone

> It may seem a strange principle to enunciate as the very first requirement in a
> Hospital that it should do the sick no harm.[1]
>
> *Florence Nightingale, 1859*

The workhouse, and the thought of ending up there, struck fear and terror into many Bradfordian hearts for many a long year, and even to this day elderly people who become ill will plead with their relatives not to be sent to St Luke's Hospital, which began its existence as just such a place. Even in June 1955, when I began my career in nursing at St Luke's Hospital, neighbours, friends and even family asked my parents what they were doing letting their daughter start her career at 'The Workhouse', the inference being that no good would come of it. So, how did it all come about?

The Bradford Workhouse in the eighteenth century.

The Act of Settlement of 1662 allowed large parishes such as Bradford to sub-divide into townships for the purposes of poor relief. Bradford parish had eleven poorhouses, situated in Calverley, Pudsey, Bowling, Bierley, Clayton, Horton, Thornton, Allerton, Shipley, Manningham and the central poorhouse at Barkerend.

A change in the law in 1834 handed responsibility for the paupers of Bradford to the Board of Guardians: thirty-two elected rate-payers who represented the Bradford Union. Their duties were varied and wide ranging and they were required to work within the Statutory Framework laid down by the Poor Law Commissioners in London, whose interference caused great conflict during the years 1837–52. For example, in 1840 the Commissioners noted that Bradford was one of thirty-six unions which failed to provide adequate accommodation for the poor. An Inspector reported 'The Workhouses of the Bradford Union are the worst I ever saw! They cannot be made to accomplish any one of the purposes of a workhouse'.[2]

In 1848 the Commissioners insisted on the creation of a Bradford Borough Union consolidating the townships of Bradford, Bowling, Horton and Manningham into one union. All other surrounding Bradford townships came under the North Bierley Union of Poor Relief.

By the end of 1851 the Bradford Guardians had responsibility for two hospitals to provide for its poorer inhabitants. The first of these was a Public Dispensary which later had an infirmary added. These institutions were mainly supported by private means but also by Benevolent & Friendly Insurance Societies and donations. The second was a Workhouse Infirmary, specifically catering for the sick and pauper population of the town.

For many years, the 'new' workhouse at Barkerend had been totally inadequate for the increasing pauper population of the town and in 1851 the Bradford Guardians erected one of the best arranged workhouses in the country, on a site at the junction of Little Horton Lane and Park Lane. The final cost of the building amounted to £7,456 and it was erected on 14 acres of land which cost £4,000, offset by the sale of the old workhouse for £2,213. When completed it contained accommodation for 350 paupers, besides a spacious infirmary for the sick and infirm.

Very stringent rules were laid down for patients and visitors. Initially visits were only allowed on one day a week and by prior arrangement. This was increased to two days a week but quickly reverted to one day because of the disruption and problems caused by too frequent visiting of inmates. The Guardians wrote 'it will be far better for the patients; it will be a great relief to the Nurses and Servants and will much increase the cleanliness of the Institution!' Visitors were requested to come clean and tidily dressed or they were refused admission and they were NOT ALLOWED TO SIT UPON THE BEDS!

By 1866 the workhouse had been greatly enlarged at considerable expense to accommodate upwards of 700 paupers and all the offices of the Union. It was provided with every convenience and formed one of the most complete establishments of its kind in Britain. It was a credit to the gentlemen who had been entrusted with the Union affairs of Bradford. They were careful in using the town's money and demonstrated considerable foresight. Further buildings were added in 1870, 1874 and 1910 when talks were already taking place about municipalisation.

In 1905 the name of the Bradford Union Hospital was adopted and on 13 November 1912 the hospital was renamed by the Board of Guardians St Luke's Hospital, in memory of St Luke, the Apostle and Physician.

It should not be forgotten that Bradford also had an infirmary situated at the junction of Westgate and Lumb Lane, opposite the Beehive public house. In March 1914[3] the infirmary was reported to have 188 inpatients and 10,168 outpatients and Bradford Corporation pledged £80,000 which, with a further £20,000 from donations, was to provide a replacement building. The outbreak of war in August 1914 postponed work on the project until the late 1920s, when the old building was literally bursting at the seams. A pathology department and X-ray department, housed in huts within the grounds, had added considerably to the hospital's role. In 1923–4 130 staff were employed, 32,796 outpatients treated, 3,115 patients admitted and 21,911 casualty patients treated. The cost of replacing the hospital had risen alarmingly, but by 1927 work began at the Duckworth Lane site and, in 1937, the Westgate building was finally closed. Readers may be aware that the site of the old hospital remains vacant and for many years it was rumoured that the treatment of smallpox patients and the effects of rudimentary control of X-rays might have contaminated the ground.

The story of St Luke's now continues using the relevant hospital minutes[4] held in the Bradford Central Library archives.

19 March 1914

A subcommittee was appointed to consider the question of the definite separation from the Poor Law Institution, of the buildings for the use of the sick and infirm. The Committee recommended that the Local Government Board issue an order constituting the following buildings at St Luke's Hospital to be separately administered by a Medical Superintendent:

Male Hospital	153 beds
Female Hospital	130 beds
Female Lock-in	20 beds
Childrens Hospital	84 beds
Maternity Hospital	40 beds
Male Phithisis[5]	47 beds
Male Imbeciles	20 beds
Female Imbeciles	20 beds
Male Lock-in/Scabies	10 beds
Male Infirm Top Floor	50 beds
Total	574 beds

This was the state of affairs when war was declared on 4 August 1914: an up-to-date, well-equipped hospital had been completed and was ready for the taking!

On 4 August 1914 the Lord Mayor, Alderman John Arnold, announced the Declaration of War from the steps at the front entrance of the City Hall. This was the accepted method of communicating important announcements affecting the lives of the citizens of Bradford at that time. It seems very strange to us in these modern times when we can hear news of world events from far away places almost as soon as they occur.

5 August 1914[6]

The following records are taken from the minutes of the meetings of the St Luke's Hospital Committee and reviewed by the Guardians in their twice-monthly meetings:

> *Chairman*: That in view of recent occurrences it is imperative that a motor ambulance should be purchased at an early date, and that a Subcommittee should be appointed to make necessary enquiries with power to purchase.

When this proposal was approved on 9 August 1914 a proviso was added that one horse be dispensed with and one Resident Chauffeur be appointed.

6 August 1914

The Lord Mayor's War Relief Fund was inaugurated and was immediately well supported and generously subscribed to by the industrialists, mill-owners and businessmen of Bradford.

A request was received from the Quartermaster of the Territorial 6th Battalion West Yorkshire Regiment enquiring whether arrangements could be made for the baking of 1,000lb of flour daily for seven days. This request was accepted and when completed work would be charged at cost price.

12 August 1914

A letter was received by the Guardians from Dr Fergus, Assistant Resident Medical Officer, stating that she had volunteered for service at the Front. Her replacement, Dr W. Lumsden, was not appointed until May 1915.

15 August 1914

A national appeal was made by the Surgeon General of the Royal Army Medical Services for the conversion of motorised vehicles to ambulances and also for volunteers to join the Nursing Services. The first designated War Hospital in the area was situated at Brighouse.

22 September 1914

A Public Inaugural Concert in aid of the Lord Mayor's War Relief Fund was held and coincided with the official opening of the Kursaal, better known to Bradfordians as the Central Baths or the King's and Queen's Halls. The former housed a large swimming pool which could be completely covered with sprung boards to turn it into a dancehall.

23 September 1914

The families and dependants of the soldiers of the Prince of Wales' Own Regiment were granted £1 9s 9d per week from the National Relief Fund if hardship could be proved by a means test. Initially many families were too proud to subject themselves to these tests, but later on had to swallow their pride in order to survive.

A scheme of training and examination of nurses in Poor Law Infirmaries was adopted by the Guardians of St Luke's Hospital, Bradford. It was resolved that certificates would be granted upon completion of training and satisfactorily passing the examinations.

7 October 1914

The Superintendent Nurse reported to the Guardians that sixteen Senior Nurses had satisfactorily passed their examinations. It was agreed that they could be granted their certificates. Two Probationer Nurses were accepted for training at St Luke's Hospital.

15 October 1914

220 Belgian refugees arrived in Bradford and were temporarily housed at Daisy Hill Institution and in four large cottages. These quarters had been annexed by the Military Authorities as a camp for the Bradford Battalion for their use at the end of October. The Office of the Lord Mayor was involved in re-homing the refugees, by setting up a War Refugees Committee. A Volunteers' Headquarters for the city was opened in Leeds Road, Bradford.

21 October 1914

Beatrice Milsom, Ward Sister, was called up to serve with the Territorials. The Guardians granted her leave of absence. Two female Probationer Nurses were appointed for a trial period of three months.

27 October 1914

First party of fifty wounded soldiers were brought to Bradford and cared for in small groups placed in Clayton Hospital, Bowling Colony and St Luke's Hospital.

A team of nurses pictured at Midland station awaiting the arrival of a hospital train.

18 November 1914

The first official approach was made to the Guardians of St Luke's Hospital, from the Surgeon General of the Northern Command, enquiring whether any hospital accommodation could be provided for sick and wounded soldiers and sailors. The reply was that a Subcommittee would consider the question and report to the Local Government Board.

It was recommended that the Nurses' Home be enlarged to accommodate a further eighteen nurses. Martha Cunningham was appointed Ward Sister at a salary of £35 per annum plus residence, rations and washing of uniform.

16 December 1914

The Guardians recommended that a system of training male nurses be inaugurated and sent a working party of three to Hackney Union Infirmary to study their methods. They reported back that, as St Luke's could not offer accommodation for men, they envisaged there would be difficulties.

10 February 1915

Three fully trained male nurses, Arthur Jackson, Fred Wilson and James Gare, were appointed at a salary of £75 per annum plus uniform and two meals daily when on duty.

Three probationer male nurses were appointed. Training allowance for the first year would be 20s a week, 22s 6d in the second year and 25s a week in the third year, plus uniform and meals when on duty.

24 February 1915

Field House was designated as an Auxiliary Military Hospital and immediately began to take sick and wounded soldiers and sailors, and continued to do so for the

Field House became an Auxiliary Hospital in 1915.

duration of the war. By 1918, 939 servicemen had received treatment within its walls.

10 March 1915

An operating table was purchased at a cost of £77 inclusive of all accessories from M. Schaerer & Co., a Swiss firm. London surgical supply firms were under such pressure in packing and sending things to the Front that they could not undertake to supply such a table for an indefinite number of months.

24 March 1915

The Guardians resolved that if the Bowling Colony was taken over by the Military Authorities, subject to the Subcommittee approval, the Master would be authorised to arrange for the transfer of 'the inmates' to the Daisy Hill Institution.

16 April 1915

The Board approved the handing over of the Bowling Colony for military purposes. The following day thirty-nine patients including sixteen stretcher cases were admitted, and trained staff from St Luke's Hospital were transferred to look after them.

The Lord Mayor published precautions against air-raid attacks.

5 May 1915

The Guardians resolved that Superintendent Nurse Marion Foggett be permitted to train nurses at St Luke's for Military Hospital purposes for terms of six months 'WITHOUT PAY', but with two meals per day provided when on duty. (Note the inequality between male and female trainees even then!) Dorothy Bentham and Catherine Peel were the first two to be appointed.

2 June 1915

It was reported that considerable damage had been done to the windows of the Daisy Hill cottages by throwing stones at the refugees living there. The police became involved.

3 June 1915

A War Subcommittee was appointed to study the possibility of providing a Base Hospital for wounded soldiers/sailors.

Marion Foggett was permitted to train nurses after May 1915. She became Superintendent of the War Hospital.

The Local Government Board approved the use of Bowling Park Colony as a Military Hospital and the following staff were appointed:

1. Superintendent Nurse Marion Foggett
2. Two Sisters and two Charge Nurses, one for each house
3. Six Probationers, three for each house, two for day duty and one for night duty
4. One Temporary Cook, three Maids and six Scrubbers.

An Armstrong Whitworth motor ambulance (20–30 horsepower) was ordered from Messrs Chalmers & Co. at a cost of £619 12s 6d. The Bradford Coat of Arms was to be painted on the exterior.

The Bradford Bowling Green Committee offered a number of sets of wooden bowls and the free use of the greens in Bowling Park for the soldiers and sailors who were mobile.

11 June 1915

The War Subcommittee met with the Lord Mayor. He promised that the Corporation would assist in providing beds for inmates dispossessed by the setting up of a Military Hospital. This was approved by the Guardians who gave the Subcommittee full power to act on their behalf.

Approximately £25,000 would be required to erect temporary dwellings at Horton and Bowling Park. The Lord Mayor was prepared to raise this sum by public subscription and this subsequently came about.

30 June 1915

A letter was received by the Guardians from the Chief Constable enquiring whether St Luke's could be used as an ambulance station in case of air raids. Permission was granted.

1 July 1915

A letter was sent from the Guardians to the Commander-in-Chief of the Northern Command following a request for accommodation for wounded soldiers at St Luke's Hospital as a Base Hospital. The War Office and the Local Government Board had reached a verbal agreement. The Guardians stated that they would agree to part of the hospital being set aside and separated from the Union House. The buildings referred to contained four large pavilions providing 544 beds and a Nurses' Home accommodating fifty nurses.

They proposed that a Committee of their own body should administer the hospital with their own Medical Officer, Dr B. Slater, in charge. His assistant would be Dr Williamson and both would be granted commissions. Mr Wheeldon, assistant Workhouse Master, would be appointed as Quartermaster. They would appoint all staff and the cost of maintenance of the patients would be at a rate to be agreed upon to cover the actual expenditure. The adoption of this proposal would involve the relinquishment of Bowling Park Colony being used as an Auxiliary Military Hospital. The Guardians advised either early acceptance or refusal of the offer due to the urgency of the question and disruption to follow. The reply to this proposal was not received for nearly four months!

An account was submitted to the War Office for the care of wounded soldiers at the Bowling Colony during the first quarter ending 30 June 1915, amounting to £320 8s 0d.

10 July 1915

Woodlands Convalescent Hospital at Rawdon received the first batch of wounded soldiers.

Several of these temporary pavilions were built in the hospital grounds in order to cope with the steadily rising numbers of wounded.

From July 1915 Woodlands at Rawdon was used as a convalescent home for wounded soldiers. In the late twentieth century it was an orthopaedic hospital.

9 September 1915

A letter was received by the Guardians from the Town Clerk enquiring what was to be done by the War Office for the provision for wounded soldiers at St Luke's. An early decision was required in order to permit proposed building schemes to go ahead to provide accommodation for displaced inmates.

The Guardians replied, 'regret that no further information can be obtained from the War Office'.

15 September 1915

The Medical Officer of St Luke's, Dr B. Slater, enlisted in the RAMC and Dr Lumsden was appointed as Assistant Medical Officer.

7 October 1915

The Chairman reported verbally that the military authorities had now decided to accept St Luke's Hospital as a Base Hospital for wounded soldiers on the conditions laid down by the Guardians. This decision was obviously prompted by the large numbers of casualties arriving daily in Bradford and district.

14 October 1915

The Subcommittee appointed to deal with the War Hospital submitted the following arrangements to the Guardians for their approval:

Transference of Patients:
1. 80 Male Sick to Barnsley at 12s per week and extras
2. 32 Old/Infirm Females to Barnsley at 8s per week and extras
3. 10 Old/Infirm Males to Settle at 7s 7d per week and extras
4. 10 Old/Infirm Females to Settle at 7s 7d per week and extras
5. Wibsey Council School, Bradford, to be lent by the Education Committee for accommodation of 100 Old/Infirm Women for which they received no payment
6. Consumptive patients to be transferred to Bierley Hall Workhouse in the care of the Health Committee

Bradford Automobile Club assisted in transferring patients to the new locations.

Cleaning and Painting Work:
1. Male Hospital   All areas require cleaning and painting
2. Male Consumptive Ward   Basement cleaning
3. Male Infirmary   Provision for Quartermaster's Office
4. Female Infirmary   Provision for Quartermaster's Office
5. Clothes racks for soldiers' old kits, new kits and hospital clothing

Tenders were accepted from Bradford firms:
Wm Pickering & Sons, Garnett Street, for 300 wooden lockers for the soldiers' belongings at 5s 6d each

Taylor & Parsons Ltd supplied 50 Lawson Tate bedsteads at £2 2s each
A Manchester firm supplied 350 Black Coir Fibre mattresses
The Empire Steam Laundry agreed to wash uniforms for 110 nurses at 2s 11d per head per week for a trial period of two months

The Guardians also made provision for the following:
· Cleaning and sanitary fittings to be provided
· Front Buildings: Administration Block to provide accommodation for Registrar's room, Medical Officer's Room, Clerical Rooms, Waiting Rooms, Messenger's Room, etc.
· National telephone to be installed in Registrar's private office
· Gateway entrance requires diverting to provide an access road to the Female Infirmary
· Committee room to be used as a nurses' dining room and trestle tables to be provided
· Future Committee meetings to be held at Manor Row in premises which were to become the Children's Clinic in later years

Accommodation had to be sought for the extra staff to be employed at the War Hospital.

Lady Powell handed over Horton Hall (later to become the residence of the Bishop of Bradford) to the Guardians for the use of the nursing staff – free of charge.

Authority was given to Matron Foggett to appoint the required number of Ward Sisters and Staff Nurses, a housekeeper and servants for the Nurses' Home.

Authority was given to the Chairman of St Luke's to appoint clerks, typists and gate attendants for the War Hospital and to have fifty keys cut for the entrance gates which would be manned by Porters' Lodges. The Chairman's Clerk was authorised to arrange terms of employment for the caretakers of Wibsey School.

The Military Authorities were requested to grant an immediate payment of £5,000 to cover the expense incurred in the setting up of a Military Hospital.

After these initial provisions were completed the painting, cleaning, electrification, renovating and restructuring began. The old building at the South Corner of the hospital, near 'A' Block, was demolished and the site cleared to make way for ambulances to turn the corner. Two rooms in the basement of 'A' Block were fitted up for Radiography Work which necessitated the installation of sundry sinks, washing appliances and an asphalt floor in the X-ray room. The space under the entrance became a sterilizing room with extra cupboards.

Dr Mitchell was given permission to purchase X-ray apparatus for the War Hospital.

The telephone system in the Porter's Lodge was fitted with a changeover switch coupled up to the Registrar's Office. This was very soon recognised to be inadequate and four Trunk Lines from the Exchange were installed with seven branches to different extensions. A new agreement had to be made with the Postmaster General by which three Trunk Lines were on the unlimited call rate and one on the measured rate. The annual increased rental rate was to be £10 5s 0d with a present war payment of £37 5s 0d.

The improvement to the electric lighting required a new main switch, new distribution fuses, new drop flexibles, lamps, holders and shades. A large part of the hospital was still lit by gas lamps.

In 'B' Block padded rooms were stripped and refitted, walls replastered and whitewashed, woodwork washed and repainted, rooms set aside for storage of kit with clothes racks installed.

In 'C' Block the basement was turned into a concert hall with the help and expertise of Mr Grant, the Stage Manager of the Empire Theatre, Bradford. The doors were enlarged and made to open outwards to accommodate beds and stretcher cases (in some areas of the hospital stretchers bearing patients had to be tilted sideways as the doorways were too narrow). A stage was erected and a base was fitted for the organ. The area was also used as a recreation, snooker and billiards hall. Messrs. Pickersgill & Co. supplied a bagatelle board and a set of balls. Fitted cupboards to store equipment had to be made rat-proof. Many concerts took place here and other forms of entertainment were organised by the men themselves as well as by visiting groups of artistes. Two dressing rooms were fitted with washbasins and screens; and toilets, a bedpan washer and sluice room were also provided.

In 'D' Block the Quartermaster's office and store was fitted with rooms for storage of kit, uniforms, hospital uniforms and a boot store. A Non-commissioned Officers' room was provided on the ground floor.

There was also a Disinfecting Station set up on 'D' Block. Wounded men arriving from the battlefields were infested with head and body lice and scabies. The verb 'to chatter' became part of the English language from the times that the soldiers sat in the trenches picking 'chats' or lice off themselves and each other while engaging in friendly banter, inane conversations or even gossip, which helped to cover their acute embarrassment. Many friendships were formed during these 'chatting' sessions.

20 October 1915

Salaries were agreed for staff appointed to the War Hospital:

1. Ward Sisters: £50 per annum plus Board and Lodging and Washing of Uniforms (usually £35)
2. Staff Nurses: £40 per annum plus Board and Lodging and Washing of Uniforms (usually £25)
3 .Ward-maids: £18 (formerly referred to as scrubbers)

28 October 1915

A request was issued from the officer commanding the Royal Field Artillery for the land behind the Daisy Hill homes to be used as a riding ménage for experimental horse trenches. Permission was granted.

3 November 1915

Matron Foggett was authorised to appoint five Ward Sisters and nine Staff Nurses to work in the War Hospital. Many other appointments were made in different categories.

Throughout October and November large numbers of casualties arrived daily in Bradford and were cared for in the city's hospitals. There was an increasing need to provide more hospital beds, particularly when the first Red Cross ambulance trains, capable of carrying hundreds of sick and wounded, came into service. The first of these arrived in Bradford on 9 December 1915.

11 November 1915

Permission was granted to alter the paving in the yard to allow the motor ambulances to gain access to the various buildings without any severe vibrations to the patients being carried therein.

The vicar of Bradford, the Revd George Atkinson, and the parish priest of St Joseph's Roman Catholic Church, the Revd T.J. Blessing, offered to officiate as chaplains to the soldiers, sailors and prisoners of war admitted to the hospital. The Guardians readily agreed to these offers.

8 December 1915

Miss Rodgers was appointed as Home Sister. In later years she became Matron of St Luke's Hospital. Hilda Dawson was appointed as a Probationer Nurse. She was a wonderful nurse who was later to become Superintendent of the operating theatres. Her kindness is remembered by the present writer who arrived as a scared and naïve student nurse to work in the theatres in October 1955 and who, thankfully, survived the experience and went on to take charge of an operating theatre suite in Africa eighteen years later.

15 December 1915

A letter was sent to the Guardians from the Superintendent of the Bradford City Fire Brigade suggesting provision of certain fire-fighting appliances at the War Hospital. Permission was granted.

Miss Rodgers was appointed as a Home Sister in 1915. She eventually became Matron of St Luke's.

16 December 1915

An advertisement was to be placed in the local press thanking donors for gifts made to the War Hospital.

December also saw the transportation of many wounded soldiers and sailors to St Luke's Hospital under Lieutenant Colonel Wrangham, the Officer in Charge. He immediately asked for more beds to be made available for military use. (The Army Lists[7] show that Dr Wrangham received his temporary appointment to Lieutenant Colonel in July 1916. Major W.H. Thompson and Major J. Phillips FRCS were appointed in November 1915.)

23 December 1915

The War Hospital Extension Subcommittee submitted the following proposal to the Local Government Board:

> It is proposed that the whole of the Horton Lane premises (except the Medical Officer's residence and the two Workhouse Casual Wards, Male & Female) be handed over for the period of the war to the Army Council, on the understanding that the Guardians retain full control of the buildings and that the alterations and additions required to the premises to bring the accommodation up to the required number be at their discretion and be carried out by them.

It was acknowledged that provision would have to be made for present inmates, namely adult male and female sick, female lunatics, short period male and female lunatics, sick children, maternity hospital, children's nursery, and male and female infirm requiring hospital treatment. The Bowling Colony was considered suitable for some of the inmates and some elderly could be boarded out, preferably in Council Schools if the Education Committee agreed.

The hospital architect estimated that the cost of erecting the temporary buildings at Horton and Bowling Park would be £25,000.

1 January 1916

The Bradford War Hospital name was used for the first time.

8 January 1916

A report from the War Hospital Chairman, the mill owner R.S. Dawson, warned that £35,000 was needed to enlarge the hospital to either 1,300 or 1,400 beds. After heated discussions with a strong division of opinion an agreement was reached that the whole of the Horton Lane premises were to be handed over to the Military Authorities as soon as was reasonably possible.

12 January 1916

A letter of complaint was received from the Administrator of the War Hospital about the poor quality of the meat supplied for patients.

20 January 1916

The Military Authorities wrote to the Administrator that they could not agree to pay for meals on duty for Boy Scouts and other volunteer workers at the War Hospital, even though they often worked twelve-hour shifts with no food or drink provided.

27 January 1916

The Military Authorities would not agree to a kitchen extension costing £300. It was agreed that an existing shed should be adapted.

28 January 1916

The reply to the War Hospital Extension Subcommittee from the Lord Mayor's Committee (who had promised the money) reads as follows:

> It is suggested that by re-arranging the beds in the present four blocks the number be increased from 540 to 600. Four other blocks now occupied by Union patients would supply another 300 beds and it is proposed to build three more blocks holding 300, thus bringing the total accommodation to 1,200. The administrative buildings would be utilised by the additional nurses and orderlies besides providing for the necessary extension of the officers' quarters. The three new buildings would be built of wood, after the Leicester pattern, if this style commends itself after inspection.

The demand for beds was to continue and is clearly shown on contemporary postcards.

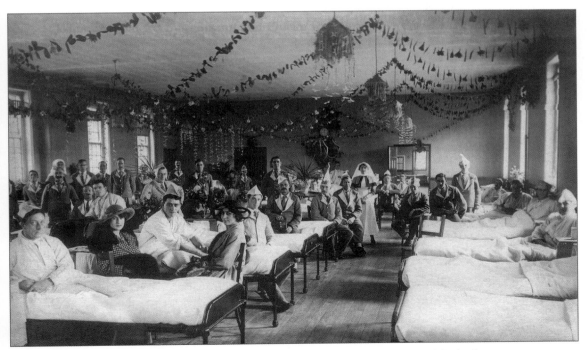

This postcard shows three lines of beds in the ward: a sign of the rising demand for bed space.

It was agreed that the Administrator of the Hospital would manage the whole of the premises after the new buildings were erected and the premises evacuated by the Union patients.

It is NOT proposed to build a recreation hall. The total cost of the new buildings, including a mortuary & post-mortem room and enlargement of the stores, with complete equipment, our architect Mr Holland estimates will be £15,500.

It was suggested that after the war the new pavilions for patients should be pulled down and the materials sold, the amount realised being returned to the Lord Mayor's Fund. In the event, this never happened.

The staff of electricians, firemen, stokers and tradesmen employed on the premises remained in the service of the Guardians by whom they continued to be paid.

The Guardians found that provision would have to be made for 800 displaced inmates. Of these they believed that 350 could be placed in other Union Houses and, with the permission of the Education Authority, in Council Schools. The remaining 450 would be removed to the Bowling Park and buildings would be erected for their accommodation at an estimated cost of £15,000. It was suggested that after the war an independent valuation be made of these premises and that the Guardians retain them, paying the amount of the valuation back to the Lord Mayor's Fund. The Guardians undertook to carry out the whole of the work as rapidly as possible. The architect issued certificates monthly and the amount due was paid directly to the contractors by the Lord Mayor's Committee which had full power to check and audit all accounts.

10 February 1916

The Guardians agreed to accept the entire proposal previously outlined and the work commenced immediately at a great pace and with great enthusiasm. The Union patients were rapidly moved out to various other abodes to enable the major changes to take place within the existing buildings and for the new buildings to be erected.

All the time this was happening patients were arriving daily from the battlefields or being sent to receive further treatment or recuperate in auxiliary hospitals or convalescent homes.

A Finance, Stores and General Purposes Subcommittee was set up specifically to deal with matters relating to the War Hospital.

18 March 1916

The Royal Certificate was granted to Bradford War Hospital Supply Depot and the Royal Charter was granted giving the hospital full military status. This has never been rescinded, and following the wonderful work carried out during the First and Second World Wars, the writer recalls St Luke's Hospital being placed on 'standby' at the time of the Falklands Conflict and the first Iraq war. Even today the red crosses painted on the two stone pillars guarding the former main entrance – which signified it as military hospital – can still be seen.

A mystery surrounds the whereabouts of the Charter today: it seems to have completely disappeared. It was a beautifully framed parchment document that hung on the wall in the outer office leading to the Matron's Office. The author remembers studying it while waiting to be summoned to the inner sanctum of Matron's Office. (I once had to confess to the crime of breaking a thermometer and, upon handing over the broken pieces, being fined 1s 6d, to be paid off at sixpence a month!)

5 October 1916

Princess Marie Louise officially opened the extensions to the hospital in a ceremony attended by the Lord Mayor and other civic dignitaries, the War Extension Subcommittees and the Guardians, who formally handed over the hospital to the Military Authorities.

The name St Luke's Hospital was dropped for the duration of the war and the designation 'the War Hospital' was adopted and kept until 1919.

From October 1916, when St Luke's was officially taken over, meetings of the Guardians ceased until after the war. Therefore no Minutes exist for this period. Under the Defence of the Realm Act (DORA) hospital records are frozen until 2019. However, a picture can be gleaned from the many memories and anecdotal accounts from Bradford people, both medical and civilian.

It was always understood by the staff at St Luke's Hospital that as well as our own servicemen some German prisoners of war were treated. They were housed in 'temporary' Blocks H and I, situated at the Holme Top end of the hospital.

These blocks were still in use for patient care during the 1950s, albeit in a poor state of repair. As a student nurse I worked in H1, a female geriatric ward, on night duty in 1955 and 1956. It was a cold and draughty place and, if it rained, buckets had to be carefully placed to catch the rainwater. Extra covers were placed on some beds to prevent the patients from getting wet. After major refurbishment in the 1960s, Blocks H and I became the Physiotherapy and Occupational Therapy Departments and the Central Linen sorting room. They continued in use until the 1980s when they were demolished and replaced by the new Horton wing of the hospital.

I remember hearing from many people that the hospital had been an important centre for treating gas victims during and after the Great War, but I have very little evidence from hospital sources to support the belief. However, there are accounts in war literature which confirm that gas cases were treated in Bradford. Sister Henrietta Hall (QAIMNS) gives an account of her experiences at St Luke's in *The Roses of No Man's Land*.[8] She describes the desperate plight of the young men who took such a long time to recover and, in many cases, the fear which being gassed had implanted in them. Breathlessness, susceptibility to cold or any changes in weather and constant coughing stayed with the victims for weeks or months. Oxygen was the only relief for some and Sister Hall describes her nurses holding the oxygen mask to the face of patients for half an hour at a time and, after a rest, returning to their bedside to continue. One young man, a farmer's son from Cornwall who had been gassed at Ypres, heated his thermometer in his hot water bottle when the Medical Officer was doing his rounds. Sister Hall said nothing even though she had observed his subterfuge. She understood the terror he had of being returned to the Front and was relieved when he was sent to a convalescent hospital with little likelihood of further service.

Corporal Ivor Watkins of 6th Battalion, Welch Guards recalls the following:

At Houplines, near Armentières, in March 1918 we were going up, by night, as a covering party for an Australian tunnelling company, which meant if Jerry came over we'd have got it in the neck before the tunnellers. We got into a house where there was a cellar, got some mattresses and a brazier and made ourselves comfortable. There were some 18-pounder batteries behind us and the Germans were going at them. On the night of the 16th of March he started shelling those batteries with mustard-gas shells. Our gas guard must have got killed because we had no warning. Gas is heavier than air and it must have got down into the cellars because when we woke in the morning, we felt our eyes burning terribly and thought it was the smoke from the brazier. We started rubbing our eyes, but what we were doing was rubbing the mustard gas into them. We soon realised with the smell, which is akin to horseradish, what we had done. We all came up and were rushed down to the casualty clearing station. Our eyes were watering profusely. Nothing but water rushing from our eyes. They were burning like hell. I could just see a mist in front of me, but I hadn't rubbed as hard as some of the others.

From the clearing station I was rushed to the 2nd Canadian Hospital. Within four days I was at St Luke's Hospital in Bradford, where they were clearing out the casualties as quickly as they could. They attached a sign to me, 'Gas Shell – Very Severe'.

When I got to Bradford I couldn't see. It was the most terrifying experience I have ever had. Was I going to be blind for life? What was I going to do? My trade, my employment gone. It hit me very, very hard. For the first month or so I couldn't recognise anything, and then there was a gradual haze. I had a Scottish Army Sister and I'll always remember the intonation, 'Taffy, I'll get your sight back, don't worry'. I was given goggles to wear to keep the glare out. I also had burns to the tender parts of my body which were treated with ointment. I had a steam kettle as well to inhale. And then I started heavy smoking as I thought to clear my chest, but it was obviously just soothing the nerves. It was fashionable to smoke. We were given cigarettes in hospital. We were treated right royally. I recovered my sight, but so many didn't. I had my 20th birthday in that hospital.[9]

In the autumn of 1958, Mr George Whyte-Watson, the Consultant Surgeon for whom I worked as a Staff Nurse on Ward A2 at St Luke's Hospital, asked me if I would like to be involved in clinical trials using Nitrogen Mustard Compounds in the treatment we now call Chemotherapy. He told me that this had largely arisen from many years of research into the after-effects suffered by the gas victims of World War 1.

Those initial trials involved three very brave women who offered themselves as the first patients to be treated with these new, potentially dangerous, drugs with as yet unknown side-effects. It was another pioneering 'first' for St Luke's Hospital.

Today, patients who undergo chemotherapy to treat various forms of cancer owe much to those three ladies who offered themselves as human guinea pigs, and also to the many gas victims of the Great War from whose suffering came the research and knowledge we have today.

Most hospitals have resident ghosts and St Luke's was no exception, as those of us who have worked night duty will testify. Tales were told about 'Grey Ladies' who appeared in the wee small hours of the morning on C, D, E, F, H, J & K Blocks. I can certainly recall strange experiences and episodes during my night duty as a student in the late 1950s which were hard to explain, and could have been put down to imagination. In 1966, when I worked as a Night Sister for six months and had to visit the wards in the different blocks three times each night, covering a lot of ground inside and out in all types of weather, I never felt unsafe. However, I often heard footsteps and felt comforting presences which I simply described as 'my Guardian Angels'.

Not all of the staff at the War Hospital were British. Albert Lester Jones BS, AM, MD, Physician and Surgeon, was born at Weatherford, Texas, on 6 April 1885, and graduated as a Doctor of Medicine in Cleveland, Ohio, in 1916. He became an intern at Cleveland City Hospital just before America entered the Great War. In July 1917, Dr Jones volunteered for service in the US Army Medical Corps and was accepted, commissioned First Lieutenant and ordered to Army Headquarters School at Washington DC where he was detailed for overseas duty with the British Army. On reaching London in October 1917, he was immediately assigned to Surgical Service at the Bradford War Hospital where he remained on active duty until he was ordered to France. There he had a seven-month attachment to the 5th Scottish Rifles Infantry Battalion, 33rd Division on the Ypres sector in Belgium. During the Battle of Metern on that sector, Dr Jones's Dressing Station was located in the Front lines. The stretcher-bearers were unable to go forward to aid the wounded so the doctor ordered his post to be advanced into the firing trenches and there they remained, attending to the wounded under heavy shell and rifle fire until ordered to the rear.

For this service Dr Jones was cited for the British Military Cross by Field Marshal Sir Douglas Haig, and later was decorated at Buckingham Palace by King George V. In September 1918, he was assigned to the American Army and finished his service with them having been promoted to the rank of Captain. He was mustered out in October 1919 and returned to Cleveland, where he set up his own practice in medicine and surgery. He married Jane Louise Anderson of Lakewood, Ohio, on 2 April 1924.

On 7 July 1917 the *Yorkshire Observer*[10] reported the opening of the Abram Peel Auxiliary War Hospital. The Surgeon General's speech served to underline the importance of the work being carried out in Bradford's hospitals, and also alluded to the mental scars of battle:

This War has brought with it new medical difficulties. The horrors of this terrible conflict could not fail to have serious effects on the delicate, intricate and elaborate machines we call men. We now have to deal with something more than shattered limbs; we have shattered nerves; the heart and its coordinating powers have lost their harmony of action. The bravest hearts are now made to tremble. The same care and same provision must be made for these sad maladies that are made for maimed and wounded men. Some of this new accommodation will be appropriated for soldiers suffering from such maladies. I trust and believe men will receive there skilful treatment and kind sympathy. It is a great thing to gain the confidence of such patients and to encourage a feeling of hope in the patient himself. My Specialist on these diseases told me of a Canadian sufferer, who was, however, a man of unbounded hope and cheerfulness. Written above his bed was the motto 'Keep smiling; Jonah came out alright.' [Laughter] And in three weeks that Canadian walked out of the hospital.

General Bedford had great pleasure in taking over the hospital on behalf of the Army. The hospital was named after a former Lord Mayor of Bradford, Alderman Abram Peel, who had been a great fundraiser for the War Relief Fund.

Private Arthur Marshall[11] was transferred to the Abram Peel Hospital on 26 August 1918. Private Marshall, born in Retford in 1898, enlisted for Army Service in September 1916 in Sheffield. However, employed at Vickers as a turner in the engineering department, his active service was deferred until the shortage of serving men became acute in 1918. Private Marshall was re-examined on 16 April and sent to York for his medical checks.

Arthur Marshall from Sheffield was treated at St Luke's. His 'hospital blues' were the uniform worn by wounded men. The revers on the tunic were pale yellow.

He received his routine vaccinations on 26 June but by the time he was due to depart from Hull in early July, Private Marshall was clearly suffering a reaction to the vaccines and was admitted to the St John's VAD hospital. After thirty-one days he was transferred to the Bradford War Hospital on 10 August and thence to the Abram Peel.

His hospital record reads, 'Patient gets easily fatigued. Occasional headaches', and the entry is signed by Captain Louis V. Lopez of the US Medical Corps. He was sent before an Investigation Board on 26 November and declared unfit for active service. As the war had ended he was immediately discharged having spent 111 of his 125 days of active military service in hospital.

Convalescent hospitals and homes provided peaceful and pleasant surroundings for the recovering wounded and helped keep beds in the main hospitals free for the

Above: Arthur Marshall's medical record shows he was ill immediately before sailing from Hull. *Above, right:* More details of Marshall's record including the signature of Louis V. Lopez, an American medic. *Right:* Arthur Marshall's family still has this Book of Psalms, given to him by Sister Rose. Who was she?

recently wounded. The Field House estate, gifted to the Board of Guardians in 1908, was one such place and Bradford was fortunate to also have Woodlands at Rawdon and the Semon Convalescent Home[12] in Ilkley.

Woodlands was strongly supported by local people who organised concert parties, provided greatcoats and boots, set up a skittle alley and shooting gallery in the cellar and provided free barber and chiropodist services for the patients. A gift of thirty pheasants was recorded and free cigarettes and tobacco came from the 'Smokes for Soldiers and Sailors Society'. Horsforth Golf Club offered free use of the course each day and afternoon tea on Thursdays, and Bradford Corporation Tramways organised free tickets for servicemen.

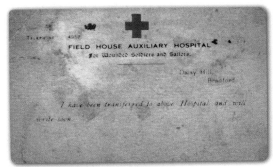

These printed postcards were a simple way by which a wounded man could notify his family of his whereabouts.

The first servicemen to be treated at Ilkley Coronation Hospital arrived after the Battle of Antwerp in October 1914. They were fifty Belgian soldiers and the Hospital Committee had to defer admissions from hospital subscribers. Indeed, in January 1915 all subscribers were notified that for the duration of the war it would be impossible to admit ordinary convalescent patients 'due to the premises being taken over by the authorities as a Military Hospital for wounded soldiers'.[13] The hospital Matron, Sister Burnley, and one nurse were seconded to the Military Authorities, who would pay their salaries. Maids' wages were increased during the war.

In January 1918 the Committee considered what would be a fair rent to charge for use of the hospital by the military and, on the handover on 1 February 1919, they received £850, being three years' rent at £150, and a sum for restitution or dilapidation.

Venereal diseases were recognised as a problem early in the war, even before the troops left the UK. Medical Officers received very little guidance on the prevention and treatment of such diseases. By 1917, the Dominion governments protested against the failure by the British government to deal with the problem, recorded as high as 287 per 1,000 with some imperial troops. This led to Regulation 40 D being added to the Defence of the Realm Act (DORA) in 1917 which made it an offence to solicit, invite or perform sexual intercourse with any member of the Armed Forces. Initially women who were found to have communicated any form of venereal disease to troops were penalised, but the government, fearing a backlash from the six million newly enfranchised women who claimed that 40 D was one-sided, appointed a royal commission to research, report and advise on how the problems could be dealt with.

Contrary to popular belief, the troops did not get off scot-free. If a soldier contracted a disease and tried to conceal it, he could be court-martialled, with a penalty of imprisonment with hard labour for two years if the case was proven. On the other hand, if he did not conceal the disease, but reported to the Medical Officer and went to hospital, he could lose all his pay and emoluments, and, if married, his wife would lose her separation allowance during the time he was hospitalised. Consequently, many men did not report such problems and they only came to light when soldiers were wounded and hospitalised on repatriation to the UK. Military hospitals in the UK had to be prepared to deal with these problems along with the more urgent and severe problems, but because of the law, medical officers who gave such treatment were considered to be committing 'crimes' by aiding and abetting. Therefore, many medical officers both at the front and at home were afraid to deal with such cases.

On the Home Front the government responded to pressure and in 1916 the Venereal Diseases Act was passed, providing free and confidential treatment for every citizen. Generous grants were given to hospitals and health authorities who were willing to provide services and accommodation to deal with patients. In April 1917 the Bradford Royal Infirmary opened a clinic for the treatment of Venereal Diseases at a time when most voluntary hospitals were refusing the requests of the Army Council to provide such clinics.

The 'special' clinic, as it was popularly known, remained at Bradford Royal Infirmary for many years until the new purpose-built clinic was opened at St Luke's in 1958. Tucked away discreetly at the rear of the hospital and approached via external doors leading on to Park Lane, patients were able to come and go with a good degree of privacy. This was of the utmost importance in gaining the trust of the people being treated. Between 1914 and 1918 approximately 400,000 cases of venereal diseases involving military personnel were treated in France and Britain. It was mid-1918 before medical officers were officially allowed the freedom to treat patients with these diseases.

Bradford's contribution to the treatment of the wounded was an enormous contribution to the war effort. The Deputy Director of Medical Services for the Northern Command acknowledged this at the opening of the Abram Peel Hospital.[14]

The Army already owes a great debt to the city for the splendid War Hospital accommodation of 1,200 beds. At York HQ is a large map marked by distinctive flags showing the situation of the hospitals. The West Riding of Yorkshire had not only given thousands of men to the Army, but had provided so many hospitals that the names of the towns could not properly be seen for the flags.

General Bedford acknowledged with grateful thanks 'the kindly thoughts and patriotic sentiment' which had prompted the Lord Mayor and Bradford Corporation to make such generous provision for wounded soldiers. On inspecting hospital premises in Bradford, General Bedford commented on 'the lightness, brightness and airiness of the wards and the wideness of the outlook obtained from the grounds of the hospital'. Those servicemen who recovered from their wounds were granted home leave prior to reporting to their Command Depot. This was the last stop before the 'Return to Hell', which so many of them feared. Despite being surrounded by suffering, the bright airiness of a Bradford hospital ward must have been preferable to the mud of Flanders.

Notes

1. Nightingale, F., *Notes on Nursing: what it is and what it is not*, Norwalk, Appleton-Century-Crofts
2. Report of the Poor Law Commissioners 1840. Available in Bradford Central Library
3. See Firth, Gary, *Bradford Charity and the Public Purse: a History of Bradford Hospitals from 1780*, Bradford Hospitals NHS Trust, 2001
4. Minutes of the Board of Guardians of St Luke's Hospital. Available in Bradford Central Library
5. Phithisis comes from the Greek for 'wasting away'. The word was applied without distinction to both atrophy of the lungs caused by exposure to dust, and to tuberculosis. The term is no longer in use
6. The following records are taken from the minutes of the meetings of the St Luke's Hospital Committee and reviewed by the Guardians in their twice monthly meetings. Available in Bradford Central Library
7. Army Lists July 1916, RAMC Serving with the Bradford War Hospital. Available at the National Archives Kew
8. Macdonald, Lyn, *The Roses of No Man's Land*, pp. 160–3, Michael Joseph Ltd, 1980
9. Arthur, Max, *Forgotten Voices of the Great War*, pp. 261–2, Ebury Press, 2002. By kind permission of The Imperial War Museum
10. Speech of Surgeon General C.B. Bedford reported in the *Yorkshire Observer*, July 1917
11. The author is grateful to the son and grandson of Arthur Marshall for permission to use details of his service and hospital records and to publish family photographs
12. Semon was chairman of the Infirmary Board in the 1850s and, along with mill owners Titus Salt and Robert Milligan, established a Committee of Operatives to provide the equivalent of a hospital fund for mill workers. Subscriptions came from employers and employees, from the Friendly Societies and from Manchester Unity of Oddfellows. The Ilkley Convalescent Home was named in recognition of the work done by Semon.
13. Minutes of the Committee of Ilkley Coronation Hospital available in Bradford Central Library
14. Speech of Surgeon General, ibid

TEN

Can We Help?

Tricia Platts

The Great War saw a greater movement of peoples than ever experienced before. In addition to the millions of troops moving across continents and oceans an almost equal number of civilians was displaced either temporarily or permanently. The needs of all these people were similar: a welcome, an offer of comforts and a safe onward journey. In Bradford it was mainly volunteer groups which provided support for people on the move and their story is one of superb organisation, typical Yorkshire warmth and personal acts of kindness.

Images of women were often used in recruitment posters. This one incorporates two ideas: the reported outrage against women in Belgium and the defence of wives and girlfriends at home.

A poignant image issued as a fundraising card by the *Bradford Telegraph*.

In the first days and weeks of the war German forces overran Belgium. Atrocities committed against civilians, the firing of public buildings such as the ancient library at Leuven and the destruction of some 16,000 homes were widely reported in British newspapers. It was not surprising therefore, that when refugees poured out of Belgium they were welcomed in England. It is estimated that in 1911 there were nearly 5,000 Belgian nationals living in England. This figure rose to over a quarter of a million during the war and had fallen to less than 10,000 by 1921. In total around two million Belgians left their homes with little more than they could carry on horse- and dog-drawn carts or handcarts.

Provision for these refugees was passed to a variety of charitable and government agencies. The War Refugee Committee[1] (presided over by Lady Lugard and with offices in the Strand) received funds from the Local Government Board from April 1916 onwards and 30,000 refugees found employment through local Labour Exchanges.

Outside London local committees were formed which, in Bradford, was led by the Lady Mayoress's War Guild[2]. This group was formed on 13 August 1914 under the then Mayoress, Mrs G.H. Robinson (leadership passed to each new Lady Mayoress on commencement of her office). To ensure that every part of the city became involved, the guild was administered through the Municipal Wards. Each formed a group with its own President, Secretary and Treasurer and all churches and clubs were asked to send representatives to the meetings of the local committee. A Central Advisory Committee met with ward representatives each month.

With the guild reaching into virtually every street, its success was guaranteed. Within weeks, parcels of new and nearly new clothing for men, women and children were dispatched to devastated areas of France and Belgium and the Bradford Cinderella Club[3] had also received parcels.

From then on, regular grants of shirts, socks and underclothing were sent to the Soldiers' Dependants' Committee, the Serbian War Relief Fund, Mine Sweepers, YMCA (France), prisoners of war, various regiments and also to individual serving men. When St Luke's became a war hospital (see Chapter 9) the Lady Mayoress's War Guild was able to help with extra supplies of towels, bed linen, dressing gowns, pyjamas,

The formidable Lady Mayoress, Mrs G.H. Robinson, who instituted a hugely successful War Guild across the city.

day and nightshirts, linen, cotton overalls, stretcher covers and grave clothes. These 'last garments' each had a card attached which had been printed by Humphries with

This postcard, dating from about 1904, shows a group of blind children being treated to an outing organised by the Bradford Cinderella Club.

the verse from John, Chapter 15: 'Greater love hath no man than this, that a man lay down his life for his friends'.

Local efforts were supplemented by gifts from abroad, especially from America. The Ladies' Sewing Party of the Greystone Relief Committee, the Pawtucket War Relief Society and the Rhode Island Club, among many others, sent regular parcels of clothing, linens, 'comforts' and whatever was thought to be of help.

On 22 October 1914, 220 Belgian refugees arrived in Bradford. They were temporarily housed at the Daisy Hill Institution and in four large cottages. These quarters had been annexed by the Military Authorities as a camp for the Bradford Battalion. Other refugees were housed in the Airedale College Chapel on Church Bank[4] and others were 'hosted' by local families.

The Lord Mayor's office became involved in the re-housing of the refugees during the following months and a Volunteers' Headquarters was opened in Leeds Road. The Lady Mayoress's War Guild was able to supplement the efforts of the government's War Refugees' Committee by providing clothing, bedding and furniture for the 220 arrivals. These refugees were maintained entirely by local funds for many months. Only in 1915 was support available from the government, and even then volunteer groups in Bradford and Ilkley received assistance for new refugees rather than for the continuing support of those who arrived earlier.[5]

A party of Belgian refugees, pictured at Windsor baths, formerly the Kursaal.

A Belgian family accommodated at East Bierley and Hunsworth in 1914.

Employment for Belgian men was found in the city, including work at the munitions factory at Low Moor. Those who were absent from work on the day of the explosion in August 1916 were questioned carefully, but sabotage was ruled out[6]. Following this incident and with a growing impatience with the shortages caused by war conditions, sympathy for the refugees dissipated. On 2 June 1915 police became involved in an incident at the Daisy Hill cottages. Considerable damage had been done to the windows by stone-throwing at the refugees who lived there.

When war ended the Belgian refugees rapidly returned to their devastated country. The National Archives contains record cards of every individual refugee, which make fascinating reading. The cards record arrival date, addresses where housed, employment, appeals for financial support and travel grants, requests for clothing, furniture and other necessities, and date of final departure. One example is Rosa Leysen (née Geernaerts) of Antwerp. She is described as an 'elderly female' and passed through Bradford in November 1914 on her way to lodgings at 9 Kelton Square, Halifax. She stayed there until 4 January 1918 and on 26 February 1919 returned to Belgium by ship[7].

Belgian refugees are remembered in Otley with a plaque on the clock tower in the market place. This was paid for by those who found a home in Otley during the war and, at the recent unveiling of the newly-restored clock tower, the Belgian Ambassador, Baron Thierry de Gruben, expressed his thanks to Otley and recalled the generous hospitality that the refugees had received in the Great War.

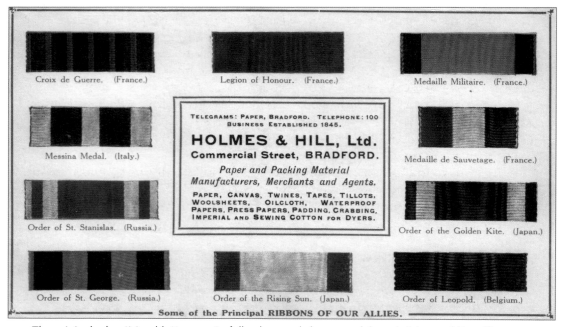

The original advertising blotter was in full colour and shows medals and ribbons of the allies: a popular image in the war.

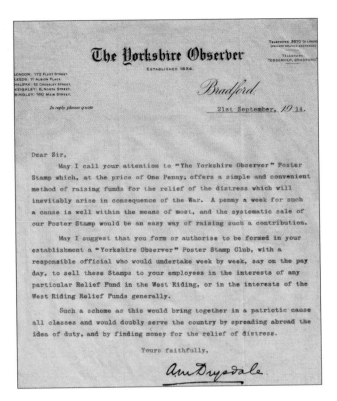

A letter promoting the penny stamp issued by the *Yorkshire Observer* which was a 'simple and convenient' way of raising funds for the war effort. A 'Poster Stamp Club' within an office or factory would ensure a good amount was collected weekly.

In Sheffield there is a 19ft-high cross based on a fifteenth-century French design which bears the names of the refugees who died in the city during the war. Three thousand Belgians lived in Sheffield and the raising of the cross was the last act of the Committee which 'had not only fed, housed and educated their children but which had sent them back to their homes again.'[8] There is no such memorial to the Belgian refugees who lived and worked in Bradford.

Companies involved themselves in fundraising projects, for example a blotter issued by Holmes Hill displays the medal ribbons of the Allies. The *Yorkshire Observer* offered readers the opportunity to buy a stamp, the proceeds of which went to the war effort.

Charity work, especially raising money through Flag Days became a major outlet for the energies of the young women of Bradford. In 1916 Charles Ogden, a historian of the war effort in Bradford, issued the Bradford War Work Souvenir in which he praised the Flag Days which had become common in the preceding years:

It is indeed, an inspiration of genius by which was established in our community the habit of purchasing, whichever organisation authority ordained it should be so, a little paper flag at any price dictated by the beguiling of fair collectors or the prompting of one's conscience and sympathy – an extraordinary illustration of the power of a trifling symbol to stimulate enthusiasm . . . in the phlegmatic masses of the population.[9]

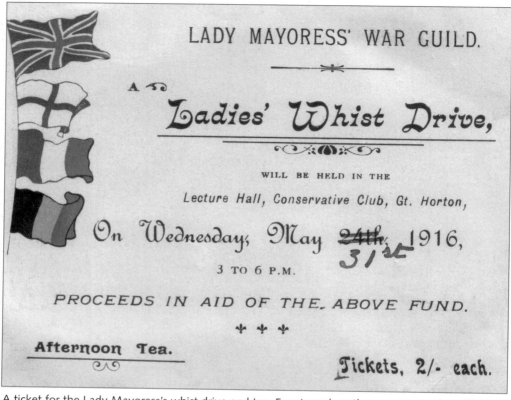

LADY MAYORESS' WAR GUILD.

A *Ladies' Whist Drive,*

WILL BE HELD IN THE

Lecture Hall, Conservative Club, Gt. Horton,

On Wednesday, May ~~24th,~~ *31st* 1916,

3 TO 6 P.M.

PROCEEDS IN AID OF THE ABOVE FUND.

❀ ❀ ❀

Afternoon Tea.

Tickets, 2/- each.

A ticket for the Lady Mayoress's whist drive and tea. Events such as these were popular with the women of Bradford. They could socialise and amuse themselves while also 'doing their bit' for the war effort.

David James[10] reports that on fourteen Saturdays in the summer and autumn of 1915, £12,000 was collected on the streets of Bradford for war objectives. In 1916 this figure rises to an astonishing £197,000. The Lady Mayoress of Bradford's War Guild was a beneficiary of some of this.

In cities throughout the land Flag Days became all too frequent and, coupled with anxieties expressed about the welfare of young women and children involved in them, pressure was put upon the Home Office for the regulation of collections across the country. This was finally introduced into the police force, factories, etc., by the Miscellaneous Provisions Act of 1916. This enabled local boroughs to regulate street collections with a series of provisions; collectors had to be over sixteen years of age, not accompanied by an animal, unpaid and with the name of the charity clearly displayed.[11] The public could now be assured that Flag Days were legitimate and they became part of the wider picture of fundraising for the war effort. An advantage of these collections was the street coverage which could be achieved: working class areas received as much attention as middle class areas and, as Lady Baddeley wrote in one of her letters to Queen Mary, 'a flag day gives the "man in the street" an opportunity of giving his mite and it is the pennies that mount up.'

This postcard shows a Bradford street party, probably in about 1916. These events helped to draw the community together, while also raising money and morale.

Street parties such as the one shown above (believed to be in the Leeds Road area in 1916), served a dual purpose in raising money while giving the population a fun-filled community occasion. Banners, bunting and dressing up could involve all those on the Home Front. Young children were prevailed upon to write poems, which were printed onto postcards and sold for the war effort.

The two examples shown feature Leonard Harrison at the age of twelve (he later became a reporter on the *Bradford Telegraph & Argus*)

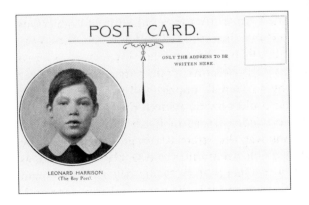

POST CARD.

ONLY THE ADDRESS TO BE
WRITTEN HERE.

LEONARD HARRISON
(The Boy Poet).

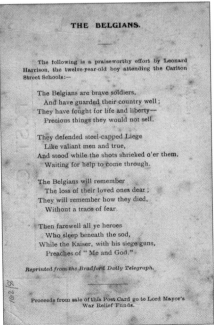

THE BELGIANS.

The following is a praiseworthy effort by Leonard Harrison, the twelve-year-old boy attending the Carlton Street Schools:—

The Belgians are brave soldiers,
   And have guarded their country well;
They have fought for life and liberty—
   Precious things they would not sell.

They defended steel-capped Liege
   Like valiant men and true,
And stood while the shots shrieked o'er them,
   Waiting for help to come through.

The Belgians will remember
   The loss of their loved ones dear;
They will remember how they died,
   Without a trace of fear.

Then farewell all ye heroes
   Who sleep beneath the sod,
While the Kaiser, with his siege guns,
   Preaches of " Me and God."

Reprinted from the Bradford Daily Telegraph.

Proceeds from sale of this Post Card go to Lord Mayor's
War Relief Funds.

POST CARD.

162/8

½d.
STAMP.

EDITH WHALLEY,
Cornwall Terrace, Manningham.

These children and their poems are just two examples of the *Bradford Daily Telegraph*'s effort at fundraising. As the most commonly used form of communication, postcards were an excellent format to adopt to raise cash.

A CHILD'S APPEAL.

MY NAME is Edith Whalley,
  A little girl you see;
I weigh just two-and-forty pounds,
  And that's something to be.

I'm a proud little helper,
  Collecting for the Telegraph Band;
And though I do but little,
  It is done with heart and hand.

I don't do half my duty,
  And then run away in fear;
But on I fight with all my might,
  Like a brave young volunteer.

So all who chance to see me,
  Just see what you can do;
And as you see me work a bit,
  Why, try to do some too.

I know 'tis hard to give to all,
  Very hard, indeed;
But don't let Bradford be behind,
  For our soldiers' cause I plead.

BRADFORD, DEC. 1914.

The proceeds from the sale of these cards will be devoted to the
" Bradford Daily Telegraph War Relief Fund ".

and an even younger Edith Whalley of Cornwall Terrace, Manningham. Edith is pictured dressed as a nurse and the card, issued in December 1914, raised money for the *Bradford Daily Telegraph* War Relief Fund.

The real *tour de force* in both organisation and service provided was the Khaki Club. Described as 'one of the most joyous pieces of war work done in Bradford',[12] its story is yet another example of the drive and determination of the women of Bradford. In March 1915 the Committee of the Bradford Women's Patrols[13] called a meeting in the Midland Hotel to which they invited the Lord Mayor and distinguished speakers and presented the case for a club for soldiers and sailors. It would provide comfortable safe surroundings for men to meet their girlfriends and would also provide wholesome food at a reasonable rate.

The entrance to the Midland railway station in Forster Square. In one of these buildings, the Khaki Club was established.

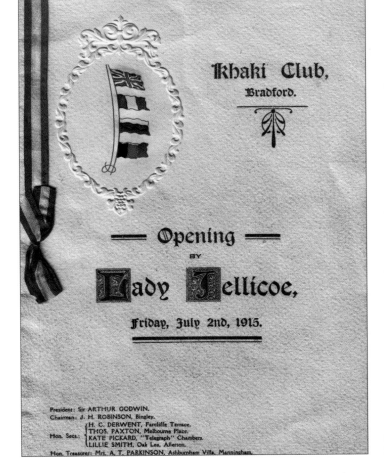

The beautifully produced programme for the official opening of the Khaki Club. The name of the author of the detailed account of the Khaki Club, Miss Kate Pickard, appears alongside the great and good of Bradford.

Lady Godwin is pictured inside the official programme.

It would seem that the response was immediate and within days premises had been found in Forster Square. The Midland Railway Co. provided a building free of charge and it was quickly refurbished to make it as unlike a barracks as possible. The upper floor had a games room with two billiard and two bagatelle tables, and a reading and writing room. On the lower floor was a café, concert room and lounge. Donations large and small, a succession of flag days and the support of Bradford companies kept the Club open until June 1919.

Lady Jellicoe (wife of the Admiral of the Fleet) performed the official opening on 2 July 1915 with reserve companies of the 16th and 18th Battalions of the West Yorkshire Regiment, the City Volunteers, Boy Scouts, Police Band and Army Service Corps in attendance. A civic reception followed and Lady Godwin unveiled the Roll of Honour.

The Committee found 200 volunteers for their rota and this enabled the club to be open throughout the day and night. It was estimated that 1,200 visitors a day came to the club including servicemen, family members and girlfriends. One and a half million meals were served, including 32,000 free meals. Concerts were organised and the Revd Mr Paxton opened a shop selling essentials, and a library. This proved extremely popular and Paxton found all kinds of sources for books both new and secondhand. He also sent parcels of books to serving men, which were returned during their next leave.

As the St Luke's War Hospital became established wounded men began arriving in large numbers. One hundred and twenty-seven convoys were met by volunteers from the Khaki Club, bringing a total of 19,244 men. Miss Pickard writes: 'Nothing was more pathetic than the way in which the most sorely wounded men appreciated the cigarettes which some would beg to have lighted for them when they were too weak or unable to do this for themselves.'[14] The Khaki Club provided concert parties at the hospital and even arranged trips out, although these had to be abandoned when fuel became scarce.

From 1917 to June 1919 volunteers from the Men's Committee of the Club met every train coming into Bradford after 10 p.m. 'to invite every weary man to the Khaki Club for a free meal and hot drink.' Miss Pickard reports that a total of 27,565 men and 1,468 of their friends were received in this way. Male volunteers

A fundraising tableau outside the Town Hall, possibly mounted by the Royal Irish Fusiliers. A tracked vehicle, gun limber, 9.3in howitzer and other weaponry behind the sandbags would have attracted considerable attention. Commemorative postcards are being sold from a rack in the foreground and the indicator on the wall of the Town Hall shows the Bradford column to have reached £2.75 million. The indicator is a model of a shell.

also drove men home, even as far as Halifax. Equal care was taken of men departing from Bradford bound for 'the battlefields' and they were seen off with a cheery wave.

It is difficult to quantify the effect such a wonderful organisation must have had on serving men and their families. For an exhausted, battle-weary man the journey home from the trenches was long and dreary. Imagine arriving on a cold dark night to be greeted by hot food and drinks and the support of willing Yorkshire volunteers; and during leave, to have the club to provide recreation, companionship and a comfortable meeting place must have been a welcome relief for the men.

Notes

1   National Archives, MH8/7 Memorandum showing purposes for which the Board advances money to the War Refugee Committee. Expenditure from the Belgian Refugee a/c from September 1914 to March 1915 was £944,088

2   The Lady Mayoress's War Guild including the Personal Comforts Fund, Report of the Advisory Committee, June 1919. Available in Bradford Central Library

3   The Bradford Cinderella Club founded in 1890 to 'reach and afford amusement' to the poor children of Bradford had also established a holiday centre at Hest Bank near Morecambe. Between April and October 1914 up to forty children at a time spent a fortnight there at a cost of £1,000 for the season. In addition to special treats and day trips, the Cinderella Club also provided footwear, usually clogs, for the children of many families. One of the club's most significant achievements was in providing meals for school children: the forerunner of the school meals service instituted by the Bradford Schools Board and Corporation under the city's Provision of Meals Act 1905

4   The Airedale College Chapel was founded in 1837 by Congregationalists from the United College at Undercliffe and was designed to seat 700

5   National Archives, MH8/7 ibid

6   Several hundred Belgians were employed at the newly built munitions factory at Birtley near Newcastle. A small town was built to house about 6,000 Belgians. It was named Elisabethville after the Belgian Queen and was run under Belgian law. Girls were taught French, Dutch and English by Ursuline nuns and the boys had Army schoolteachers to lick them into shape

7   National Archives MH8/66

8   Canon Dolan, Bishop of Sheffield at the unveiling of the cross at City Road Cemetery, Sheffield

9   Charles Ogden, *The Bradford War Work Souvenir*, Bradford 1916

10   David James *Bradford*, Ryburn Press Town and City Histories Series, 1990

11   PRO HO 45/10827/321759

12   See The Khaki Club: Romantic Story of a Great Voluntary War Effort 1915–1919 by Miss Kate Pickard. Available in Bradford Central Library

13   The Bradford Women's Patrols aimed to provide a safe environment for women who were, by necessity, in the city at night, going to and from shift work, meeting friends or attending meetings

14   The Khaki Club ibid.

ELEVEN

Women, Peace & Politics

Mike (and Angela) Woods & Tricia Platts

The service and sacrifice of fighting men in the Great War was matched by the service, and possibly sacrifice, of a whole population of anonymous women who emerged from Victorian and Edwardian society into a rapidly changing world. While 'change' characterises the whole of history, the pace of change had never been so rapid as in the period before the war. Mechanisation of factories, the speed of communication between cities and continents and increasing mobility led to changes in the role of women from all social classes equal in significance to the widening horizons of their men folk.

One of the most immediate effects of war experienced by women is colourfully described in the newspaper of the Independent Labour Party, the *Bradford Pioneer*:

> Dear Sir,
> Now that the terrible calamity – war – is upon us, I should like to bring before the notice of your readers who are, or ought to be, collectivists, what the City of Bradford Co-operative Society have done during the first two weeks of the war. When war was declared, a war that was absolutely unnecessary, a war begun not by us but in spite of us, prices of food stuffs were advanced immediately by nearly every dealer, outrageous prices were demanded for flour and all other necessities. . . .[1]

The financial circumstances of the woman at home became even more difficult if her husband was killed or wounded. No government allowances (dependants' benefits) were paid as-of-right. Indeed, Kitchener maintained that by paying all the 'widows', the country might be paying the dependants of cowards. 250,000 women were 'on relief at this time and there was real suffering in the industrial cities including Bradford'. In January 1915, it was proposed in Bradford that where the family income was less than 2s per head in a family when rent had been deducted, school dinners should be provided.[2]

National policies were also changing and by May 1915 allowances were paid to legitimate dependants such as wives and children. It was now agreed to pay mothers, sisters and other relatives where it could be established that 'a real home' had been established.

Female clerks pictured in the offices of John Speight & Sons.

Whether working outside the home or not, women were no strangers to the endless domestic drudgery of their lives. Those women already in paid work were generally low skilled (domestic service, shop work, factory hand, etc.) and rarely had professional training. The onset of war and departure of men to the battlefield extended opportunities for women. By filling the gaps in the workforce in the service sector, in factories supplying the war effort (including heavy manufacturing) and in munitions, women had the opportunity for higher wages while fulfilling a service to the nation.

Help for women was regarded as of increasing importance and by 1918 the Bradford Chamber of Commerce[3] had laid on a management course for women who had been left by their men to manage fish and chip shops. The chamber saw a real potential crisis and the traditional Yorkshire diet was in jeopardy. The women had been struggling on the business side with shops going bankrupt. Fish and chips must get through!

The changing role of women is a book in itself but we will quote two examples of the way in which the traditional male dominance was being challenged in Bradford.

Firstly, women wanted to serve and the shortage of labour in textile mills plus the new industries of munitions and plane making provided opportunities for factory work. Men reluctantly allowed 'dilution' into skilled crafts but only on the basis that the women would make way for the returning men when the war ended. By then the women had proved their point: they were equal to any job, subject to rational constraints.

The second example is from transport in the city. In July 1915 the General Manager of Bradford Tramways, Mr C.J. Spencer, spoke on the proposals to allow women conductors on 'his' trams:

Full consideration must be given to the proposal to allow women conductors on Bradford trams. I have not said in NO circumstances will we make the innovation, but in the interests of public safety we do not intend to employ women unless it has become absolutely necessary. In Bradford as you know, the gradients are severe and occasionally emergency duties devolve on the conductor and generally these duties have been well performed. What would happen in similar circumstances if we have women conductors? I do not know because the experiment has not been tried. It would all depend on the sort of women who occupied the conductor's platform.

Strongly opposed by C.J. Spencer, bus conductresses eventually made their appearance on the city's public transport.

In September 1915 Huddersfield took on women conductors and in the same week Bradford Tramways showed signs of labour shortages. In November 1915 the Bradford Tramways were paying £6,000 a year as make-up pay for the serving men and the services were deteriorating. Mr Spencer was still not ready to respond to pressure:

Female conductors have been accepted in a good many towns and according to the reports of the managers of the various undertakings, have been satisfactory. It is entirely out of the question and impossible under any circumstances in Bradford.

Tunics and skirts are uniform, but shoes, stockings and blouses seem to be left to the individual choice of these conductresses.

By December a compromise had been reached. Kiosks were to be set up to sell tram tickets. Conductresses were on their way and by July 1916 three of Maggie Newbery's sisters were conductresses on the trams.[4] Mr Spencer joined the Navy and returned after the war.

Mrs Annie Walker of 2 King Street, Eccleshill, was one of many women who found employment delivering the post. Annie's husband was a journeyman joiner and their fifth child had been born in 1912, the eldest being barely eleven years old. Fortunately Annie's parents-in-law lived in the same street which made it possible for her to contribute to the war effort by taking over a man's role. Annie's granddaughter, Mrs Jean Cook, discovered that Annie's fine looks and busy family life belied her trying circumstances. Her own mother had died when Annie was only four and, as a sufferer from diabetes, Annie herself died at the early age of fifty in St Luke's Hospital in 1924. Annie is buried in Norman Lane Cemetery, Eccleshill.

Mother of five Annie Walker joined the war effort as a postwoman.

Elizabeth Heaton pictured with her soldier husband and two sons. She delivered both post and babies, and also worked in the War Hospital in the afternoons.

Elizabeth Heaton[5] of Lidget Green, mother of two young boys and with a husband in the 16th West Yorkshire Regiment (Bradford Pals), also delivered post but, in addition, she volunteered as a member of the Voluntary Aid Detachment. Having delivered post in the morning, she was employed at St Luke's (locally referred to as the Gas Hospital) in the afternoon. Her main duties were performing 'last offices', that is the laying out of the sick and wounded men who had died. Her father-in-law constructed a wheeled cart in which she could transport the bodies to the local undertaker, Joseph Hey of Great Horton. In addition, Elizabeth acted as a midwife to families at home. Her son Jim recalls that after the war ended Elizabeth was presented with a parchment scroll in recognition of her work at a special ceremony at City Hall.

Nurses, skilled and initially unskilled, served at home and in virtually all theatres of war, but again not without opposition. In July 1915, Shipley Education Committee accepted the proposal that some primary school teachers could be released for service as nurses in France and Flanders. (The pragmatic solution the Committee came up with was that classes for the under fives should be stopped.) However the Chairman, Mr C.E. Learoyd, opposed the proposal that the Committee should make up the pittance paid to nurses to the equivalent of teacher's pay on the grounds that 'if her patriotism was of the right sort, she would still want to go.' It must have been an acrimonious meeting as Mr Rhodes went on to say, 'If her patriotism is like that of the majority of this committee it will be of a very poor kind indeed'.

However, not all young women felt equipped to take up traditionally male employment. Middle class women in northern industrial cities found it difficult to accept work on the buses and trams or factory work, whether in worsted, woollens or munitions. Florence Lockwood of Huddersfield, a Quaker woman of considerable energy described the lot of these women in her diary in 1915:

> For the ordinary housewife, there seemed nothing but to join in flag days, knitting and sewing teas, whist drives, dances, concerts, getting money for the Red Cross, warm clothing and comforts for the soldiers, eggs for wounded soldiers, parcels for prisoners, working in hospitals for the wounded, looking after Belgian refugees and collecting money for their repatriation, or making sandbags and gas masks as well as lending money to the Government with which to carry on the war.[6]

Certainly the number of 'knitting circles' and fundraising parties recorded in Bradford's papers is remarkable and Florence Lockwood caught the rhythm of the times. She was a remarkable diarist and social reformer and was also involved with the Union of Democratic Control, the Colne Valley Liberal Women, the Prince of Wales Fund, the War Distress Committee and the Poor Law Guardians. It was in this last function that, in September 1914, she had noticed the complete lack of maternity provision for working women beyond being confined to the workhouses. She set about finding alternative, decent maternity provision and fought successfully for the provision of pre- and postnatal care.

From the outbreak of war the British Army recognised that women could play an important role in persuading men to join the forces. Some recruitment posters were specifically aimed at women of all ages, such as 'Is your Best Boy wearing khaki?' and 'If you cannot persuade him to answer his country's call and protect you now, discharge him as unfit'.

TO THE
YOUNG WOMEN OF LONDON

Is your "Best Boy" wearing Khaki? If not don't **YOU THINK** he should be?

If he does not think that you and your country are worth fighting for—do you think he is **WORTHY** of you?

Don't pity the girl who is alone—her young man is probably a soldier—fighting for her and her country—and for **YOU.**

If your young man neglects his duty to his King and Country, the time may come when he will NEGLECT YOU.

Think it over—then ask him to

JOIN THE ARMY TO-DAY

A recruitment poster which appeals to the consciences of young women. The message is plain: 'the time may come when he will neglect you' if he has neglected his duty to his country.

The Mothers' Union followed this example and published posters reading 'My boy, I don't want you to go, but if I were you I should go' and 'On his return, hearts would beat high with thankfulness and pride'. Baroness Orczy (author of *The Scarlet Pimpernel*) founded the Active Service League and urged women to sign a pledge:

> At this hour of England's grave peril and desperate need I do hereby pledge myself most solemnly in the name of King and Country to persuade every man I know to offer his services to the country, and I also pledge myself never to be seen in public with any man who, being in every way fit and free for service, has refused to respond to his country's call.

Baroness Orczy supported Admiral Charles Fitzgerald's movement, the Order of the White Feather. Young women across the country were encouraged to hand a white feather to any young man who had not joined the British Army. Such was the enthusiasm with which this was taken up that the government had to protect men employed on state business, and the Home Secretary, Reginald McKenna, issued badges confirming that the bearer was serving 'King and Country'. There was a suspicion that the feathers were not always handed out for the right reasons. Compton Mackenzie complained that some 'idiotic young women were using white feathers to get rid of boyfriends of whom they were tired' although it seems unlikely that straight-talking northern girls needed such a stratagem.

Fenner Brockway claimed to have been given enough white feathers to make a fan and the campaign was gradually abandoned as wounded men in civilian clothes repeatedly embarrassed the young women. Neil Oliver[7] recounts the story of Private Norman Demuth who was handed a white feather on a bus. He used it to thoroughly clean his pipe and handed it back saying, 'You know, we didn't get these in the trenches'. The young woman's embarrassment was heightened by the barracking she received from other

The white feather given out in thousands, but indiscriminately.

passengers indignant at the soldier's humiliation. Arthur Skelly (see Chapter 3) was handed a white feather while walking along Manningham Lane. He was home recuperating from wounds and was none too impressed!

Until 1914 large numbers of women, including active groups in Bradford, were involved in the suffragette movement. Two days after the outbreak of war the National Union of Women's Suffrage Societies (NUWSS) announced that it was suspending its activities until the war was over[8]. By 10 August, the government had agreed to release from prison all suffragettes, in return for which the movement threw its weight behind the war effort. In fact the government allocated a grant of £2,000, with which the women organised a demonstration in London with banners reading 'We Demand the Right to Serve', 'For Men Must Fight and Women Must Work' and 'Let none be Kaiser's Cat's Paws'. Emmeline Pankhurst addressed a crowd estimated at 30,000 and called upon trade unions to allow women to take on the work of men. The zeal of these women led to them describing Ramsay MacDonald (the future Prime Minister) as 'more German than the Germans' for his anti-war speeches and Arthur Henderson, who was in favour of a negotiated peace, was accused of being in the pay of the enemy.

Unlike her sister, Sylvia Pankhurst, along with another suffragette Emmeline Pethick-Lawrence, opposed the war. These two played active roles in the Women's Peace Party which, in the north of the country, was matched by the Women's Peace Crusade founded by Helen Crawford. As organiser of the Glasgow rent strikes and campaigner for women, Crawford had the experience and determination to turn the WPC into a national movement in the summer of 1917. The time was right: the mounting death toll, food shortages, queues, high prices and the repressive effects of the Defence of the Realm Act (DORA) had led to a Great War weariness.

In Bradford a strong Women's Peace Movement already existed among Independent Labour Party members who now began to demonstrate under the banner of the Women's Peace Crusade. Florence Lockwood of Huddersfield found the WPC 'most encouraging'. A diary entry reads:

> Heaps of women awaking from the opium of false propaganda . . . went to the first public meeting of WPC in Huddersfield . . . our meeting was hopeful – young married working women are now beginning to see it.[9]

The WPC printed nine pamphlets that were distributed door-to-door. Titles included 'Casualties', 'A call to Socialist and Labour Women', 'Questions to Clergymen and Ministers', 'Lost Opportunities for Peace'. However, under the terms of DORA, in November 1917 it became illegal 'to print or distribute leaflets on the subject of war or peace'.

The Bradford Women's Humanity League held its first meeting on 17 March 1916. The *Bradford Pioneer* publicised the resolution passed at the meeting:

> that this meeting of Bradford Women protests against the inflicting of militarism on this country through the passing of the Military Service Act and calls for its immediate repeal. It further protests against the manner in which the Act is being administered by the tribunals and the unfair treatment of Conscientious Objectors who are not receiving their legal rights from the Act. [10]

Those most active in the foundation of the BWHL were Esther Sandiforth of 12 Hope View, Windhill, and Fanny Muir of 4 Highfield Road, Frizinghall. They were both members of the Shipley Branch of the Independent Labour Party and of the Shipley Council Against Conscription. Hilda Wilson, the daughter of the curator of Bethel Methodist Church on Ryan Street, Bradford was also very active in speaking, singing and reciting poetry at women's peace demonstrations.[11]

The BWHL concentrated its activities on:
- Opposing conscription
- Campaigning against the 'crucifixion' of conscientious objectors (Field Punishment No. 1)
- The problems of food queues
- The provision of pensions for disabled servicemen

In pursuit of their aims the group attracted speakers of national standing. The *Bradford Pioneer*[12] advertised a meeting of the BWHL to be held at the Friends' Meeting House, Fountain Street on 10 October. William Leach chaired the meeting and the guest speaker was Charlotte Despard, sister of General Sir John French. The meeting was preceded by a procession which left Westgate at 2.30 p.m. Members were scathing about Christabel Pankhurst who was 'tucked up in her pretty little flat in the Arcade Trocadero, Paris'. Elsie Guest, a frequent contributor, wrote in the *Pioneer*:

> Women, rouse yourselves! It is in your power to protest. If you refuse, then you are partly responsible for all the casualties of this war.[13]

The women also lobbied local MPs, councillors and churchmen and canvassed signatures for the petition to the Peace Negotiations Committee as reported in the *Bradford Pioneer*:

> The memorial asking the Government to take the earliest steps to open negotiations . . . is being extensively signed. The ILP, UDC, NCF and WHL[14] are all actually at work obtaining signatures.[15]

Esther Sandiforth wrote several articles for publication in the *Bradford Pioneer* including one entitled 'Motherhood' in which she robustly championed the role of women:

> The power of women today is enormous. On women is thrown the burden of keeping alive the industries of the nation . . . but they must refuse. . . . We have one great common platform. Motherlove is universal. Nothing but Motherlove will save the world from its madness.'[16]

As we shall see, Fanny Muir was imprisoned for her beliefs and Sarah Coulson, Headmistress of Bowling Back Lane School, is reported as coming into conflict with the education authority for showing her support. The *Bradford Daily Argus* and the *Bradford Telegraph* both reported on Miss Coulson's stance. As an active Quaker and pacifist, Miss Coulson objected to any form of militarism in her school and, in a letter to the Education Committee, she vowed not to spread war propaganda by refusing:

> teaching the songs of the Allies, making sacks or other sewing, urging or having anything to do with war savings, taking the children to war films, teaching the necessity of economy in food as a means of helping the war, taking part in flag days, giving lessons upon Nurse Cavell or Jack Cornwell or Trafalgar Day from the usual point of view.[17]

The Education Committee members were impressed by her stand and particularly noted that she only wore her pacifist badge outside school and did not raise the topic of pacifism with her pupils. However, when the Education Committee minutes went before the full City Council, members were not so sympathetic. The Education Committee was instructed to take a stronger anti-pacifism line and required to instruct all teachers that 'they must carry out all instructions of the Committee unless they apply for exemption'.[18]

The imprisonment of Fanny Muir followed a public meeting in Shipley market place. She was arrested after addressing the meeting and was charged later under the Defence of the Realm Act, accused of making false statements about the conduct of the war. With her only witness (Esther Sandiforth) she disputed the accuracy of the reporting of her statements and criticised her judges as 'elderly men who are not of military age' and who had no right to sit in judgement on her. She was found guilty and given the choice of a £50 fine or three-month imprisonment. She chose Armley gaol.[19]

The Bradford Womens' Humanity League held a protest meeting as Fanny Muir's sentence began and wrote to the magistrates

> with righteous indignation against elderly men passing such a sentence upon a widow who spoke the truth while young men were giving their life's blood to protect these women and secure freedom in speech and action.

On her release, Fanny Muir took a short holiday in Ilkley before attending a 'Welcome Home' social organised by the BWHL in the Textile Rooms on 18 September. Refreshments, music and a warm tribute paid in which Esther's sacrifice was revered. The meeting was fully reported in the *Bradford Pioneer*. On the following Sunday Fanny and Esther addressed a public meeting, after which they disappear from the history books.

A very active and personalised opposition to war came from the men of Bradford who, as a matter of religious belief, political scruple or personal conviction chose the difficult path of the conscientious objector and refused to serve. In the first two weeks of the war in August 1914, 20,000 casualties were recorded. The early rush of volunteers would clearly not be sustained and conscription began to be a real possibility. The No-Conscription Fellowship (NCF) began in the autumn of 1914 when Fenner Brockway, at the suggestion of his wife, wrote a letter inviting all who were prepared personally to resist conscription to communicate with him; this letter was published in the *Labour Leader* and by November 1914, the NCF was launched. (In 1916 Fenner Brockway was imprisoned in Pentonville and later the Tower of London for refusing to be conscripted.)

The Military Service Act introducing compulsory conscription was eventually passed in 1916. A clause providing exemption on conscientious grounds was included. There had been suggestions that exemption should be limited to those of the Quaker faith, but with the help of pressure from the NCF, the term was not defined and thus men had the right to claim exemption from military service on grounds of conscience. In total, over 16,000 made such a claim and were required to attend a tribunal which examined the sincerity of their claim.

In Bradford members of the Quaker movement, the Labour Church and the Independent Labour Party established a branch of the NCF. Fred Jowett MP supported conscientious objectors and spoke against the powers given to government under the Defence of the Realm Act. The limitations on freedom of speech and expression which the Act imposed made it difficult for individuals to resist the orthodoxy of conscription. NCF activities were reported widely and members of the Bradford branch were constantly pursued. In March 1915 twelve applications were refused in Shipley and nineteen in Halifax.

Revis Barber, son of the Secretary of the Bradford Trades Council, was imprisoned as a conscientious objector in 1917. He served two years, including time at the Dartmoor Work Centre. Mrs Barber[20] of 204 Upper Woodlands Road formed the Mothers and Wives of Bradford Conscientious Objectors Group. Meetings were advertised in the *Bradford Pioneer*. On Monday 10 December 1917 a series of 'teas' began which were to raise funds to provide a present for 'every Bradford lad in Works Centres and Settlements at Christmas'.[21] In September 1917, 3,000 women gathered for a demonstration against the treatment of conscientious objectors[22]. Revis Barber later went on to become a Bradford Alderman (as his father had been) and a hall of residence at Bradford University today bears his name.

In June 1916 Edward Driffil was arrested by the police. In addition to being an NCF member he was also the Literature Organiser of the ILP in Bradford and his rooms were raided by the police in the search for seditious pamphlets. In August the police confiscated all his copies of a pamphlet by Bertrand Russeell entitled 'Rex v. Bertrand Russell', which was a verbatim report of his trial at the Mansion House. Russell was fined £100 for being the author of the Everett leaflet which had publicised the case of a conscientious objector in terms which were regarded as seditious under the Defence of the Realm Act.

In September 1916 Edward Driffil was fined £10 and, through the *Bradford Pioneer*, donations were sought to help pay off the fine (£11 7s 9d had been raised by December). In July 1917 Driffil was summoned again for selling a pamphlet at the Leeds Convention of NCF entitled 'Why? A Question and Appeal to British Labour'. Written by E.D. Morel, a leading anti-conscriptionist, the pamphlet 'unlawfully prejudices the recruiting, training, disciplining or administration of HM's Forces.' Driffil's case was heard at Leeds Town Hall and, while being fined, he continued to be classed as having 'absolute exemption' from military service. Despite this, he had recruiting papers sent to him twice and responded with a column in the *Bradford Pioneer* on 14 September headed 'The British Bunglers Unlimited':

> You blood-thirsty orphan-makers have had your fling and dismally failed . . . let the anti-militarists have the job of wiping up the mess you've made.[23]

Edward Driffil continued to distribute Labour Party and Socialist literature and wrote regular accounts of his work in the *Pioneer*, usually in colourful language. In March 1917 he was able to report that in the preceding three months nearly £100 of literature had been sold and 'every penn'orth of it a mental bomb guaranteed to explode the cobwebs out of the brains of a bishop'.[24]

This intriguing picture inscribed 'Bradford and District NCF at DCP Sept 1917' bears no names. What was DCP?

This photograph of a large group of NCF members bears no names and it would be particularly interesting to learn the identity of the woman. Could she be Ethel Snowden, wife of Philip Snowden the Bradford MP? An active member of the Women's Peace Crusade, Mrs Snowden became Honorary Treasurer of the National Council against Conscription which was closely allied to the NCF, only more political in its objectives. Edith Ellis, the first wife of Havelock Ellis, was also active within the Independent Labour Party and peace campaigning circles. Katharine Conway was a member of the small group who founded the Independent Labour Party in Bradford in 1893. Her husband, Bruce Glasier, the veteran Socialist propagandist, wrote an impassioned ILP pamphlet entitled 'The Perils of Conscription' in the summer of 1915.

Local councils assembled the members of the tribunals which summoned anti-conscriptionists. The membership was almost entirely male and drawn from the professional classes and the recently retired. Each tribunal was required to include a military representative who had the right to cross-examine the applicant while also holding a mandate to swell Army numbers. Newspaper readers might have thought that, sometimes, objectors were dealt with in a comic nature. This transcript of a local tribunal[25] was held in March 1916. The military representative expressed 'regret that in this country, unlike France, there is a right of appeal' for conscientious objectors.

The local tribunal met on the evening of Friday 30 June 1916. Councillor Thomas Hill (Chairman) presided, and others present were Cllr F.F. Rhodes, C.E. Learoyd, T.F. Doyle, Mr Ernest Illingworth, Mr J.A. Burton, (military representative), and Mr Isaac Lindow (clerk). The minutes were recorded thus:

Chairman: (addressing the applicant, who spoke with a foreign accent): You are appealing as a conscientious objector?

Applicant: Yes.

Mr Burton: You object to taking up arms against Germany?

Applicant: Yes.

Mr Burton: Why do you object?

Applicant: My parents are living in Germany.

Mr Burton: But you are a naturalised Englishman?

Applicant: Yes.

Mr Burton: And you have sworn allegiance to the King?

Applicant: Yes, and I have kept it.

Mr Burton: But you do not desire absolutely to keep it now?

Applicant: I am willing to do anything else that is required of me except take up arms.

Mr Burton: You have been naturalised since 1912?

Applicant: Yes.

Mr Burton: Now you say you have a conscientious objection to taking up arms against the German nation?

Applicant: Yes, against my own people.

Mr Burton: What do you mean by 'my own people'? You must belong to one side or the other.

Applicant: I have nothing to do with the German Empire. I renounced all rights to being a German twenty-one years ago.

Mr Burton: Have you renounced your rights in the proper form?

Applicant: Yes.

Mr Burton: Then they would put you in prison if you were in Germany now?

Applicant: Yes.

Councillor Rhodes (after examining the applicant's form): He does not say he objects to taking up arms against his own people, but that he objects to taking up arms against the nation.

Applicant: I did not make the application form out myself.

Mr Burton: What is the real meaning to be attached to your words? Does your filial affection to your progenitors prevent you from taking up arms, or your loyalty to your old nation?

Applicant: I am loyal to England, and nobody can prove anything different.

Mr Burton: No, no, I am only asking your view. You say you object to fight against the Germans. Every Englishman now is anxious to do everything he can to beat Germany. You say you are willing to do anything but fight. But why should you not fight? You know you are not likely to meet your father and mother on the battlefield.

Applicant: I hope not.

Mr Burton: Well, your argument does not apply in the sense in which you put it. You will not fight your father and mother in the field.

Applicant: I might meet them on the road to Berlin. [Laughter]

Mr Burton: Yes, but in that case you can step to one side. [Laughter]

Mr Burton expressed the hope that the road to Berlin would shortly be opened by the Allies, and added that the applicant was evidently quite prepared to do anything he could except take up arms. The Chairman observed that the sentiments now expressed by the applicant had certainly done something towards modifying the statements contained in his original appeal and as he had professed his willingness to do anything but fight, the tribunal had decided to give him a certificate for non-combatant service. The Non-Combatant Corps was subject to military authority but many COs refused to take orders or participate in any way with military activities.

At the end of June 1916 six 'Conchies' were fined in Bradford and taken to Recruitment Offices. On the way they were jeered at by passers-by. It must be noted that once recruited into the Army they were subject to military discipline and court-martialled for refusing to take orders or participate in the war in any way. The *Observer* reports thirty-four death sentences in France that were commuted to Penal Servitude under the Army Act. It is not recorded how many of these were press-ganged men who had their objections rejected. The hatred remained.

In November 1916 the *Bradford Pioneer* carried a report by J. Crawshaw on the year's work of the Bradford Branch of the No-Conscription Fellowship. The membership had increased from fifteen (who had met in Laycocks Café in Tyrrel Street) to 250 during the year and three Yorkshire conventions had been held in Bradford. Some fifty arrests had been made. These men had been fined 40s and costs and then

> been handed over to the Military Authorities, court-martialled, imprisoned on sentences ranging from 112 days to two years, with or without hard labour. This has failed to break them down and most of this number had already been taken before the Central Tribunal and judged by it to have been genuine conscientious objectors and released from prison for work of national importance, sent home on indefinite furlough or released unconditionally.[26]

The report goes on to describe another 'diabolically unfair' method of pursuing CO's. Some forty or fifty men were currently affected viz:

> Preventing these men following their usual or other employment with a view to starving them into submission or demoralising them for further resistance. Some have been kept out of employment six months – most of them over three months.

The group prided itself on saving men from the heel of militarism and establishing a national policy for the future where right would be the only true might.

Mr Graham, a Wakefield Councillor, objected to conscientious objectors making use of Wakefield Library and asked 'if any steps were being taken to mitigate this evil. They get sugar and jam while soldiers' wives and families are often without sugar.' He referred to his quarry as 'contemptible curs'. No action was taken. Asquith Archie Dalton of the 5th Reserve Battalion West Yorkshire Regiment became a NCF member. He was held in Wakefield prison after appearing before a tribunal in February 1917. Records of his case can be viewed in the Liddle Collection at Leeds University.[27]

The Quakers in Bradford, represented by families including the Hustlers, Peckovers and Harrises, had provided the backbone of the nineteenth-century peace movements, opposing the Crimean War in the 1850s, the Bulgarian Atrocities Campaign and the campaigns in Afghanistan in the 1870s. Most crucial was their opposition to the Boer War at the turn of the century when they proved to be a small but vocal community. The 'extended Quaker family' included the Priestmans of Bradford who were key figures in both the Liberal Party and the emerging Independent Labour Party.

Along with the Independent Labour Party, or at least part of it, other anti-war groups flourished in Bradford. The women of Bradford proved to be excellent organisers, fiery speakers and indomitable promoters and defenders of their cause. The anti-war agitation seen in Bradford as in other cities reflected complex views. The clarity of thought from the non-conformists before the war had been shattered as had the certainties of society generally. Bradford's special trading position, with its massive reliance on contracts in mainland Europe, and its non-conformism, was changed forever.

Between 1850 and 1880 Bradford dominated the world markets with its cheaply mass-produced but high quality worsted fabrics, and this prosperity dimmed the class war. The belief that international commerce brought international peace dominated radical thinking. After 1880 the threat of recession brought what we would now call 'cost cutting' which led to an increase in industrial confrontation with the low-waged. Old beliefs faded and at the 7th Annual Conference of the ILP held in Leeds in April 1899 the Bradford Branch proposed:

That this conference while recognising that enduring peace between nations can only be secured by the establishment of international cooperation for the production and distribution of wealth, welcomes any and every endeavour which tends to bring about concord between nations, and trusts that the cause of international arbitration as opposed to brutal war may be materially advanced by the International Conference which the Czar [*sic*] has convened.

The motion was defeated largely because of its reference to the Tsar who was regarded as a bogeyman against which socialists felt they had to protest.

J.A. Jowitt[28] (who is unrelated to Fred Jowett MP) records that the peace movement and peace protestors from 1899 to 1912 were largely ignored by the local press and it took the intensification of the international crises from 1912 onwards to bring them back on the agenda. When war came however, there was confusion among the anti-war groups arising from the conflicting messages within the dominant but hitherto largely ignored pull of nationalism and patriotism: the pull of the flag.

Fred Jowett, Independent Labour Party MP for Bradford West said,

> Let us who are Socialists keep our minds clean, our hearts free from hate, and one purpose always before us – to bring peace as soon as possible on a basis that will endure.

His words signal an acceptance of the inevitable. Jowett remained as a voice of the middle ground along with the future Prime Minister, Ramsay MacDonald, both of whom spoke in support of moderation in the halls and meeting rooms of Bradford during the war. Both accepted that to swim against the tide of patriotism (and later, grief) would be fatal to their influence and probably downright dangerous. Fred Jowett supported President Wilson's suggestions for peace while objecting to the German offers of terms. The problem for the Radicals and Independent Labour Party was that there were five sets of opinions:

· Those who opposed war and killing as such – largely represented by the non-conformist religious groups, Quakers and Christadelphians
· Sturdy Socialists who saw the war in the terms of a class struggle where workers were being exploited to fight fellow workers to defend capitalism
· Those who were patriotic to Britain and the flag and though in theory opposed war, in practice wished to defend British interests and defend Britain while vigorously opposing the Machiavellian clandestine treaties that had brought the world to such a sorry state
· Those who felt that the war was necessary to defend British interests – that Prussian domination was a real danger and that the qualms of class division and even religion needed to be shelved while the danger existed.
· Those who felt the call of the flag above anything else

The government shamelessly exploited the views of the last two groups, with the Tory and Liberal press attempting to gain political capital from the overwhelmingly patriotic attitudes of the masses by labelling the ILP as a pacifist organisation. This was far from the truth.

Even Philip Snowden and Fred Jowett, both considered to be local political heroes, were not fully-committed pacifists. They stood with the No-Conscription Fellowship, supported by the Quaker manufacturer Arthur Priestman. William Leach pressed his views from the editorial seat of the *Bradford Pioneer*:

> We hate all war, especially the present one. This is a pacifist or peace journal [the *Bradford Pioneer*] conducted among other purposes, with the objective of stating as well as we can the ILP position on this hideous tragedy now being enacted in Europe. . . . Human life is the most sacred thing we know, and its preservation, its development, its best welfare, must therefore be our religion on this earth.

Two of the Independent Labour Party MPs for Bradford. Fred Jowett (left) and Philip Snowden, were thorns in the side of the government throughout the war. Snowden was a Cabinet member in the short-lived Labour government of 1924.

Leach had been editor since 1915 and used the *Pioneer* to support the pacifist cause, quoting Morel and Bertrand Russell. Leach was once stoned in the street for his views and, when he stood for Parliament as an ILP candidate he came low in the polls. Eventually he was elected in 1922 and in the short-lived Labour government of 1924 was made Minister for Air. Sidney Webb described this as a 'peculiar and unfortunate' appointment of one who had been known as 'an extreme Pacifist'[29].

The total opposition to war among ILP members was being diluted. Fred Jowett MP believed Germany had to be defeated before the nations could progress. The Revd R. Roberts had written in the *Pioneer* in October 1914:

Through 40 years of public life I have preached peace . . . I have never believed humanity would so far break down as to make it necessary to pay the extreme price of waging a war to preserve peace. Yet for my sins, I have lived to see that . . . we are threatened with the ruin of civilised society. The success of Prussia in the awful tussle for life means that humanity will sink into a smoking ruin. . . . Better to die than to be Prussianised.

> We must take up the Fiery Cross and carry it to the remotest hamlet in the country, call every man and woman to the colours. 'Down with militarism'. That is our cry – as it is also the cry of our comrades all over Europe. Blazen it on the banners. Write it on the pavements. Sing it in the streets.[30]

Only the Quakers maintained a coherent anti-war attitude, believing that it was morally wrong to take human life. When conscription was introduced in 1916 even the Quakers could no longer hold their position. They were forced to make choices according to the conscience clause of the Act. Some volunteered to fight, others acceded when forced to choose and still more appeared before the tribunals as conscientious objectors.

In October 1915 the Germans issued the first of their 'terms for Peace' to the French. The terms, even in hindsight, could be described as preposterous. They demanded all French Colonies, the area stretching from St Valery to Lyon including the resident 15 million people, indemnity of £400,000 and the demolition of all forts. The terms were of course rejected. The 1916 German overtures for peace were less arrogant. In December 1916 Ramsay MacDonald spoke against the Kaiser's proposals in the Bradford Friends' Meeting House:

> Germany makes overtures for peace which are regarded as 'sheer impudence'. The mere suggestion that negotiations should be opened is not an offer for peace. The putting forward by the Imperial Government of a sham proposal, lacking all substance and precision, would appear to be less of an offer for peace but a war manoeuvre.[31]

The *Pioneer* continued to press for Peace by Negotiation[32]. A 'just and lasting' peace was unlikely to come about if terms were imposed. The enemy would feel it had been unjustly treated and prepare for revenge so the peace would not be lasting. While some would say it is for the defeated to open negotiations, the *Pioneer* urged the government to show that

> the Nation is truly strong and to have the courage to take the first step without fear of seeming weak . . . could anything be more awful than to think that our men's lives were being sacrificed just because the politicians of the different countries, like sulky children, were refusing to be the first to speak.

Immediately beneath this was a call for its readers to sign a memorial to be presented to the Prime Minister, and under a headline 'The Home Secretary on War', the *Pioneer* prints an excerpt from 'Liberalism; its Principles and Proposals' by Herbert Samuel. While vividly describing the reaction of the majority to the call to arms (including the majority of Bradfordians despite the efforts of the *Pioneer*, the Women's Humanity League and all the other local activists for peace), could there be a stronger contrast between the pro- and anti-war lobbies?

> If warfare continues it is largely because, even in an age of enlightenment, wars are popular. The cheering crowds in a time of war, lining the streets while the

troops, bands playing, colours flying, march through on their way to embark; the hot excitement of the packed audiences in the music halls, shouting the choruses of patriotic songs . . . and while war invokes these elemental passions among the masses . . . the leaders of public opinion in the Press, on the platform and even in the pulpit, are often found justifying war by elaborate and plausible sophisms.

Notes

1 *Bradford Pioneer*, 14 August 1914
2 From the *Yorkshire Observer Budget*, 6 January 1915
3 Records of the Bradford Chamber of Commerce 1918 available in West Yorkshire Archives
4 Maggie Newbery, *Reminiscences of a Bradford Mill Girl*, City of Bradford Metropolitan Council Libraries Division, 1980
5 The information about Mary Elizabeth Heaton is kindly and proudly donated by her grandson Stanley Heaton of Bradford
6 Florence Lockwood's diaries, available in the West Yorkshire Archives
7 Neil Oliver, *Not Forgotten*, Hodder & Stoughton, 2005, p. 134
8 Pankhurst, C., *Unshackled: the Story of how we won the Vote*, Cresset, London, 1959. War was the only course for our country to take. This was national militancy. As Suffragettes we could not be pacifists at any price. Mother and I declared support of our country. We declared an armistice with the government and suspended militancy for the duration of the war. We offered our service to the country and called upon all members to do likewise. . . . As Mother said, 'What would be the good of a vote without a country to vote in!'
9 Florence Lockwood's diaries, available in the West Yorkshire Archives
10 *Bradford Pioneer*, March 1917
11 For a full account see Finola Doogan: 'Chalk Marks in the Rain: a Study of British Women's Opposition to the First World War', Bradford University Peace Studies Dept, 1992
12 *Bradford Pioneer*, 29 September 1916
13 *Bradford Pioneer*, 3 November 1916
14 ILP: Independent Labour Party, UDC: Union of Democratic Control, NCF: No Conscription Fellowship, WHL: Women's Humanity League
15 *Bradford Pioneer*, 9 June 1916
16 *Bradford Pioneer*, 14 April 1916
17 Elementary Education Subcommittee minutes 12 December 1917 WYAS
18 *Bradford Telegraph*, 31 December 1917
19 *Bradford Daily Telegraph*, 30 May 1918, *Bradford Pioneer*, 7 June 1918
20 Mrs Barber was the wife of Alderman Walter Barber who was to become Lord Mayor of Bradford in 1918
21 *Bradford Pioneer*, 7 December 1917
22 *Bradford Pioneer*, 7 December 1917
23 *Bradford Pioneer*, 14 September 1917
24 *Bradford Pioneer*, 23 March 1917
25 *Shipley Times and Express*, 1 April 1916
26 *Bradford Pioneer*, 10 November 1916, p. 6
27 University of Leeds, GB 0206 Liddle Collection CO 023
28 Jowitt, J.A. and Taylor, R.K.S., Bradford 1890–1914: The Cradle of the Independent Labour Party. University of Leeds Department of Adult Education, 1980, outlines the local, social and economic background to the development of socialism in Bradford, and gives detailed accounts of the Bradford and Keighley Independent Labour parties
29 Webb, Sidney, *The First Labour Government*, 1924. See Political Quarterly reprinted at: www.blackwell-synergy.com
30 Quoted in Jowitt, A., *The Patterns of Religion in Victorian Bradford*
31 Editorial in the *Yorkshire Observer*, 6 January 1917
32 *Bradford Pioneer*, 23 June 1916, p. 2

TWELVE

Aftermath

Tricia Platts

Dear Mrs Barraclough,

Before you get this letter you will no doubt have received from the War Office the sad news of the death of your son. He was brought on board the 'Valdivia' at Salonika and was very ill from heat stroke. Notwithstanding every attention from the doctor and nursing sister, he grew weaker and passed away on 7 July. I am the Church of England Chaplain and I was with him just before the end. He was conscious and spoke of you. I took the body ashore and the funeral – a Military Funeral – took place in the British Army Cemetery at Salonika. The site of his grave is 205. Every respect was paid. We were met by the guard and firing party and after the funeral service the bugler sounded the Last Post. I am sorry to be writing such sad news to you. I wish we could have saved him for you.

Revd J.H. Darby[1]

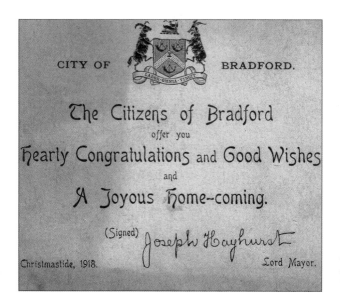

Lord Mayor Joseph Hayhurst (after whom the fire engine featured earlier in this book had been named) issued this 'Welcome Home' Christmas card in 1918.

This is just one of countless letters written to bereaved families during the four years of war, but for Mrs Barraclough it was an experience repeated several times, as the newspaper describes:

Mrs Barraclough, a widow of 73 Tong Park, Baildon, has lost four sons and a grandson in the war. Private Joe Barraclough, Royal Defence Corps, aged twenty-eight, was drowned on the Leinster[2] on 10 October 1918. Private Fred Barraclough, Royal Army Service Corps, aged 29, died of sunstroke in Salonika on 7 July 1917. Corporal Herbert Barraclough died on the same day in France. Private Willy Barraclough, Labour Corps, died of influenza in West Hartlepool on 10 December 1918. Her grandson Private Ernest Hird was killed on 18 April 1918.[3]

Left: Memorial plaque bearing the names of the four Barraclough brothers from Tong Park.

Right: Fred Barraclough wearing his hot climate headgear.

Left: Herbert Barraclough was killed in France on the day Fred died in Salonika.

Right: Willie Barraclough died of flu after the war ended, but while still in service.

Left: Joe Barraclough with his wife and daughter.

Standing in the fields overlooking Tong Park cricket ground is the war memorial. There are no houses left today.

Today, all that remains of the village of Tong is its war memorial, the houses having been demolished in the 1950s because of the lack of piped water to the village. Of all the memorials scattered around the communities which make up the City of Bradford, this lonely structure is the most poignant. Its isolated position in the fields somehow reflects the loneliness of those left. The names it bears include a family decimated. Mrs Barraclough and her daughters inserted memoriam messages in local papers for many years subsequently. In 1917 she wrote:

> Not dead to those who loved them,
> Not lost, but gone before;
> They live with us in memory still,
> And will for evermore.
> 'They fought the good fight.'

It is difficult at this distance to comprehend the range of emotions engendered when the shooting stopped at 11 a.m. on 11 November 1918. While thousands were celebrating in the streets others mourned; relief and joy were matched by despair and loneliness. In the days immediately following the Armistice news of peace celebrations in the local papers was scarce: the black-edged pages of recorded deaths were still to be seen and a whole page advertisement from the Bradford Dyers Association was the only good news. Jobs were being offered to men returning from the war. The people of Bradford had to wait until the *Bradford Weekly Telegraph* was published on 15 November to see how the peace was celebrated. The front page carried a cartoon from *Punch* showing a distraught Kaiser contemplating his ruin. 'The Sands Run Out' was the caption. On page three there were numerous unillustrated reports.

One report described the scene in front of the City Hall where, on the Monday evening, a floodlit rostrum was constructed. From here, the newly elected Lord Mayor, Alderman Joseph Hayhurst, accompanied by his wife the Lady Mayoress and representatives from the Labour, Liberal and Conservative parties, gave speeches of thanks for the peace. Two rockets were fired after each speech and a band played 'Pack Up Your Troubles'[4].

Before the Monday evening show, the manager of the Theatre Royal addressed the audience and the National Anthem was sung. On behalf of his audience he immediately sent a congratulatory telegram to Earl Haig. Outside the YMCA in Forster Square people flocked to an open-air celebration. Massed choirs and a brass band led the singing of popular hymns, and messages from prominent people were flashed onto a large screen on the side of the YMCA building. There were services

A crowd gathered to welcome home returning servicemen.

of thanksgiving at Bradford Cathedral and Eastbrook Hall where the Hallelujah Chorus was sung. The minister warned that the next job would be to feed the German people: the conscience of the world would not let them starve.

However, on page eight of the same paper there were 104 photographs of Bradford soldiers killed or wounded in action. Connie Galilee[5], in her mid-nineties when this book was compiled, recounts the feelings at the time:

> News was slow to spread in those days and even after 11 November 1918, the official end of the war, men were dying in Mesopotamia for a week or so. There was less a sense of rejoicing – too many widows and orphans for that – more a sigh of relief. Nobody knew then what was to become of the men who had fought so well and hopelessly and did return for the families left ill-provided despite their sacrifice. I have seen men with no legs begging in the street, propped up on a wooden 'go-cart' – home-made of course – what a reward!

When the war ended men slowly arrived back in Bradford over many months, some not being discharged from service until the end of 1919. Employment patterns had changed considerably and work in the textile mills, carried out by women during the war, now reverted to men. These mills were to see a steep decline: the war had merely artificially raised the need for cloth and previous signs of diminishing demand quickly returned. However, the real problem was for men who had been disabled by their wartime service, and it was in response to this that the King's Roll National Council was set up under the chairmanship of Earl Haig. The City of Bradford King's Roll Committee was chaired by the Lord Mayor and asked citizens, particularly employers, 'to consider the urgency of the unemployment problem among Disabled Ex-Service Men'.

The Lord Mayor, while listing some thirty firms currently employing a proportion of disabled men, estimated that a thousand firms had not yet enrolled in the scheme. They were 'specially invited to contribute in some small way by stating what they are prepared to do in the direction of employing at least one disabled man.' He estimated that 300 men were looking for work and, to help stir the imagination of employers, he gave examples of the kinds of jobs which had already been filled by the disabled. Of the two dozen on his list, twelve had amputations of fingers, hand, foot, or one or two limbs. Examples included:

Condition	Previous employment	Suitable for	Regiment
Fracture of skull Subject to dizziness	General Labourer	Any light work away from machinery	Pte, Labour Corps
Amputation of right foot	Dyer's labourer	Light employment in the dyehouse	Pte 1/4th KOYLIs
Gunshot wound in left leg/Gassed	Hairdresser	Watchman/ caretaker	Pte, 18th Hussars
Gunshot wound in left hand, all fingers amputated	Drop stamper	Wool warehouseman or packer	Sapper Royal Engineers
Gunshot wound in face/Fractured jaw	Carter	Indoor work (away from machinery)	Private 7th Yorkshire's

The Welfare State was still thirty years in the future and these men, many of them in their early twenties, would have had little financial support for themselves and whatever family they might have. Elderly people today can still recall the hawkers of the 1920s and '30s who walked country lanes selling ribbons, sewing threads and sundries from a tray hanging from their neck. Some of these men would be the casualties of war who might have chosen an open-air way of life, being unfit for enclosed work, or might have accepted this as the only way of scraping a living. Some paternalistic employers were able to create positions for the disabled and others succumbed to pressure from the King's Roll Committee and thus helped acknowledge the debt the country owed to servicemen. Sassoon writes in 'Aftermath' (1919):

> Have you forgotten yet?
> Look up, and swear by the green of the spring that you'll never forget.

How could society cope with the wounded and bereaved alongside returning soldiers and their families? What had it all been for? Ideally, British society stood for decency, order, peace, fairness and social harmony and the maiming and loss of life in defence of these values had to be justified. But within society, class and racial differences ensured the response of each individual was unique, and Bradfordians represented a northern industrial workforce with divisions and ideals quite different from those of the national rhetoric. How often do we hear, 'He never spoke about the war, y'know'? This was perhaps more true of working-class men than of the returning officers as memories were tucked away in an attempt to heal the mental scars of trench warfare, the spilling of blood and guts and inexpressible grief at the loss of comrades. It is significant that silence was chosen as an act of remembrance.

City of Bradford.

CIVIC WELCOME
:: TO ::
BRADFORD SAILORS AND SOLDIERS
Who have served in
the European War,

At "The Windsor," Morley Street,"
On October 6th, 7th, 8th and 9th, 1919.

RECEPTION BY THE RIGHT HON. THE LORD MAYOR

(Councillor Walter Barber, J.P.), at 7-30 p.m. each day.

DANCING—Lieut.-Col. GADIE (Chairman).
WHIST DRIVE—Major TAYLOR (Chairman).
ENTERTAINMENTS—Herbert GILL, Esq., J.P. (Chairman).
REFRESHMENTS—Lieut. and Quartermaster Geo. SMITH. (Chairman).
TRANSPORT—Fred PICKERING, Esq., J.P. (Chairman).

TOWN HALL,
BRADFORD.

FREDERICK STEVENS,
Town Clerk.

A programme for a four-day Civic Festival held in October 1919. A year after the war ended, the men were not forgotten.

In October 1919 the national government hastily made plans to commemorate the Armistice. The idea came from Sir Percy Fitzpatrick in a memorandum to Lord Milner for the attention of the War Cabinet. Fitzpatrick, High Commissioner in South Africa throughout the war, recalled the 'three minute pause' observed at noon each day during which people could:

> concentrate as one in thinking of those who had pledged and given themselves for all that we believe in . . . Only those who have felt it can understand the overmastering effect in action and reaction of a multitude moved suddenly to one thought and one purpose.[6]

Thus was a tradition 'invented' and, at this distance, it is interesting to read the reasoning of Fitzpatrick which won such immediate approval from the Cabinet:

> It is not in mourning but in greeting that we should salute them on that day. When we are divided it may serve to remind us of the greater things we hold in common. When we are gone it may help to bring home to those who come after us the meaning, the nobility and the unselfishness of the great sacrifice by which their freedom was assured.[7]

Fitzpatrick went on to describe not only the women and children for whom the silence would be kept as a reminder of the freedoms bought but, above all, the men, both living and 'especially those who gave their all – our Glorious and Immortal Dead whom we can never repay'.

After discussion, the Cabinet decided two minutes would be the appropriate length and the King readily approved the plan. On 7 November 1919 newspapers carried a personal request from the King:

Tuesday next, November 11, is the first anniversary of the Armistice, which stayed the world-wide carnage of the four preceding years and marked the victory of Right and Freedom. I believe that my people in every part of the Empire fervently wish to perpetuate the memory of the Great Deliverance. And of those who have laid down their lives to achieve it. To afford an opportunity for the universal expression of this feeling it is my desire and hope that at the hour when the Armistice came into force, the eleventh hour of the eleventh day of the eleventh month, there may be for the brief space of two minutes a complete suspension of all our normal activities.

At a given signal . . . I believe that we shall all gladly interrupt our business and pleasure . . . and unite in this simple service of Silence and Remembrance.

The following day, the *Yorkshire Post* reported some of these first Acts of Remembrance:

Just before eleven o'clock, the boys of Bradford Grammar School assembled in the main hall and members of the school O.T.C. were drawn up on the terrace. The King's proclamation was read and upon the first maroon being fired from the Town Hall, the cadets were brought to attention [and] their officers saluted as the Union Jack was dipped. After the period of silence the boys sang the National Anthem.[8]

The same newspaper also described the wider impact on citizens:

He must have a strangely cold heart who was not moved by the impressive scenes witnessed yesterday. As eleven o'clock drew near there was a certain hesitancy in the movements in the streets. The centre of the city was thronged but, at the signal, immediately men uncovered their heads and women bowed their faces and all stood silently until the two minutes had passed.[9]

The following year, in November 1920, the cenotaph in Whitehall was unveiled as a part of the Armistice Day commemoration. After the laying of wreaths, the King and Prime Minister moved to Westminster Abbey for a second solemn unveiling. This was the Tomb of the Unknown Warrior, the inspired idea of an Army chaplain, David Railton, who was to hold the living at St James's, Bolton in Bradford for part of his career. The story of David Railton – a man with a great idea – is told in Horace Hird's book, *Bradford Remembrancer*.[10] The great idea came to Railton in

1916 when he was serving near Armentières where, in the small garden behind his billet, there was a grave marked by a cross of white wood. In deep black-pencilled letters the inscription read: 'An Unknown British Soldier [of the Black Watch]'. Not until 1919 when Railton returned home did he decide to pursue the idea, but not knowing which of the 'great men would be likely to heed the request of an ordinary padre at such a time'. Many years later, at the insistence of family and close friends, Railton wrote a short memoir of the events leading up to the unveiling.

Urged on by his wife, Railton eventually wrote to Bishop Ryle, the Dean of Westminster in August 1920 asking if the body of an unknown comrade could be buried in the Abbey and suggesting that his own 'war flag' be used at the burial rather than a new flag with 'no service experience'. Bishop Ryle took the idea to the War Office, Prime Minister, Cabinet and Buckingham Palace and, on 19 October, was able to tell Railton that the proposal had been accepted. In carrying forward the idea Bishop Ryle added details which matched Railton's vision. French soil was brought in a hundred sandbags and a Belgian marble slab was chosen to cover the tomb, edged with five maxims of faith:

> The Lord knoweth them that are His
> In Christ shall all be made alive
> Greater love hath no man than this
> Unknown and yet well known
> Dying and behold we live.

Railton's flag remained at the foot of the tomb, with the King's wreath resting on it, for twelve months after the unveiling and was then placed in its present position by men of his old regiment, the 141st Infantry Brigade. The inscription inlaid on the tomb used brass made from cartridge cases retrieved from British lines after the Armistice and was devised by Bishop Ryle[11] who, when criticised for its length, replied 'People have such short memories. In years to come, they would probably have been asking who on earth the Unknown Warrior was.'

This was, of course, David Railton's point. So many 'unknowns' had been lost, each remembered by their family. Selection of the body to be interred in the Abbey was cloaked in secrecy. Brigadier General L.J. Wyatt, the director of the War Graves Commission (which had another Bradford connection) was instructed to disinter six unidentified bodies of British soldiers, one from each of the great battle areas; Aisne, Arras, Cambrai, Marne, Somme and Ypres. They were brought to an Army hut near Ypres and set out on a dais, each covered with a Union Jack. At midnight on 9 November the Brigadier entered the room, was blindfolded and then moved along the row of bodies and selected one at random. This body was then placed in a coffin made of Hampton Court oak bearing the inscription 'A British Warrior who fell in the Great War 1914–1918 for King and Country'. A French military wagon drawn by six horses and accompanied by French troops took the coffin to Boulogne, where people lined the streets to see 'Tommy Anonyme'. The British destroyer *Verdun* (chosen for its significance for French allies) brought the cortège to Dover which was then carried by train to Victoria station.

The band and drums of four regiments of Foot Guards and the pipers of the Scots Guards followed by detachments from all the armed forces as well as 400 representatives of ex-Servicemen's Organisations provided an escort to Westminster on the morning of 11 November. The route was not direct so that more people could witness the procession and, as it passed the cenotaph in Whitehall, the King and government ministers joined it after the Service of Remembrance. At the Abbey, fifty-nine holders of the Victoria Cross of all ranks provided the Guard of Honour and David Railton stood with them. Few people knew him: the idea was ascribed to 'an army padre' and it was not until after his death that his identity became known. How many Yorkshire folk have stood by the tomb since 1920, unaware of its connection with a one-time Bradford resident.

Fabian Ware was a schoolmaster in Bradford for four years. At the outbreak of war in August 1914 he discovered he was too old for military service at the age of forty-four. Instead he managed to secure a position with the British Red Cross Society and was based in France from September 1914. Through his efforts in dealing with the wounded he quickly realised that there was no official organisation responsible for marking and recording graves. He rapidly created one and, in 1915, it was transferred from the Red Cross to the Army. By the end of the war, Ware had reached the rank of Major-General and had twice been mentioned in despatches. He was awarded the Légion d'Honneur and made a Commander of the Order of the Crown of Belgium in addition to many British honours.

In May 1917 the Imperial War Graves Commission was established with the Prince of Wales as its President and Fabian Ware as Vice-Chairman. He held this post until he retired in 1948. Ware's vision was that every serviceman, irrespective of rank, race or creed, would have his own grave with identical headstone in a setting

The Ramparts Cemetery at Ypres, one of the most beautiful of the dozens of cemeteries established by Fabian Ware.

reminiscent of an English garden. He obtained advice from the Royal Botanical Gardens at Kew as to planting appropriate to the location of every graveyard, and to ensure that the landscaping and monuments were of the finest he engaged the most distinguished designers and architects. Ware also obtained formal agreements with foreign governments to ensure that graveyards could be managed by the Commission in perpetuity but he ensured that local labour was employed in their initial preparation and subsequent upkeep.

Record keeping, publishing of registers and responding to requests for information from relatives were a high priority and the work of the Commission today in providing an interactive website (www.cwgc.org) is a reflection of the high standards which Fabian Ware set for himself and his team. The Commission is always active. On 12 June 2006 the grave of Lance-Sergeant Edward Hartley of Leeds was dedicated. He was reported missing in action but his remains were identified by the Dutch Army Recovery team. Lance-Sergeant Hartley's family will now have the comfort of a named grave.

1922 was the year of war memorials. They rose all over the country and Saturday 1 July 1922 was the date chosen for the dedication of Bradford's memorial, which stands adjacent to the statue of Queen Victoria near the Alhambra Theatre. The date marked the sixth anniversary of the Battle of the Somme in which the Pals' Battalions raised in the city had suffered so greatly. A crowd of 40,000 people (only 3,000 more than the 37,000 names on the City's Roll of Honour) witnessed the unveiling.

The architect's drawing of the Bradford Cenotaph, which was unveiled on 1 July 1922.

The official programme printed for the unveiling ceremony. Lieutenant-Colonel Anthony Gadie was prominent throughout the war and beyond as a supporter of the uniformed men of Bradford and instigator of memorials.

A crowd of 40,000 gathered at Bradford Cenotaph on 1 July 1922.

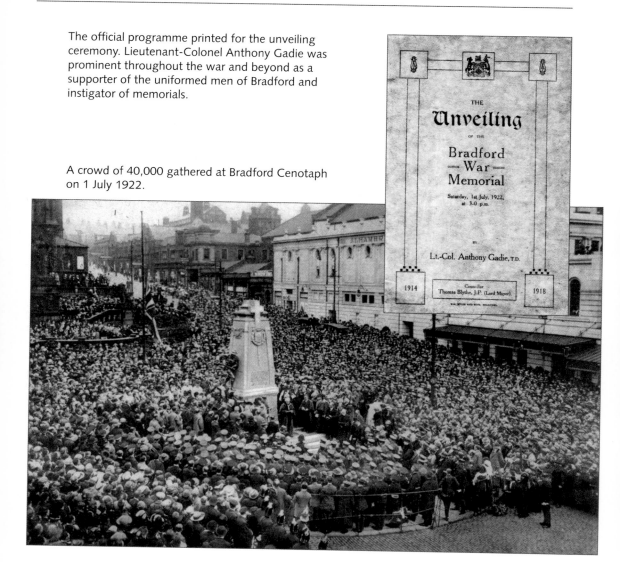

The memorial was designed by the Bradford City architect, Walter Williamson, and used stone quarried from Bolton Woods. The cross symbolises sacrifice and the wreath, containing the words Pro patria mori, symbolises grief. At either side are two bronze figures, one a soldier and the other a sailor, lunging forward with their rifles. The original bronze bayonets have long since been removed but the stance of the two figures remains aggressively war-like.

Harold Brownsword was the architect of memorials at Eccleshill, Greengates, Allerton and Thornton and each of these are full of symbolism and more reflective in style. The figure of Peace at Eccleshill, the winged figure of 'Peace through Sacrifice' at Greengates and the elaborate structure at the entrance to Ladyhill Park seem to communicate a different image to the memorial in the centre of Bradford. The Greengates memorial has been mentioned in the preface of this book. The

The highly symbolic memorial erected by the people of Allerton and Daisy Hill.

Allerton memorial, unveiled in July 1922 by Sir James Hill and Lieutenant-Colonel Gadie (both of whom were Lord Mayors, MPs and Aldermen of the City), demands closer examination.

The memorial depicts 'The Tribute of Posterity to Fallen Heroes' and has three bronze figures. A youthful male figure symbolising posterity offers a laurel wreath to a soldier who is held in the arms of the cowled figure of Death. The soldier's heel rests on a snake's head (representing evil) but his left arm hangs helplessly, pointing down at the snake as a reminder to future generations that the snake is not dead. At the rear of the pedestal are inscribed lines translated from the Greek which were written at Marathon in 490 BC on the defeat of the Persian army:

> The land they loved shall wear
> The fadeless crown her warriors gave her
> When, wrapped in death's dark cloud
> They laid themselves down dying to save her.
> Yet, being dead, they die not, in the grave though they be lying.
> These be the souls to whom high valour gave glory undying.

Beneath the foundations of the memorial is buried a lead-lined casket which holds a contemporary newspaper and other documents. The unveiling of this, as with the many other memorials around the city of Bradford and the country as a whole, presented the population with a focus for remembrance. The Bishop of Bradford presented a stirring address on 11 November 1921 which linked Christian sacrifice with imperial destiny. His address was reported in the *Yorkshire Post*:

> The Bishop asked what was England's highest title to immortality? It was not her wealth, he said, nor the vast extent of her Empire . . . it was the measure of her service to humanity. Of late years this had been her ideal. On this Day of Remembrance we thanked God that England's sons were true to this ideal and that He called us, as we believed, to serve humanity and save the world from tyranny and domination of material force. We mourned the dead but it was with hearts aflame with thankfulness and pride, and not despairingly we mourned.[12]

It was clearly important that the loss of lives could be acknowledged and accounted for. The bereaved sought consolation as well as a sense of reassurance that the sacrifice was not without reason or meaning.

Local newspapers continued to carry detailed accounts of remembrance services for many years. In November 1925 the *Bradford Daily Telegraph* published lists of forthcoming memorial services including a Toc H service at St Wilfrid's, Lidget Green, attended by Mayor J.H. Palin MP, himself a member of Toc H, the meeting of the Bradford Council of the League of Nations at Horton Lane Congregational Church and a Special Armistice Service at the People's Church, Kirkgate, where Revd C.J. Tribe's topic was 'Have we Forgotten?' and where members of the congregation were urged to sign the Peace Letter to the Prime Minister. It was reported that about fifty signatures were collected, declaring that they refused to take part in settling dispute with any nation by means of massacre and destruction, for the good of their country, for the well-being of their fellow men all over the world and for the protection of civilisation.[13]

The *Telegraph* also reported the service of remembrance at the Bradford Cenotaph on Wednesday 11 November 1925 under the headline 'The Great Silence in Bradford'. The address given by the Lord Mayor's chaplain was quoted in full, his theme being 'the fruitful sacrifice':

> I call it a fruitful sacrifice and I would emphasise the word because there is an unthinking and dangerous tendency in some quarters to say the sacrifice was in vain. Postwar conditions in Europe and of this land, to the poverty, the unemployment, the class conflicts, the industrial unrest at home, to the international rivalries, jealousies and hatreds abroad which so far have been the outstanding legacies of the Great War. I do most earnestly hold that we do not honour our dead by depreciating the value of the unspeakable benefits they purchased for us at such cost. Are our national liberties nothing? . . . we are here today as a commonwealth of nations, unbroken and intact . . . we must conserve and perfect the work they made possible . . . we must honour those who won the war by winning the peace.[14]

The reporter then described the scene as wreaths were laid, and was especially moved by those ordinary citizens who mounted the steps after the official party:

> Weeping mothers, their hands clasped in those of fatherless little children, laid flowers in this sacred place in memory of loved husbands; aged couples sorrowfully mounted the steps, their hearts aching with poignant yet proud remembrance of heroic sons.[15]

While the Great War was still being fought, ex-servicemen's organisations began springing up. The first of these was the National Association of Discharged Sailors and Soldiers (NADSS) founded in 1916 under the auspices of the Trade Union movement. The National Federation of Discharged and Demobilised Sailors and Soldiers (NFDDSS) quickly adopted a bias against officers and, to counteract this, the Comrades of the Great War was founded in August 1917 with the support of conservative and coalition politicians. The Independent Labour Party encouraged the formation of the National Union of Ex-servicemen in 1919 which was openly committed to class politics.

By 1921 the first three of these organisations had amalgamated to form the British Legion under the leadership of Douglas Haig. Membership grew from only 18,000 in 1921 to 117,000 by the end of 1922, reaching a peak of 500,000 (men's and women's branches combined) in 1938. In Bradford, the Waddilove family, reputed to be the richest in Bradford, had lost their only son Norman on the first day of the Somme[16]. He was shot as he climbed out of a trench. In memory of him, they gave their substantial house, 25 Claremont Villas, as a resource for returning servicemen. The Blighty Club was established there and in 1928 the Bradford Pals Comradeship Association. The Royal British Legion now has its Bradford Headquarters on the same road.

Right: The grave of Norman Waddilove who was killed on 1 July 1916. His family gave their house as a centre for returning servicemen.
Below: An advertising leaflet for the Blighty Club, which shows some of the attractions it had to offer.

The Bradford Blighty Club, Ltd.

Club House
25, Claremont Villas

Bowling Green & Tennis Court

Lobbying for benefits and pensions was only part of the work of these associations. The chief activity of the British Legion was winning public support and recognition of the most serious cases of hardship. Artificial poppies were first made in northern France and offered to the British Legion as a means of fundraising. Inspired by John McCrae's poem In Flanders Fields,[17] the Legion ordered 1.5 million poppies for sale prior to 11 November 1921. The *Yorkshire Post* reported a slow start:

> The appeal made by the Lord Mayor of Leeds ten days ago for volunteers to take collecting boxes and sell poppies on Armistice Day in aid of Earl Haig's Fund for ex-servicemen, has met with an extremely disappointing response, and last night only three or four offers of such help were stated to have been received.[18]

The report was answered by a reader's letter a few days later:

> Perhaps if a little more generosity were shown by the moneyed classes in this country there would be no necessity to appeal to children to contribute their pennies to assist other children left unsupported through the war. This letter may smack rather too much of Socialism for publication in your paper, but nevertheless it is hard facts, and at the present time to appeal to the working class to contribute further funds seems ridiculous.[19]

Despite the slow start, poppy buying proved extremely popular. The red flower in the buttonhole seemed to have mass public appeal and the British Legion established their own workshops (staffed by severely disabled veterans) in order to meet demand. The *Yorkshire Post* attempted to explain the significance of the poppy thus:

> This is Armistice Day, the day on which Germany acknowledged the defeat of her great and threatening armies. This is a day therefore of remembrance, gratitude and sympathy, a day on which we should all pay homage to the sign of the Red Poppy in token of our sentiments.[20]

Emma Talbot, great-aunt of Eric Bosher (see Chapter 4) lost her son at Gallipoli and her husband had survived the Boer

Poppy-seller Emma Talbot wearing the medals of her husband and son.

War. When selling poppies Emma wore the medals awarded to her menfolk. The important aspect of the poppy appeal was that it raised funds for the survivors of war and thereby gave Remembrance Day an added dimension. The presence of maimed, permanently scarred ex-servicemen was not always comfortable but the British Legion ensured that they were not sidelined and even today the Poppy Day Appeal remains a major charity fundraiser.

Memorials are still being created today, including one to the Bradford Pals. On 1 July 1916 the stepping-off point for the Pals was from trenches in front of a pattern of woods dubbed with the names Matthew, Mark, Luke and John near the village of Serre. The wood Matthew, behind the Bradford lines, has been ploughed up while the others remain as a cemetery complex known as Sheffield Park. Probably the most striking of the memorials in Sheffield Park is dedicated to the Chorley Pals. Before 2001 certainly the least dignified was to the Bradford Pals: a small home-made notice pinned to a tree.

The World War I Group based at the Mechanics' Institute Library in Bradford, led by Mrs Joan Kenny, decided that something had to be done. The obvious site for a memorial to the Bradford Pals was in Sheffield Park itself but this was not possible. The second choice was the village of Hébuterne and in 2001 a plaque was dedicated with full civic honours. Each year members of the group return to place new wreaths and in 2004 the Lord Mayor of

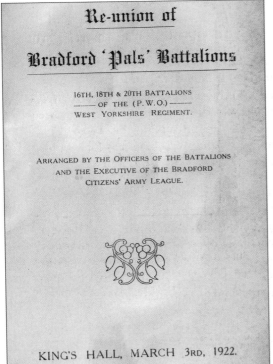

Above, left: The programme for a reunion of three West Yorkshire battalions of 'New Army' volunteers. The King's Hall was part of the Kursaal, which had been renamed at the beginning of the war.
Above, right: The memorial to the Bradford Pals' regiments in the village of Hébuterne on the Somme. Members of the World War I Group at the Mechanics' Institute Library organised for the plaque to be unveiled in 2001.

The stone in Centenary Square which commemorates the men of the West Yorkshire regiments. The inscription ends with the words: 'And lo, a mighty army came out of the North'.

Bradford, Councillor Allan Hillary, and the Mayor of Hébuterne, M. Tabary, attended a service conducted in French and English which remembered those of both nations who served and died near that spot.

Bradford City Council has also erected a memorial stone to commemorate all the servicemen of West Yorkshire who lost their lives in the Great War. 'And lo, a mighty army came out of the North' is the inscription across the foot of this memorial in Centenary Square.

This book has been compiled by members of the World War 1 Group in the ninetieth year after the Battle of the Somme. All the people of Bradford played a part in the Great War and it is their efforts and their lives which have inspired the authors in their task. We hope that readers will share the sense of pride and respect for those citizens of Bradford who contributed so much to the victory.

> Now to be still and rest, while the heart remembers
> All that it learned and loved in the days long past,
> To stoop and warm our hands at the fallen embers,
> Glad to have come to the long way's end at last.
>
> Then – with a new-born strength, the sweet rest over,
> Gladly to follow the great white road once more,
> To work with a song on our lips and the heart of a lover,
> Building a city of peace on the wastes of war.[21]

Notes

1   Quoted in *Shipley Times and Express*, 27 December 1918

2   The *Leinster* was a hospital ship which went down off the coast of Ireland while transporting those recovering from wounds

3   *Shipley Times and Express*, 27 December 1918

4   'Pack up Your Troubles' was composed by George and Felix Powell who had performed in music halls in Ilkley and Bradford before the war. George was a pacifist but Felix enlisted and was to hear his song used many times as men went 'over the top', an experience which was to prey on his mind in later years. On completing the original song it had been 'shelved' by the brothers but a competition was launched for a marching song for the troops and Pack up your Troubles was declared the winner. It became one of the best-known songs of its era and survived into the Second World War. Felix continued to stage shows around the country but during the Second World War the Luftwaffe bombed the London theatre where his show was being staged. Felix embezzled money to keep the business afloat but his wife refused to tour with the show and Felix was found dead on the stage. He had shot himself with a rifle while dressed in the 'Dad's Army' uniform of the Peacehaven Home Guard

5   For a full transcript of Connie Gallilee's Recollections see Appendix 1

6   National Archives CAB 24/CP45, 4 November 1919

7   National Archives, ibid

8   *Yorkshire Post*, 12 November 1919, p. 9

9   *Yorkshire Post*, 12 November 1919, p. 8

10 Hird, Horace, *Bradford Remembrancer*, The MacDonald Book Co. Ltd, 1972, pp. 160–70

11 The inscription reads: Beneath this stone rests the body of a British Warrior, unknown by name or rank, brought from France to lie among the most illustrious of the land and buried here on Armistice Day, 11 November 1920 in the presence of his Majesty King George V, his ministers of state, the chiefs of his forces and a vast concourse of the nation. Thus are commemorated the many multitudes who, during the Great War of 1914–18 gave the most that man can give – life itself – for God; for King and Country; for loved ones; home and empire; for the sacred cause of justice and the freedom of the world.

12 *Yorkshire Post*, 12 November 1921

13 *Bradford Daily Telegraph*, 17 November 1925

14 *Bradford Daily Telegraph*, ibid

15 *Bradford Daily Telegraph*, ibid

16 Hudson, Ralph N., *The Bradford Pals*, Bradford Libraries, 2000, p. 35

17 John McCrae was a Canadian doctor who came to Europe as a gunner in 1914 and later transferred to the medical service. 'In Flanders Fields' appeared in *Punch* in December 1915 having been written during the Second Battle of Ypres. McCrae was working in a dressing station on the banks of the Ypres Canal which was no more than a hole in the ground 'into which men literally rolled when shot'. The poem became instantly popular and begins:

> In Flanders fields the poppies blow
> Between the crosses, row on row
> That mark our place; and in the sky
> The larks, still bravely singing, fly
> Scarce heard amid the guns below.
>
> We are the Dead. Short days ago
> We lived, felt dawn, saw sunset glow,
> Loved and were loved, and now we lie
> In Flanders fields.

18 *Yorkshire Post*, 5 November 1921

19 *Yorkshire Post*, letter, 10 November 1921

20 *Yorkshire Post*, 11 November 1922

21 From 'Now to be Still and Rest' by P.H.B. Lyon, born 1893, served with the Durham Light Infantry, MC 1917, wounded 1918, Headmaster of Rugby 1931–48.

Appendix 1

Transcript of Connie Galilee's Recollections

1.   Dreadful stories were put about (and never repudiated by the media or the government) of the bestial 'Huns' who spitted babies on their bayonets and raped the women etc., etc. Men volunteering almost en-masse – they would beat the Huns by Christmas!

Meanwhile there was comradeship and free travel. Fighting talk everywhere, and white feathers given by silly females to any apparently fit men in mufti. This continued for about two years, with resident Germans' shop windows broken and sometimes attacks on people who had lived here for years, and vilification in the press.

2.   Women took men's places in the mills. The town was prosperous because of the manufacture of khaki for the troops and worsted for the officers.

Many people had allotments and grew vegetables, also kept hens and rabbits. There was no rationing at the start of the war and not a lot of obvious food shortages. A belligerent and confident air prevailed.

Much changed in 1916 when the submarines took their toll on Merchant Shipping. Food became scarcer and there was some rationing. Instead of butter there was dreadfully poor quality margarine – bad enough to make those with delicate digestions ill. On production of a Doctor's Certificate these people were granted a butter ration (not always eatable because it had been kept for too long for the highest bidder). One shop only in Bradford – on Manningham Lane – dispensed the rations. Women baked their own bread.

3.   Everything changed after the second battle of the Somme. Virtually all the young, fit men in Bradford were wiped out. Inch wide black borders in the local paper were filled, page after page after page, with the names of the casualties. 'Ee – that's Joan's lad gone!' 'Look, four in that family; whatever will she do?' I vividly recall women hanging over the paper and an atmosphere of horror and incredulity,

and many tears. Men began to appear in 'Hospital Blue' with legs or arms missing. One woman (Kate Kennedy) who lived in White Abbey lost four sons and her husband in one day. From being a very respectable, house-proud wife she became an hopeless alcoholic who said, 'They have taken all my men folk, now the government can look after me.' The Stipendiary Magistrate refused to jail her for being drunk and disorderly, and the wealthy wool men frequently gave her money on market day (Thursdays). Gloom hung over the city like a thick fog.

4.   By this time everyone was sick of the waste and mismanagement, and 'Haigh' was a dirty word. The 'family' and older men were training to replace the Bradford Pals. Known as the Pals' Fathers they were issued with uniforms and arms and drilled regularly. Once a week they marched to Baildon and did a day's rifle practice on a range on the moor. They were saved by the war's end, but news was slow to spread in those days, and even after the war men were dying in Mesopotamia for a week or so.

There was less a sense of rejoicing (too many widows and orphans for that) than a sigh of relief. Nobody knew then what was to become of the men who had fought so well and so hopelessly and did return, or of the families left ill-provided for despite their sacrifice. I have seen men with no legs begging in the street, propped up on a wooden 'go-cart' (home-made of course): what a reward.

N.B. I remember my Mother being furious because two men of German extraction were at starvation point as their customers deserted them. One was a blind piano tuner. The other was Mr Henty the tea man who wore a typical German slouch hat and Ulster and was very lame. A german toyshop owner changed his name to Atkins (Tommy Atkins) to try to overcome prejudice, but still never appeared at the shop counter because of abuse.

Appendix 2

Timeline of Events in Bradford

1914

4 August	Declaration of war from the steps of the City Hall
6 August	Lord Mayor's War Relief Fund inaugurated
15 October	220 Belgian refugees arrive in Bradford
26 October	City Volunteers headquarters on Leeds Road opened
27 October	First party of wounded soldiers, fifty in all, brought to Bradford

1915

15 January	Bradford 1st Pals' Battalion march to camp at Skipton
24 February	Military Hospital opened in Field House
15 April	1/6 Battalion departs for France
16 April	Lord Mayor publishes precautions against air raid danger
12 May	Bradford 2nd Pals' Battalion into camp at Bowling Park
2 July	Lady Jellicoe opens the Bradford Khaki Club
20 September	Women employed in Bradford as letter carriers
22 September	Sir Arthur Godwin opens Bolling Hall as museum
23 September	1st and 2nd Pals' Battalions leave Ripon for Salisbury Plain
9 December	The first Red Cross train arrives in Bradford
14 December	Women tram conductors employed

1916

1 February	Lord Mayor's War Relief Fund Trust Deed adopted
25 February	Two 'enemy' firms in Bradford ordered to be wound up

4 March	Sergeant Meekosha receives his Victoria Cross from the King
5 March	First alarm of Zeppelins in Bradford
28 March	Royal Certificate granted to Bradford War Hospital Supply Department
7 June	Final day for Voluntary Enlistment
29 June	Bradford Conscientious Objectors tried by court martial
1 July	The first day of the Battle of the Somme
21 August	Low Moor explosion
5 October	Princess Marie Louise opens Bradford War Hospital extensions

1917

6 April	Food hoarding prohibited

1918

29 May	HM King George V and Queen Mary visit Bradford
31 August	Bradford heroes decorated by General Maxwell in Lister Park
11 November	Armistice proclaimed from the steps of City Hall

1919

15 March	Belgian refugees leave Bradford
19 April	Return of 2nd Battalion West Yorkshire Regiment from France
19 July	Peace Day celebrations in Bradford
6–9 October	Civic welcome to Bradford Sailors and Soldiers
11 November	First anniversary of the Armistice

Appendix 3

Websites

www.1914-1918.net
The Long, Long Trail. This is the best Great War resource on the internet. Lots of useful information about all manner of Great War subjects. If you are researching a soldier the best starting point is to read the section 'How to research a soldier in WW1'. Studying this site thoroughly before going onto the associated forum is recommended. The next step is to click on View/Subscribe (no cost) and go to the Pals Forum. This presents material which is at the forefront of amateur historical research into the Great War.

www.cwgc.org
Commonwealth War Graves Commission. This site lists all who died in wars involving the UK. Information about the location of graves is given for each person and, for those who want to visit, clear directions for finding the war cemeteries is also given.

www.nationalarchives.gov.uk
The online Medal Index Card database is searchable for anyone entitled to the 1914/15 Star, Victory and War Medals, Silver War Badge and Gallantry awards. An image can be downloaded for £3.50 and will lead to the reference number of the Medal Roll if you are visiting the National Archive in person.

www.gazettes-online.co.uk
The *London Gazette* contains news of promotions and awards to servicemen which can help trace the career of officers.

www.naval-military-press.com
This is a commercial bookseller specialising in Great War titles, including British and Commonwealth military histories.

www.abe.co.uk
A second-hand antiquarian book site which has bibliographical information on books relating to the search for war records.

www.westernfront.co.uk
The Western Front Association
The site is dedicated to remembering and researching all those who served. The Association also produces 'Stand To!' which is one of the best periodicals on Great War matters.

www.iwm.org.uk
The Imperial War Museum site offers a wealth of information on every aspect of war and easily searchable.

www.armymuseums.org.uk
This is a 'gateway' site to all regimental museums, each of which has its own style but all are equally informative.

www.bl.uk/collections/newspapers
The British Library collection of newspapers is searchable for local titles and local availability.

www.firstworldwar.com
This is a well organised site with plenty of variety in its content.

www.fordham.edu
This site, the Internet Modern History Sourcebook, provides access to thousands of public domain and copy-permitted war-related texts.

www.bradfordtimeline.co.uk
Belle Vue Grammar School for Boys is the host to this website. The timeline gives an excellent overview of the history of Bradford and sets it alongside national and international events, inventions, 'firsts', sporting and cultural events, music and books.

Bibliography & Further Reading

BOOKS

Aggett, W.J.P., *The Bloody Eleventh: the History of the Devonshire Regiment*, Devonshire and Dorset Regiment, 1988

Arthur, Max, *Forgotten Voices of the Great War*, Ebury Press

Baker, Kenneth, (ed.), *The Faber Book of War Poetry*, Faber & Faber

——, *Poems of the Great War*, Penguin

Bilton, David, *The Home Front in the Great War*, Pen & Sword

Blackwell, R., *The Low Moor Explosion*, Coventry Lanchester Polytechnic Press, 1987

Brome, Vincent, *J.B. Priestley*, Hamish Hamilton, 1988

Collins, Diana, *Time and the Priestleys*, Sutton Publishing, 1994

Cook, Judith, *Priestley*, Bloomsbury, 1997

Cooper, Susan, *J.B. Priestley: Portrait of an Author*, Heinemann, 1970

Dobson, E.P., *The Garnett Story 1831–1962*, William Sessions, York, 1962

Duckett, R., *Aspects of Bradford* (vols 1 and 2), Wharncliffe Books

Firth, G., *Bradford Charity and the Public Purse*, Bradford NHS Trust

Fisher, J.J., *History of the Duke of Wellington's West Riding Regiment (The Iron Duke's Own) during the first three years of the Great War*, Whitehead, 1917

Graves, Robert, *Goodbye to All That*, Jonathan Cape 1929

Grogan, P., *A History of the St Mary's Roman Catholic Church, Bradford*, 1975

Hird, Horace, *Bradford Remembrancer*, The MacDonald Book Co. Ltd, 1972

Hudson, Ralph N., *The Bradford Pals*, Bradford Libraries, 2000

Jackson, John C., *The Low Moor Explosion*, Raw Nook First School

James, David, *Bradford*, Ryburn Press Town and City Histories Series, 1990

Le Fleming, H.M., *Warships of World War 1*, Ian Allan Ltd

Lingard, D. and Nicoll, C. and J., *Low Moor in Times Past*, Countryside Publications Ltd

Macdonald, L., *The Roses of No Man's Land*, Penguin

Marlow, J., (ed.), *The Virago Book of Women in the Great War*, Virago

Myers, Constance M.H., *Low Moor The Story of a Village*, July 1971

Neillands, R., *The Old Contemptibles*, John Murray

Nudds, Percy, *Low Moor and District Past and Present*, 1973

Ogden, Charles, *The Bradford War Work Souvenir*, Bradford, 1916

Oliver, Neil, *Not Forgotten*, Hodder & Stoughton, 2005

Pankhurst, C., *Unshackled: the Story of how we won the Vote*, Cresset, London, 1959

Priestley, J.B., 'At the Verdun film', reprinted in *The Balconinny*, Methuen, 1929

——, *Benighted*, Heinemann, 1927.

——, *Bright Day*, Heinemann, 1946.

——, *English Journey*, Heinemann, 1934.

——, *Letter to a Returning Serviceman*, Home & van Thal, 1945.

——, *Lost Empires*, Heinemann, 1965

——, *The Lost Generation: an Armistice Day Article*, Friends Peace Committee, 1932.

——, *Margin Released*, Heinemann, 1962

——, *Postscripts*, Heinemann, 1940

——, *The Town Mayor of Miraucourt*, Heinemann, 1930

Tempest, Capt. E.V., *The History of the Sixth Battalion West Yorkshire Regiment* Volume 1: 1/6 Battalion. Percy Lund Humphries & Co. Ltd, The Country Press, Bradford, 1921

OTHER SOURCES

Documents held by West Yorkshire Archives Service, Canal Road, Bradford
Bradford City Library

NEWSPAPERS

Bradford Daily Argus
Bradford Pioneer
London Gazette
Shipley Times and Express
Yorkshire Observer
Yorkshire Post
Yorkshire Observer Budget